To the Hon.
Josette Sheeran

With warmest regards
and all good wishes

Praise for Jewels of Allah

"A well-documented and persuasively written examination of the change in Iranian women's status under the country's secular and religious governments...maintains an engaging tone that makes it easy for casual readers to follow the arguments."

– KIRKUS REVIEWS

"Knowing our history is knowing ourselves. Nina Ansary expertly reveals largely untold stories of the multifaceted women of Iran and their perseverance to overcome considerable obstacles."

– ALISA MILLER, CEO, PUBLIC RADIO INTERNATIONAL (PRI)

"I am a big fan of women speaking out, telling their stories, using their voices—and author Nina Ansary has used hers in an astonishing, important way. Her *Jewels of Allah* is brave, authentic and riveting. What a compelling example of why women NEED to tell their stories. Read this."

– KATHY NAJIMY, ACTRESS/ACTIVIST

"This must be included within the Essential Reading lists of all schools—it is a vital historical account, a necessary and refreshed analysis particularly for our 21st Century culture of fear climate."

– MARCELLA KARAMAT, CURATOR/ FREELANCE WRITER, *THE HOLLYWOOD REPORTER*

"Nina Ansary's book is a must-read for anyone hoping for a fuller understanding of the role of women and the women's rights movement in Iran. It is a much needed antidote to Western misconceptions."
– SAN FRANCISCO BOOK REVIEW

"The women of Iran have no greater champion than Nina Ansary, nor does anyone equal her in explaining the seemingly paradoxical expansion of women's education since the Iranian Revolution."
– RICHARD W. BULLIET, PROFESSOR OF HISTORY, COLUMBIA UNIVERSITY

"Nina Ansary, with clear and precise language, laser-like focus and deep knowledge, lifts the veil of news media neglect and ignorance hiding the experiences of women and girls in Iran. *Women's eNews* is delighted she regularly shares her insights and inside knowledge with its readers."
– RITA HENLEY JENSEN, EDITOR IN CHIEF *WOMEN'S ENEWS*, NEW YORK

"This is essential reading on Iran, and feminism, human rights, and social movements. The book turns itself into a archive of all the relevant figures, publications, and eras related to the history of women in Iran, and as a researcher and writer, I know I will refer back to it in the future."
– MAHSA ALIMARDANI, INTERNET RESEARCHER AND IRAN EDITOR, *GLOBAL VOICES.COM*

"This is a remarkable book. Nina Ansary explodes some of the myths and prejudices held about Iranian women across the centuries. This volume is an invaluable addition to the existing literature on the subject and a must read for all those who are interested in understanding Islam and feminisms and in the celebration of differences and diversities within the feminist movements."
– BARONESS AFSHAR OF HESLINGTON, PROFESSOR, ACADEMY OF SOCIAL SCIENCES, UNIVERSITY OF YORK

"*Jewels of Allah: The Untold Story of Women in Iran* is an important journey through time, amplifying the powerful voices behind the Iranian women's movement. Author Nina Ansary highlights the courageous women and their progressive steps forward throughout history. The book is an eye opener, from a misunderstood story to how women's empowerment really advanced. It's an enlightening and fearless journey that's important for women around the world to learn."

    — DEIRDRE BREACKENRIDGE, AUTHOR, SPEAKER AND
       CEO, PURE PERFORMANCE COMMUNICATIONS

"Nina Ansary takes a fresh look at the women's movement in modern Iran; a century-long struggle for equality in a historic civilization, and one of the most vibrant feminist movements in the Middle East."

    — NEGAR MORTAZAVI, IRANIAN AMERICAN JOURNALIST AND ANALYST

"An elegant and enlightening experience—*Jewels of Allah* contains critical talking points, facts, and research that will empower its readers to more effectively understand the winds of change that are contributing to the empowerment movement of Iranian women."

    — YASAMIN BEITOLLAHI, DIGITAL MEDIA PROFESSIONAL
       & *HUFFINGTON POST* CONTRIBUTOR

"You can wrap them up in cloths not of their choosing but their powerful spirit still shines through. The Iranian women have always found a way to express themselves, make their presence felt and impact the society. This all comes through Dr. Ansary's book which expertly highlights the challenges and the opportunities facing Iranian women during the secular Pahlavi dynasty and during the various presidencies of the current theocracy."

    — DR. FIROUZ NADERI, DIRECTOR FOR SOLAR SYSTEM
       EXPLORATION AT NASA'S JPL

Jewels of Allah

THE UNTOLD STORY
OF WOMEN IN IRAN

Nina Ansary, Ph.D.

Revela Press
Los Angeles, California

The images contained in this book are provided for commentary, example and reference as to the content herein. Every reasonable effort has been made to assess the identification and source of those images displayed throughout this book, and they are included for the reader's reference and information where the same has been ascertained. In many cases the images are out of copyright or otherwise in the Public Domain. In all cases identification of the source or rights holder is attributed wherever possible, or unless the source was otherwise unable to be determined. Any information pertaining to the identification of those images which otherwise may have been unavailable by the author is welcomed, and every effort will be made to include the same where verified.

Cover art: Morteza Pourhosseini
Cover design: Yolanda Zuniga
Indexer: Under the Oaks Indexing

Publisher's Cataloging-in-Publication Data
    Ansary, Nina.
        Jewels of Allah : the untold story of women in Iran /
    Nina Ansary, Ph.D.
        pages cm
        Includes index.
        LCCN 2015932626
        ISBN 978-0-9864064-0-9 (hardcover)
        ISBN 978-0-9864064-1-6 (paperback)
        ISBN 978-0-9864064-2-3 (eBook)
        1. Women--Iran--History.   2. Feminism--Iran--History.
        3. Women's rights--Iran--History.   I. Title.
        HQ1735.2.A76 2015   305.420955
                    QBI15-600085

Revela Press LLC
RevelaPress.com
Los Angeles, California U.S.A.

This book is dedicated to my family, friends,
those who worked on and supported this book
(you know who you are), and every individual
who has been oppressed by discriminatory ideology.

100% of all proceeds from the sale of the book will
go to charitable organizations and institutions, with
the primary recipient being the OMID Foundation, a
501(c)(3) registered organization that has been empowering
disadvantaged young women in Iran for over ten years.
For more information on the OMID Foundation, please visit:
OMIDFoundation.com

The day we lose our ability to show compassion and tolerance is the day we have effectively lost our humanity.

—Nina Ansary

Contents

Introduction

AUDACIOUS GRANDMOTHERS

I grew up in Iran with two very different grandmothers. As a young girl, I took at face value the fact that one of my grandmothers was a devout woman who never left her home without wearing a head scarf, and the other was a Western-educated progressive-minded woman who didn't think twice about swimming topless in the family pool. Yet both women were forces to be reckoned with and by no means subservient.

My maternal great-grandfather believed in the value of education and sent all of his daughters to foreign-language schools, refusing to marry them off before their twentieth birthday at a time when sixteen was thought to be almost too old for a girl on the marriage market. My maternal grandmother was not only fluent in English, but also a very independent, feisty lady who used to walk miles every morning on her own in an era when women were expected to be wary of wandering out alone. She was an inspiration to her daughters, nieces, and granddaughters.

What was amazing about my paternal grandmother was that she had three sons and one daughter, yet she valued an education for all her children. Despite being a devout woman, she was not only *not* averse to sending her daughter to school in Iran's newly westernized climate, but in fact later came to the United States with her daughter so that my aunt could attend university. Unlike my grandmother, my aunt is not a religious woman, nor has she ever worn a head scarf. She is very fortunate to have been raised by a strong-willed, devout woman who was not opposed to having her daughter attend college in the United States. Granted, my grandmother accompanied my aunt to the United States, but this was during an era in Iran when a young woman going abroad to get an education was definitely not standard practice. So this audacious grandmother was also an inspiration to me.

It was during my scholarly journey into the Iranian women's movement that I began to reflect on how my grandmothers personified very different lifestyles and beliefs. In the course of my academic research, I came to realize why women from disparate backgrounds in Iran have more in common than is widely assumed. With my audacious grandmothers in mind—as well as generations of Persian women who have longed for equality—my commitment to a woman's right to determine her own destiny was intensified. It was also these factors that strengthened my belief that attire does not and should not define any woman if it is by choice and not mandatory.

I left Iran with my family when I was twelve years old and have been living in the United States ever since. I am humbled and grateful to reconnect with the history of the women in my country of origin. It is my hope that I will contribute in some small way to their ongoing struggle for empowerment. In fact, their struggle has become my own passionate cause.

Why did I choose to entitle this book *Jewels of Allah?* This book is based on my doctoral thesis on the women's movement in Iran, written in 2013 for Columbia University. I have rewritten the manuscript solely as an homage to all Iranian women who for centuries have struggled and continue to struggle against a discriminatory gender ideology imposed and justified by hardline conservative factions as the will of "Allah" (God in the Muslim world). The title is meant to convey that women, who have been ordained as inferior, are in fact the jewels of the Creator.

In researching the feminist movement in the West, I came across a quote by American suffragist and women's rights activist Alice Stokes Paul (1885-1977). She believed in the importance of women joining together collectively in order to advance the cause of women's equality. In 1923, she described the women's movement in this way:

> I always feel that the movement is sort of a mosaic—each one of us puts in a little stone, and then you get a great mosaic at the end.[1]

Inspired by the mosaic image, I recognized that it also reflected what is occurring in Iran. Like my two grandmothers, Iranian women have different perspectives and attitudes, yet they are united in the desire to be free to follow their own path. Every woman is a unique gemstone, and I have faith that together they will change the course of history in their homeland.

Chapter One

VEIL OF HALF-TRUTHS

It is difficult to find many bright spots in the lives of Persian women.... Their liberty of movement, of action, and of speech is curtailed.... In the prevailing social condition ... they could not do anything unless [they were] helped by men.... But some of the women maintain, and I agree with them, that their wisest plan is to go ahead and show what they can do. The day will come when the men will ask for their help.[1]
Clara Colliver Rice, American missionary, 1923

Here is the inconvenient truth: a flourishing, unwavering feminist movement is an unanticipated consequence of the Islamic Revolution.
Nina Ansary

So much of this was unknown to me....
Reader's comment on Nina Ansary's Facebook page

The historical narrative of the "woman question" in Iran is an intricate labyrinth. It is not a story that can be accurately recounted by portraying women as "oppressed" or "liberated" during a particular historical period. The audacious history of women in Iran is a maze, with unexpected twists and turns, gains and losses, triumphs and defeats.

When assessing Iranian women's history, the inconvenient truths that arise are striking: The Islamic Revolution that was explicitly antagonistic to the modernizing initiatives of the Pahlavi monarchy gave rise to a flourishing of powerful female voices. At the same time, the spirit of the progressive Pahlavi era influenced popular-class women (religious conservative women of the middle class who constitute the majority of women in Iran), despite the eradication of numerous "liberating" laws and institutions.

The women of Iran have been struggling for centuries to achieve equality; however, there have been periods throughout history when they were relatively free to determine their own lives. In this opening chapter, my intention is to enumerate the key misconceptions or half-truths concerning Persian women—from ancient history to the present—and to briefly explain why these statements fail to represent their authentic narrative.

Let me begin by submitting what I believe to be the *popular* narrative about women's lives in Iran over the last forty years. It goes something like this:

> During the Pahlavi Monarchy, women were on an upward trajectory. In a nation on the cusp of modernity, women actively participated. They were given the right to vote and were free to be in public without veils; they wore miniskirts on university campuses. Then came the Islamic Revolution in 1979, with Ayatollah Khomeini at the helm. The burgeoning freedoms for women were extinguished. The veil was required and institutions were segregated by gender. The Islamic Republic had thus achieved its goal of resurrecting the image of the traditional Muslim woman.

The problem with popular narratives of historical events is that despite their seemingly convincing half-truths, the real story is usually much more complicated, nuanced, and less tidy. The dramatic and surprising story of the women's movement in Iran certainly is.

As a historian born in Iran, I was surprised to come upon certain essential facts about women's history in my native country that starkly contradicted my previous assumptions. For example, when I first began to conduct my research on the history of the women's movement in Iran, I was struck by this fact: a majority of traditional, religious women, and even some educated women who had benefitted from changes under the Shah, supported Ayatollah Khomeini and were a contributing factor in the 1979 collapse of the Pahlavi monarchy. I found this piece of information not only counterintuitive but also deeply puzzling and difficult to reconcile, given the fact that the Pahlavi regime was solely responsible for emancipating the Iranian woman.

Everything in my background had led me to adhere to the commonly understood view of women in Iran: they were emancipated under Reza-Shah Pahlavi and his son Mohammad Reza Pahlavi; then their rights were revoked with the dawn of the Islamic Revolution. But my years of research and study have resulted in the discovery of a number of unanticipated truths that will be explored throughout this book.

The following are popular misconceptions about women in Iran that fail to accurately portray the real, often audacious, story.

Misconception I: *Before the Pahlavi monarchy, Persian women were always suppressed by the religious and political establishment.*

In the story accepted by many, Persian women are depicted as unceasingly under the power of male authority. Because this narrative leaves out the dramatic roles played by female leaders, as well as the fact that women were perceived to be equal to men centuries ago in ancient Persia, many assume that prior to the Pahlavi monarchy, women were confined solely to the domestic sphere. If they figured into public life at all, they were merely in the shadows.

Granted, ancient history is not a subject that everyone has studied in depth. College curricula at even the most prestigious institutions probably don't require courses in Etruscan civilization, the Zhou Dynasty, Vedic India, or ancient Persia unless one is majoring in a particular branch of history. If one is not a history major or a history buff, he or she may never discover how various early civilizations held beliefs and adhered to practices that would be deemed progressive even by twenty-first-century standards.

This can certainly be said of the Zoroastrian culture of ancient Persia. Zoroastrian ideology reflected the equality of men and women to the extent that women often occupied the same professions as men and received equal payment for their work. Female leaders ruled in a number of Persian cities and states in the sixth century BC, and female commanders controlled the armies. The authority and independence of women were part of the accepted social system.

Similarly, the nomadic cultural traditions of the Turko-Mongol tribes in medieval Persia endowed women with rights and privileges that extended beyond the confines of the home. Thus, in some ways these thirteenth- and fourteenth-century women had more freedom than women who lived hundreds of years later.

Acknowledging these and other early instances of female empowerment in Persia widens the cultural perspective of women's status in society and serves as inspiration for the current ongoing struggle in Iran. These feminist role models will be explored in Chapter Two.

Misconception 2: *Iranian women didn't advocate for their freedom until recently.*

There may be a common tendency to believe that meaningful progress occurs only in the present tense, that efforts to improve society are stronger now than in our grandparents' or great-grandparents' era. Again, our sense of historical precedent is not always as sharp as it could be.

Securing women's rights is not a cause born recently; it has been ongoing for hundreds of years. Persian trailblazers include Qurrat al-'Ayn, also known as Tahirah (1817–1852), an activist, intellectual, poet, and advocate of women's equality in Iran, referred to as the "the first suffrage martyr"; and Bibi Khanum Astarabadi (1858–1921), who produced "The Vices of Men" (*Ma-ayeb al Rejal*) in 1895, considered to be the first declaration of women's rights in the history of modern Iran.

How many are aware of the professional, political, academic, and artistic contributions made by Iranian women in the early nineteenth century? Is it commonly known that during the era of the Constitutional Revolution (1906–1911), a nascent women's movement was emerging in Iran that included women's secret societies? Amidst an austere environment in which the reigning presence of Islam continued to dictate the seclusion and subservience of the female population, a handful of progressive-minded women began to courageously challenge the principles of a patriarchal order, founding schools for girls as well as women's periodicals advocating greater female participation in society.

Acknowledging the historical roots of the women's movement in Iran, highlighted in Chapter Two, serves to strengthen and inspire those currently challenged by oppressive policies.

Misconception 3: *During the Pahlavi era, all women were liberated.*

The Pahlavi era undoubtedly ushered in progressive change in Iranian society, including policies that brought about modern dress, education for girls, women's increased participation in society, more freedom of the press (including women's magazines), and the enfranchisement of women.

However, the rapid transition toward a westernized way of life was largely unfamiliar to many women, as was a more secular culture after centuries of religious customs. Most of the Pahlavi-era changes affecting women were not embraced or accepted by the majority of females from traditional backgrounds. Their families were vehemently opposed to the new standards, finding them offensive and in conflict with cultural mores. Thus, wives, sisters, and daughters were prohibited from partaking of the new freedoms.

It is the contention of some analysts and historians that the cultural shift during this time was too precipitous and excessively focused on westernizing the society rather than giving more consideration to the cultural context into which the Pahlavi policies were incorporated. In other words, these changes were considered by some to represent a cultural violation.

The Pahlavi years brought welcome liberation for a small sector of female society, but many others were unable to adapt to such a sudden and dramatic cultural transition. Chapter Three will explore the underlying conflict that ensued as a result of such noble, visionary, yet drastic changes.

Misconception 4: *During the Khomeini era, women were totally oppressed.*

The partial truth is that women *were* limited or restrained by patriarchal laws and standards. They were forced to wear the veil, prevented from attending elementary and secondary schools with male students because coeducational facilities were converted into same-sex institutions, and subject to many additional exclusionary policies. The whole truth, however, includes this critical fact: many of the seemingly discriminatory policies, such as the imposition of the veil and eradication of coed schools were initially a welcome alternative for the majority of traditional families. Why? Because wearing the veil was what their families had been accustomed to for centuries, and same-sex education meant that girls could comfortably attend classes and thus gain an education. Previously, during the Pahlavi era, most traditional families would not allow their daughters to be in the same classroom with the opposite sex or to leave home without the proper head covering.

Chapter Four will delve into Khomeini's surprising "blunders" involving policies pertaining to the veil, same-sex schools, and educational materials. The inconvenient truth is that owing to rules that many Western women and men may consider archaic and sexist, girls in Iran became educated and liberated.

Misconception 5: *There is a lack of common ground between secular and religious women in Iran.*

Throughout the world there seems to be a widening divide between religious and nonreligious perspectives, each resorting to labels such as *fanatic* and *infidel*—or worse. There is also a more encouraging phenomenon: progressive religious groups are bridging the gap between religious and nonreligious thinkers by forming coalitions to combat injustice, poverty, and violence against women. Women in Iran are building such bridges due to their common belief in women's rights. While some may not use the word *feminist,* they agree that women deserve equal rights and freedom from oppressive yet sanctioned practices.

Some Westerners may assume that Iranian women who were forced to conform to Islamic practices after the revolution and those who essentially approved of those practices would have absolutely nothing in common. In fact, the truth belies that assumption. While it is indeed counterintuitive, the fact is that religious and secular women in Iran are working together to advocate for women's rights.

The traditional female population in Iran is now highly educated, worldier and open-minded, more eager for equal opportunities, and more outspoken about being held back by discriminatory practices. While some would label it heresy, many traditional Muslim women are posing a radically earnest question: Could a reinterpretation of passages in the Koran that are used to justify the inferior position of women be a means to women's emancipation?

The unanticipated alliance between religious and secular women, and the challenge of "Islamic feminism," will be explored in Chapter Five.

Misconception 6: *There is not much of a women's movement in modern-day Iran.*

In Western countries, one can Google "women's movement in Iran" and a number of credible articles, websites, organizations, and references appear. One is then able to read about recent developments relevant to the struggle faced by women in Iran, written by journalists, academics, and feminist advocates. But are these materials available to women in Middle Eastern countries or in Iran itself? And even in the West, how extensive is the coverage by mainstream media of women's advocacy and achievements in Iran?

The reason that some might think there is not much of a women's movement in Iran is that there may be insufficient coverage of women's activism there. The fact is, however, that the women's movement in Iran is thriving. During the repressive administration of Mahmoud Ahmadinejad, which eliminated many reformist organizations and resulted in drastic setbacks for activists, women's resolve remained intact. It was in 2006 that countless female activists staged the One Million Signatures Campaign, a grassroots movement aimed at ending legalized discrimination against women in Iran. The feminist magazine *Zanan (Women,* 1992–2008), flourished in the years prior to Ahmadinejad's tenure (2005-2013), was shut down during his administration, and reinstated in May of 2014.

Countless artists, journalists, academics, filmmakers, bloggers, students, and professionals—women from all walks of life in Iran—are engaging in the struggle for women's rights. They are up against formidable challenges, but they persist in their efforts.

Chapters Five, Six, and Seven pay tribute to the many remarkable women who are at the forefront of a movement to make women's equality in Iran a reality.

Today, in a country where the Islamic regime continues to debilitate women in almost every aspect of society, Iranian women are forging ahead as part of a vibrant, inclusive movement.

LIFTING THE VEIL OF MISUNDERSTANDING

If this book shatters many of the stereotypical assumptions and the often misunderstood story of women in Iran, it will have succeeded. The objective is to reveal how a full-blown feminist movement developed and grew in the patriarchal climate of post-revolutionary Iran. What were the concealed components that made such a movement possible? What are its historical roots? And who are the women—throughout history and in Iran today—making the resurgence of women's advocacy a reality?

The story of women in Iran is audacious because throughout history they have struggled against entrenched patriarchal regimes and never relented. They are not relenting now. Against formidable odds and despite prohibitions and arrests, their movement is unexpectedly thriving. Women from across the social, religious, and cultural spectrum are joining together. With resilience and tenacity, they persist.

Chapter Two

CLIPPED WINGS

You can kill me as soon as you like, but you cannot
stop the emancipation of women.
Qurrat al-'Ayn, aka Tahirah (1817–1852), first suffrage martyr in Iran

I will never forgive anyone who visits my grave veiled.
Sadiqeh Dowlatabadi (1882–1961), early pioneer of women's rights in Iran

---

The insistent cry for women's freedom has been heard for centuries in Iran. Twenty-five centuries ago in ancient Persia, women were in some ways more liberated than they are in modern Iran. That is because there is often an ebb and flow to popular movements such as women's liberation: enlightened progress appears inevitable until political, religious, or social forces turn back the tide with just as much fervor.

Three steps forward, four steps back? While that may seem to be the case for women striving for equality in Iran and elsewhere, when the powers that be push against women's objectives, it is possible to employ the knowledge of the past to invigorate the forward stride toward progress.

Knowing that women decades ago—even centuries ago—struggled for what women are still fighting for today can't help but be invigorating and inspiring. Who would want Tahirah's fervent efforts on behalf of women's empowerment to have been in vain?

This chapter will explore women's labyrinthine history from ancient Persia through the early twentieth century. Women's equality soared in ancient Persia, was severely diminished with the Arab invasion in the seventh century, and revived only sporadically via the Turko-Mongol cultures of the thirteenth and fourteenth centuries. More recent voices of heroic women like Tahirah and Sadiqeh Dowlatabadi validate the truth that even with clipped wings, those who passionately seek freedom never abandon the will to fly.

MODERN WOMEN IN ANCIENT PERSIA

The First Persian Empire, also known as the Achaemenid Empire (550–330 BC), was founded in the sixth century BC by Cyrus the Great. During that time, the Zoroastrian faith was the predominant ideology and reflected a clear belief in the equality of men and women. This belief was evident in the divine "primal creation" of six immortal beings:

> Of the six Immortal Beings created by God, three are feminine and three are masculine.
> The sky, metal, wind, and fire are male, and are never otherwise;
> The water, earth, plants, and fish are female, and never otherwise ...
> The remaining creatures consist of male and female.[1]

Simply put, male and female are seen as being equally represented in Earth's creation.

One of the world's oldest religions, Zoroastrianism (also called *Mazdaism*) was the ancient pre-Islamic religion of Persia. Founded by the prophet Zoroaster (Zarathustra), Zoroastrianism contains both monotheistic and dualistic features. Zoroaster's teachings emphasized an egalitarian creed, not only where men and women were concerned, but also with regard to rich and poor, young and old. Human beings were seen as God's helpers here on Earth. The fundamental basis of the religion focused more on moral ethics and good deeds, and less on ritual worship. Its sacred text, the *Avesta (Book of the Law)* was compiled over centuries and was completed during the Sassanid Dynasty (AD 226–641).

According to Kaveh Farrokh of the University of British Columbia, women during this era were afforded similar rights and privileges to those of their male counterparts:

> The rights of women in Achaemenid Persia were remarkably "modern" by today's standards: Women worked in many "male" professions (e.g., carpentry, masonry, treasury clerks, artisans, winery working), enjoyed payment equity with men, attained high-level management positions supervising male and female teams, owned and controlled property, were eligible for "maternity leave," and received equitable treatment relative to men in inheritance.[2]

Maternity leave and equal pay for equal work would seem to belong on a twenty-first-century-agenda, but perhaps the Zoroastrians were indeed progressive.

Although very little is known about specific women of this era,[3] it is important to acknowledge that centuries ago in ancient and medieval Persia, women were viewed as equal to men. Women were military and political leaders. For example, in 559 BC, Pantea Arteshbod was a high-ranking commander in the Persian military, as was Apranik centuries later in 632 AD. And Queens Pourandokht and

Azarmidokht ruled, albeit briefly, over the vast Persian Empire.[4]

Empress Pourandokht (also known as Buran) was the first woman to become Queen of the Persian Empire (629–631). Daughter of Khosrow Parviz II, king of the Sassanian Empire (590–628), Pourandokht, who preached egalitarianism, wrote in a letter to her troops: "A monarch, regardless of being queen or king must defend his or her land and treat the people with justice." Her sister, Azarmidokht Sassanid, was the second Empress of Persia (630–631). She ruled over the empire after her cousin, Shapur-i Shahrvaraz, was deposed, as he was not recognized in an official capacity by some factions.[5]

Pantea Arteshbod (559 BC) was one of the greatest Persian commanders during the reign of Cyrus the Great (559–529 BC). The wife of General Aryasb (Achaemenid's Arteshbod), she played an important role in maintaining law and order in Babylonia after the conquest of the

Irdabama (488 BC)

Pantea Arteshbod (559 BC)

Azarmidokht Sassanid (631 AD)

Neo-Babylonian Empire in 547 BC by Cyrus the Great.

In Sassanian times, Apranik (AD 632) served as a high-ranking commander of the army. The daughter of Piran, the great general of King Yazdgird III, she fought tirelessly to defend her nation against outside aggressors, including the Arab oppressors, whom she referred to as "the desert rats." A legend in her own right, Apranik's motto was "No retreat, no surrender."

Pourandokht Sassanid (632 AD)

Apranik 632 AD

Women held other influential positions as well. One such individual was a successful landowner in 488 BC known as Irdabama, who oversaw a flourishing wine and grain business that employed a large workforce.[6] She was only one of a number of accomplished businesswomen in ancient Persia whose achievements provide evidence of an equal social system that accepted the authority and independence of women.

Owing to the egalitarian beliefs of Zoroastrianism, women during this period of Persian history were represented in various endeavors and leadership roles outside the home. Feminists would look back at such flourishing of women's empowerment nostalgically as the tide began to turn.

With the Arab invasion of Persia in the seventh century, egalitarianism was significantly transformed. The conversion to Islam and the shift in cultural mores was not an overnight occurrence. It took many years for the religion to spread throughout the vast Persian Empire; however, Islam clearly emphasized strengthening and safeguarding the family unit by assigning guardianship and authority to the male head of the household.[7] Thus, women's roles were severely restricted.

LIMITED OPPORTUNITIES

The gradual decline of Zoroastrianism and the eventual infusion of Islamic values into the social infrastructure meant substantial changes in the everyday lives of Persian women. The religious clergy (*ulama*) were now entrusted with presiding over all judicial, political, educational, and social matters. Women were no longer of equal status with men in any sphere of public or private life. Women and men were also socially separated both inside and outside of the household.[8]

With regard to educational policy, the principal form of elementary education was the *maktab* (elementary school) system. These institutions were primarily funded by private contributions or religious foundations commonly affiliated with a mosque.[9] The instructional curriculum among the middle- and upper-class male urban youth, government officials, and business owners typically consisted of reading, writing, classical Persian prose, and basic knowledge of the Koran—with emphasis on moral and sacred teachings. As for elite families, they usually had their own personal family *maktabs* and used the instructional services provided by an in-house tutor. Referred to as *mu'allim-i sari-khaneh* or *mirza*, these instructors were commonly lower-ranking mullahs—educated Muslims trained in religious sciences, vested with the essential academic qualifications for undertaking this assignment.[10]

Young men who wanted to continue their education at a higher level could attend a religious college or *madrasa* and focus on theology, philosophy, literature, and Arabic. The number of years one was required to attend these religious colleges was unspecified, and completion of studies was determined by the instructor.[11]

As for young women, conventional assumptions deprived them of any type of formal education. Some, but not all, daughters from elite families received sporadic lessons through either paternal or private instruction,[12] but for non-elite Persian girls during this period, educational opportunities were virtually nonexistent.

There was an overall social stigma attached to women receiving an education, as the general belief among clerical leaders was that education for girls was not only against Islamic teaching but a threat to society as well. Many also believed that women did not have the capacity to become educated because their brains were incapable of retaining knowledge.[13]

Between the ninth and thirteenth centuries, the Islamic caliphate declined and was replaced by a series of Iranian and Turkic dynasties. In 1220, the Mongol forces of Genghis Khan overran Persia, and descendants of Genghis's grandson, Hulagu, ruled. During the thirteenth and fourteenth centuries, the Turko-Mongol tribes infused into the culture their nomadic traditions of a more inclusive role for women. Thus, Persian women were woven into the fabric of public life to a greater extent than under Islamic rule.

When compared to Irano-Islamic customs, women had greater social and political standing in the Turko-Mongol tribes. This is partially due to the personal convictions of Genghis Khan (1162–1227), who elevated the status of women by having his own daughters play a crucial role in his empire.[14]

In his book *The Secret History of the Mongol Queens: How the Daughters of Genghis Khan Rescued His Empire*, author Jack Weatherford writes about the impact and legacy of Genghis Khan's daughters and other Mongol queens:

> The royal Mongol women raced horses, commanded in war, presided as judges in criminal cases, ruled vast territories, and sometimes wrestled men in public sporting competitions. They arrogantly rejected the customs of civilized women of neighboring cultures, such as wearing the veil or hiding in seclusion.[15]

The new order didn't last forever, and Persian women were again forced to comply with patriarchal restrictions.

In 1501, Shah Ismail I became the first ruler of the Islamic Safavid dynasty (1501–1722), and Shiia Islam was declared the official state religion. In their quest to transform a primarily Sunni tradition, Safavid monarchs imported *ulama* (clergy) from Arab-speaking countries to enforce a Shiite juridical system.[16] The declaration of Shiism as the official state religion granted clerical authority over all public and private matters. The ruling dynasties legitimized their right to rule by claiming that they were the representatives of the Hidden Imam on Earth.[17] State and clergy thus became effectively interconnected. Monarchs were obligated to pay homage and often defer to the high-ranking Shiite clergy in all matters of the state, as they needed them as a source of legitimacy for their right to rule.

In their enhanced position of power, the clergy now determined the role and rights of women. The newly established clergy-state alliance mandated a patriarchal order that included veiling, early marriage, polygamy, and the seclusion of women.[18]

While both Sunni and Shiites[19] viewed women as inferior, the advent of state-sanctioned Shiite Islam implanted into the society at large the notion that women were subordinate to men. This ideology was reflected in Shiite theologian Muhammad Baqer Majlisi's influential manifesto, *Oceans of Light (Bihar-al-Anwar)*. The document represents Shiite thought on all aspects of life, including family law, the status of women, and the need for women's veiling and seclusion.

With regard to educational policy, girls continued to be effectively banned from education.

Female confinement to the home continued under succeeding rulers, including the Qajar Dynasty, which reigned from 1785 until 1925. The dominant practice of isolating women from public life had become firmly embedded within the fabric of society, leaving the female population crippled by entrenched mores and shackled to laws that were based on patriarchal interpretations of religious teachings.[20]

Meanwhile, cultural changes affecting the status of women were taking hold among Iran's neighbors. Mustafa Kemal Ataturk (1881–1938), founder of the Republic of Turkey, instigated a succession of radical and ambitious changes, which included the adoption of European practices and institutions relating to education, attire, and most notably the emancipation of the Muslim woman.[21] On Iran's other borders, King Amanullah of Afghanistan (1919–1929) favored reforms that included secular schooling, a ban on child marriage, and discouragement of the veil.[22] The influence of Western thought and practices was being felt in the Near East, and it was impacting the treatment of fifty percent of the population.

Where were the voices of change within Iran?

DEFIANT AND DETERMINED

One of the first activists to speak out against unjust treatment of women in Iran was the celebrated Babi theologian Qurrat al-'Ayn, also known as Tahirah (1817– 1852).

Qurrat al-'Ayn's quest for the truth began at an early age with her study of theology, jurisprudence, and literature. Her father was a cleric, and although the family was conservative, she was allowed to listen to his lectures

Qurrat al-'Ayn (Tahirah)

from behind a curtain in their home, asking pertinent questions when they arose. Upon marrying her cousin at the age of fourteen, she moved to Karbala, Iraq, where she pursued the teachings of Shaykh Ahmad al-Ahsa'i, a philosopher and religious thinker, and his successor, Siyyid Kazim-i Rashti.

Rashti and his students, including Qurrat al-'Ayn, believed in the coming of a messiah, and in 1844, Sayyid'Ali Muhammad of Shiraz claimed to be the Messiah, or Bab. Qurrat al-'Ayn was among the first eighteen believers in the Bab, who named her one of his primary disciples. There were divergent factions within the new religious group. Some remained faithful to established Sharia or Islamic law; others, including the Bab, wanted a radical break with Islam and incorporated egalitarian values into their belief system. Qurrat al-'Ayn clearly belonged to the latter group. She gave lectures espousing her views, which were widely attended by both women and men, but which also drew the attention of critics who deemed her promiscuous. The Bab defended her, giving her the name Tahirah ("pure one"), which became the nickname by which she was known.

At a gathering in 1848 in support of a new Babi religion that supported the equality of women, Tahirah appeared without a veil, shocking many of those who attended. It was not long afterward that the government crushed the Babi movement and executed the Bab. Tahirah was placed under house arrest and put to death in 1852.

Revered by members of the Baha'i faith, the religion that succeeded the Babi movement after her death, Tahirah is remembered as an important spiritual figure, a martyr for the Babi cause and for women's emancipation.[23]

Considered the first suffrage martyr in Iran, Tahirah's revolutionary spirit is hauntingly captured in her final words prior to her strangulation with a silk scarf: "You can kill me as soon as you like, but you cannot stop the emancipation of women."[24]

A THORN AIMED AT WOMEN

Sometimes the most powerful statements of protest are uttered with an incisive sense of satire and wit. *The Vices of Men* can certainly be counted among such rebellious proclamations.

Written by Bibi Khanum Astarabadi (1858–1921) in 1895, one of the earliest pioneers of women's rights, *The Vices of Men* (*Ma'ayeb al Rejal*) was a critical response to the anonymously written *The Education of Women* (*Ta'deeb al-Nesvan*). Considered to be the first declaration of women's rights in the history of modern Iran, Astarabadi's book was a penetrating yet satirical response to what she called the "nonsensical argument" in the anonymous piece on female education that spoke of the "slavish subservience" of women.

The following are remarks from Astarabadi about "anonymous's" book as well as her own book:

When I perused these pages ... I found that the author has put forth an unrealistic criticism, senseless and more biting than the thorn of a thistle aimed at women. I did not like the book; I threw it aside.... I wrote a book in answer to this evil-natured man, so that men would know that among women there are still those who are of high standing and whose force of speech may benefit from their eloquence.[25]

While *Ta'deeb al-Nesvan* may have been written by an anonymous man, it is rumored to have been penned by one of the princes of the Qajar court, "who must have feared his wife so greatly that he has not had the courage to put his name on it as its author." The following provides a short summary of the main recommendations of his book aimed at the "edification" of women:

1. Woman is a being who, similar to a child, must be educated by a man.
2. Salvation of woman is conditional upon her absolute obedience to her husband.
3. The duty of a woman at home is provision of conditions that are conducive to her husband's tranquility.
4. The aim of matrimony consists of gratification of the husband's sexual desires.
5. Woman must at all times be abashed, except in bed.
6. Woman must not speak during meals.

Would the "anonymous" prince allow women to speak in bed? Bibi Khanum's answer to his ludicrous mandates:

He should have first corrected his own vices and then given us advice.... He regards himself as "Westernized" and "civilized," but in fact he is not even "half-civilized."[26]

In her book, Astarabadi also denounced the respected religious figure Muhammad Baqer Majlisi by pointing out his decision to censor certain portions of the Koran for fear that they might corrupt the female mind:

> The great Shi'ite theologian even makes the teaching of the Koran to girls subject to censorship, leaving out the amorous story of Joseph and Potiphar's wife....[27]

A highly regarded figure of the early women's movement, Bibi Khanum Astarabadi founded the School for Girls (*Madreseh-ye Doushizegan*) in 1907. She ran the school from her home, providing a formal education to young girls with classes in reading, writing, arithmetic, history, law, religion, geography, and cookery. As a staunch advocate of universal education for girls, Astarabadi wrote numerous articles expressing her views, which were just beginning to be accepted by a handful of forward thinking citizens.

Another outspoken voice during this era was that of a woman raised in her father's harem.

Taj al-Saltaneh (1884–1936), daughter of Qajar King Nasser al-Din Shah (who reigned from 1848–1896), wrote about the plight of women restrained by the bonds of tradition in her book *Crowning Anguish: Memoirs of a Persian Princess from the Harem to Modernity.* Despite her life of privilege, she chooses words that vividly express a woman's dark fate and describe the unfortunate reality faced by her female peers:

Taj al-Saltaneh (1884-1936)

Alas! Persian women have been set aside from humankind and placed together with cattle and beasts. They live their entire lives of desperation in prison, crushed under the weight of bitter ordeals....[28]

In this heartbreaking quote, Taj poetically expresses how she would rather be dead than alive and shrouded in black:

The lives of Persian women consist of two things: the black and the white. When they step outdoors to take a walk, they are frightful images of mourning in black. When they die, they are shrouded in white. I am one of those ill-stated women, and I much prefer the whiteness of the shroud to that hideous figure of mourning. I have always demurred from putting on that garb. The counterpart to this life of darkness is our day of white. In a corner of my house of sorrow, I comfort myself with the thought of that day; yearning for its advent with incalculable joy, as though it were an eagerly awaited lover.[29]

The Veiled Women of Iran—circa 1900

Taj exposed the sheltered, decadent world of her father's harem while also revealing the personal challenges posed by a changing Iran. Her views reflect, in a penetrating and personal way, her desire to break with the stifling bonds of tradition. What is most powerful about Taj's memoir is her innate desire for women's liberation at a time when such notions were considered scandalous and taboo.

A witness to the stultifying lack of freedom that Taj described, American missionary Clara Colliver Rice spoke poignantly of the plight of Iranian women in the early 1900s. Her book *Persian Women and Their Ways* offers insight into the lives of women in Iran during that time and sheds light on how they were "handicapped from the beginning to the end of life...."[30]

> The laws of Persia are founded on the Qu'ran: the minutest details of life and conduct are enumerated in the Traditions: Islam has truly permeated the life of the Persian.... The greatest weakness in the social and National life of Persia has been its estimate of women. The seclusion and swaddling of her life has been a religious command and a political policy, and the wastage of a nation's greatest asset has kept Persia in a backwater.[31]

She goes on to observe:

> Mercifully, many of them do not realize this and even look upon their veils as protection and a privilege.[32]

Colliver Rice also commented here as well on the lack of educational opportunity for females:

> Education, like everything else ... has been controlled by Islam, whose prophet said in regards to girls, "Do not teach them the art of writing." ... A common adage in Iran is that a woman who is taught to write is like a serpent who is given poison to drink. For centuries religion and public opinion has[sic] been against the education of girls.[33]

The courageous actions of Taj al-Saltaneh, Bibi Khanum As-tarabadi, and a few upper middle class and upper class urban women were not part of an organized women's movement in Iran. And yet they signaled early signs of opposition to an imposed social order that deprived women of a formal education, political participation, and their overall freedom.

Many women began to acknowledge that education was the key to expanded opportunities and that educating girls was paramount in combating women's oppression. One of today's most prominent women's rights advocates, Guity Nashat, commented on the struggles of women from that earlier era:

> The greatest obstacle to removing the injustices from which women suffered was their ignorance.... Devoting their energies to enlightening Iranian women, they began their efforts by opening schools, and hoped that a good education would teach the younger generation of women to use their minds and not waste their intelligence in the pursuit of men.[34]

In fact, a growing number of Persian women—dedicated and tenacious activists—were unleashing their power as they began to organize, educate, and publish.

TRAILBLAZING SCHOOLS, PUBLICATIONS, AND SECRET SOCIETIES

The opening of Bibi Khanum Astarabadi's School for Girls (*Madreseh-ye Doushizegan*) in 1907 marked a new beginning.

At a time when women were not even allowed to walk in the streets after certain hours in various parts of the capital,[35] a handful of progressive women realized that education was an essential ingredient if females were to succeed in breaking through the barriers of sexism and patriarchy. For these women, schools for girls became a priority.

Prior to the Constitutional Revolution (1906–1911), which will be explored later in the chapter, separate schools for boys and girls in and around Tehran were founded and operated primarily by foreign missionaries—including those from the American Presbyterian Church; the British Anglican, French Catholic, and Russian Orthodox churches; as well as *Alliance Israélite Universelle,* an international Jewish organization.[36] As of 1896, a government decree allowed Muslim girls to attend these schools alongside Christians, Jews, and Armenian young women.[37] The missionary schools, sponsored and run by Europeans and Americans, were an early sign of Western penetration into Iran—a growing influence that Islamic hardliners would be critical of for decades to come.

There were also a number of semi-official Baha'i schools for girls, including the well-known Tarbiyat School, all of which were

Students at Tarbiyat School

founded on the Baha'i's egalitarian belief that all individuals should be free to pursue knowledge, regardless of gender.[38]

With Astrabadi leading the way in 1907, other Persian women who were equally committed to female education began to open schools for Muslim girls in Tehran. Touba Azmudeh inaugurated Namus in 1907, Safiyeh Yazdi established The Effatiyeh School in 1910, and Mahrokh Gowarshenas opened Tarraqi School *(Girls' Progress School)* in 1911. Gowharshenas opened the school without her husband's knowledge, and when he found out, he posed this rhetorical question to her:

> In the next world, when your father asks me why I let his daughter participate in activities contrary to religion and virtue, what shall I say?[39]

Mahrokh Gowharshenas's husband's remarks aside, it is important to note that the progressive efforts by Persian women, which included opening schools for girls and other advocacy activities, enjoyed the support of a number of progressive-minded and intellectual men, as well as like-minded women.

Certainly the girls who attended the new schools must have been thrilled to have the opportunity to learn, but the schools were labeled by clerics as "centers for prostitution," and students often faced various forms of hostility, causing some parents to resort to home schooling.[40]

Despite blowback in the wake of these enlightened educational endeavors, the movement toward empowerment forged ahead. One of the most distinguished advocates for female education was Sadiqeh Dowlatabadi (1882–1961).

The daughter of the leader of the Babi community, Sadiqeh was born in the city of Isfahan and educated at home. She opened the first school for girls in Isfahan in 1918. Unfortunately, it was forced to close after only three months, due to the fact that the overall mind-set of that time was that educating females was against the established order and therefore improper. Girls were to be taught only household chores, and adult women were expected to remain in se-

clusion. Undaunted by the establishment, Dowlatabadi opened another school specifically for poor girls, called Ummulmadares.

In 1919, Sadiqeh began publishing the magazine *Zaban-e Zanan* (*Women's Voice/Tongue*), which advocated educational opportunities for girls and other progressive changes affecting women. The magazine also featured articles emphasizing Sadiqeh's commitment to the Constitutional Revolution (which sought to free

Sadiqeh Dowlatabadi (1882-1961)

Iran from government corruption and foreign dominance)—and the role women played in bringing it about. In an editorial entitled "The Enemies Drew Their Guns," she expressed her belief that education for women would lead to the country's independence from foreign powers:

> It was love for Iran and the desire to see the constitutional government [succeed], as well as the thought of honoring and protecting the independence of Iran that brought [women] into the field of education. [Women] took up the pen to free Iran, to save our forsaken daughters and to help our nation. [Women] are not only unafraid to die but [women] consider it as an honor to make

sacrifices for the good of the country and [women's] freedom. Long
live Iran. Down with the dictatorship and the enemies of Iran.[41]

Not surprisingly, the publication faced strong opposition from
Mullahs in Isfahan.[42] Having cast women in a subservient role for
centuries, their patriarchal culture was not about to change. When
it came to their attention that Sadiqeh's magazine was publishing
articles by and for women, and that schools were being established
to educate girls, the authorities recognized a new women's movement
being born in their midst, and they did not hesitate before shutting
them down.

But Sadiqeh refused to concede. When *Zaban-e Zanan* was forced
to cease publication in Isfahan, she went to Tehran and began publishing it there. In 1921, she also established an association called
Anjuman-e Azmayeshe Banuwan (Society-Testing Women).[43] In
1922, she moved to Paris, where she received her BA at the Sorbonne
and wrote articles for European women's publications.[44] Studying
abroad was not a common practice even among Iranian men in those
days; for a young woman, it was audacious.

In the spring of 1926, Sadiqeh represented Iranian women at the
International Alliance for Women's Suffrage, the first time that an
Iranian woman was present at an international conference.[45]

Upon her return to Iran in 1927, this heroic woman fearlessly
appeared unveiled on the streets of Tehran. It wasn't until 1942,
during the reign of Mohammad Reza Pahlavi, that she once again
began publishing *Zaban-e Zanan.* A revered crusader until the end, she
avowed on her deathbed, in 1962 at the age of eighty, "I will never
forgive anyone who visits my grave veiled."[46]

Along with Sadiqeh's innovative magazine *Zaban-e Zanan,* other
women's publications during the early years of the twentieth century
in Tehran tirelessly campaigned for reform in academia and openly

condemned the practice of early marriage and enforced veiling.[47] These included *Danesh* (*Knowledge,* 1910) published by Mrs. Kahal and *Shokoufeh* (*Blossom,* 1913) edited by Maryam Amid Mozayyen ol-Saltaneh. Their activist perspective was viewed as a flagrant violation of the Islamic establishment and its ordained code of morality. Riots, threats, and even arrests and imprisonment often resulted. Despite such harsh repercussions, however, women persisted in getting out the word through their feminist-oriented periodicals. Sometimes such well-intentioned publications were extremely short lived. *Nameh-ye Banovan* (*Women's Letter,* 1920), edited by Shahnaz Azad, ceased publication after only three days, presumably for publishing the following statement in its inaugural issue:

> The shroud of superstition and traditional confinement have blocked the vision of men and women in this country....[48]

The magazine was permitted back on the scene only after it agreed to print a retraction clarifying that the word "shroud" did not in any way signify the veil. Nevertheless, Azad and her husband were harassed, arrested, and even imprisoned until the magazine was ultimately shut down.

Another well-known periodical, *Jahan-e Zanan* (*Women's World,* 1921), published by Afagh Parsa in Mashhad, faced such intense hostility that it was also forced to cease publication.

While most periodicals had a short life, *Alam-e Nesvan* (*Women's Universe*), published in Tehran from 1920 until 1934, was possibly the longest running of its kind due to its close affiliation with the Association of the American Girls School. Edited by an Iranian graduate of the school, it dealt with a variety of issues, including the value of education, health, and literacy. It also included articles about the international women's movement.

Throughout this period of Iranian women's drive toward emancipation, the power of the pen had a potent effect on those who were able to obtain the groundbreaking publications. Having access to the published words of women who were so passionately committed to changing the status quo meant that readers discovered they were not alone in their quest to change their own lives.

Another important path toward securing women's rights was that taken by women's societies or *anjomans*. These groups were engaged in deliberating and organizing around the issues that mattered most to women in the early 1900s. Among the most prominent organizations of the day were The Women's Freedom Society (Anjoman-e Azadi-ye Zanan, 1906), the National Ladies Society (Anjoman-e Mokhadarat-e Vatan, 1910), and the Patriotic Women's League (Jamiat-e Nesvan-e Vatankhah, 1922).[49]

Author Eliz Sanasarian relates in her book *The Women's Rights Movement in Iran: Mutiny, Appeasement, and Repression from 1900 to Khomeini* that "since most of these organizations and societies operated in secrecy there is little information about them." However, she does offer the following intriguing and inspiring specifics.

The Women's Freedom Society was created to address the second-class status of women. In order to help build women's confidence, only females were allowed to lecture at the gatherings. Membership consisted of male and females; however, single men could only attend if they were accompanied by a female relative. Meetings were held in secret outside Tehran, and yet at one point a male who had been refused entrance informed the mullahs about the organization. A group of men soon disrupted the meeting, the members were forced to flee, and the Women's Freedom Society was disbanded.

The National Ladies Society was established in 1910 in order to organize women to take action against the Qajar monarchs who maintained their extravagant lifestyle by granting economic concessions to foreigners, namely the Russians and the British. Members were primarily protesting the inferior status of women, but they blamed it on the exploitation of Iran by foreign interests.

The Patriotic Women's League, a well-known radical organization in Tehran, had as its objectives the schooling of young girls, the education of women, the protection of orphan girls, and the establishment of hospitals for poor women.[50] They published a magazine called *Patriotic Women*, which dealt with the issues of women's rights, social reform, the dangers of early marriage, and nationalizing the nation's industries. Its publisher and chief organizer was Mohtaram Eskandari.

Patriotic Women's League of Iran

Members of these groundbreaking organizations shared a fundamental common objective: attaining equality for Persian women.

WOMEN, THE CONSTITUTIONAL REVOLUTION, AND TOBACCO

The Constitutional Revolution (1906–1911) sought to compel Iran to break free from British and Russian economic exploitation, as well as to combat corruption within the Qajar monarchy.[51] Those who supported this transformation insisted that foreign ownership of Iran's resources should cease.

Granting economic concessions to foreigners, which had begun during the reign of Nasser al-Din Shah (1848–1896), continued with his son and successor, Mozzafar al-Din Shah (1896–1907). As foreign dominance over Iran's resources grew, some members of the bureaucratic elite and some religious elite demanded a curb on royal authority.

The constitutionalists were led by an alliance of enlightened clergy, members of the bureaucratic elite, and merchants who wanted to draw up an enduring document that would mandate a system of checks and balances so that Iran's monarchs could not freely exploit the country's resources by selling concessions to foreigners. The clergy were divided on this issue; some felt there was no need for supervision of the monarchy, while others believed it was sorely needed. This was the first time that such regulations were to be instigated, and since the Qajar monarchs were financing their lavish lifestyles by offering concessions to foreign capitalists, they obviously were opposed to these monumental changes.

The monarchy's granting of economic concessions to Western interests was also an issue that women took upon themselves to protest. In fact, women played a critical role in the defeat of the tobacco concession granted to Great Britain (1891–1892). (It was even rumored that women of the royal court refused to serve their husband's water pipes!) Their participation in defeating that important economic concession, along with their overall support for Iran's nationalist struggle, created momentum for women's defiance against the social order.[52] In order to protest the tobacco concession, support Iran's self-sufficiency, and demonstrate their patriotism, a number of women came out of their homes for the first time. As various women's groups took to the streets in support of the Constitutional Revolution, their actions represented an unexpected shift. The constitutionalist cause became a fortuitous opportunity for females to come out of seclusion and into the public sphere.

As author Mangol Bayat-Philipp describes in Eliz Sanasarian's book, women played an unforeseen role during the constitutional struggle:

> Their participation in the 1905–1911 political events seems to have been a spontaneous, free move on their part. There was neither a historical precedent nor a social tradition for such organized, politicized women's action to inspire and guide them. Seen in this context, the role of women clearly reveals not only a new nationalist feeling that suddenly overwhelmed them and spurred them to action, but also a nascent, though strong, desire for official recognition.[53]

One historical account, written by W. Morgan Shuster, an American official appointed as the treasurer general of Persia in 1911, attests to women's dramatic participation in support of the nationalist cause:

> Out of their walled courtyards and harems marched three hundred of that weak sex.... They were clad in their plain black robes with the white nets of their veils dropped over their faces. Many held pistols under their skirts or in the folds of their sleeves. Straight to the Majlis (Parliament) they went, and, gathered there, demanded of the president that he admit them all.... the president consented to receive a delegation of them. In his reception hall they

confronted him, and lest he and his colleagues should doubt their meaning, these cloistered mothers, wives and daughters exhibited threateningly their revolvers, tore aside their veils, and confessed their decision to kill their own husbands and sons, and leave behind their own dead bodies, if the deputies wavered in their duty to uphold the liberty and dignity of the Persian people and nation.[54]

Although the Constitution of 1906 failed to stipulate any rights or entitlements for women, women played a significant role in its acceptance. For all their brave activism, women gained little beyond their own experience in organizing for a just cause.

Unfortunately, the inferior status of women continued to be enshrined in the 1906 Constitution, placing women in the same category as other perceived second-rate beings who were also deprived of the right to vote, including "fraudulent, bankrupt, beggars, and all those who earn their living in a disreputable way...."

In 1911, Speaker of the House Shaykh Assadollah justified the misogynist decree using these words:

> The reason for excluding women is that God has not given them the capacity for taking part in politics and electing the representation of this nation. [They are] the weaker sex, and do not have the same power of judgment that men have.[55]

WHAT WOULD SADIQEH SAY?

A recent comment on my Facebook page referred to the brief biography posted beneath a photo of Sadiqeh Dowlatabadi. The reader posed this pointed question: "What would Sadiqeh Dowlatabadi say today about the treatment of women in 'modern' Persia?"

As someone who was in the vanguard of women's advocacy in early twentieth century Iran, Sadiqeh's valued perspective would certainly be enlightening. She would likely be incensed and discouraged by the backward steps that Persian women have been forced to take during the late twentieth and early twenty-first centuries. Perhaps she would also be tremendously hopeful, and encouraged by the thousands of activists, artists, writers, educators, and others who continue to advocate for women's rights.

From ancient Persia through the early twentieth century, Persian women made meaningful gains but also suffered depleting losses. The egalitarian beliefs of the Zoroastrians meant that women were often on equal footing with men; women during the centuries following the Arab invasion were subjugated to religious codes that deprived them of a life outside the home; and trailblazing women like Sadiqeh, Bibi Khanum Astarabadi, and Qurrat al-'Ayn (Tahirah) advocated for female equality, education, and political participation, despite gaining little in the way of constitutional reform. Their aspirations still resonate with those seeking freedom and equality for the women of Iran, and it is likely that Sadiqeh might advise today's activists to *keep up the fight!*

The next chapter will highlight women's impressive progress and advancement during the stunning changes of the Pahlavi era.

Chapter Three

SEEDS OF CHANGE

The Pahlavi dynasty did for Iran what Daniel Boone
and the man on the moon did for America.
Reader's comment posted on Nina Ansary's Facebook page

Despite numerous bold initiatives and the unwavering dedication of a handful of progressive individuals to alter the status quo, the over-riding traditional mind-set persisted in dictating the inferior status of women who "behind the veil of doors, behind the curtain indoors, left out of every social function, public or private, in which men play any part, were seldom educated, trusted, valued or respected."[1]

But dramatic changes were about to take hold. In 1925 a new frontier opened up in Iran that would prove as transformative to its citizens as U.S. trailblazing exploits were to Americans.

In 1921, Reza Khan, a relatively unknown commander in the Persian Cossack Brigade,[2] staged a coup that deposed Ahmad Shah, the last king of the Qajar Dynasty, and in 1925 led to the establishment of the Pahlavi monarchy.

The Pahlavi era ushered in westernized education, modern dress, increase in the minimum age of marriage, women's enhanced participation in public and professional life, the flourishing of women's magazines, the enfranchisement of women—and more. You could say, to paraphrase the man-on-the-moon comment posted on my Facebook page, that the Pahlavi regime represented "one giant step" for womankind.

But not all women were able to take advantage of the freedoms offered to the female population at large, and in this chapter we will learn why. We will explore the multitude of drastic changes that took place over the fifty-plus years that the Pahlavis were in power—profound and noble changes that benefited many, yet had unintended negative repercussions for others. We will also pay tribute to those Iranian women whose achievements during that era continue to inspire and motivate us all.

EDUCATING GIRLS THE MODERN WAY

On the eve of Reza Shah's rise to power, Iran's education system was manifestly inadequate, and adherence to religious codes of conduct meant that Iranian women remained second-class citizens.[3]

The discovery of oil in the early twentieth century added considerably to Iran's economy, enabling the inauguration of numerous socio-economic and structural improvements. The first decade of Pahlavi rule witnessed the dilution of British and Russian power; the enactment of drastic reforms, including secularization and centralization; development of education along western lines; and expansion of women's role in society.[4]

A fundamental component of the regime's monumental task of departing from centuries of religious domination entailed secularizing and restructuring the country's education system—a daring excursion into new territory. The most challenging and controversial aspect of creating a modern education infrastructure was the inclusion of girls, as many young females were still shrouded under the veil of ignorance. Educating girls was considered crucial to bringing women into mainstream society and to dismantling the outdated customs that Reza Shah believed inhibited and stood in the way of the nation's progress.

Despite reforms and the rise of new schools, illiteracy was rampant at the time of Reza Shah's ascension to the throne. Only 50,000 students were enrolled in state-run and private institutions. In addition, the 1906 Education Act providing free and compulsory education through the sixth grade remained unenforced; state regulations for instructor qualification were practically nonexistent; higher education was significantly underdeveloped; and the antiquated *maktab* (religious schools) system still prevailed.

Between 1921 and 1941, far-reaching reforms were initiated by the Ministry of Education (inaugurated in 1910). These included restrictions on the opening of new *maktab*, which led to a drastic reduction in the number of these religious institutions and further lessened the powers of the clergy.[5] Ministry policies also resulted in a revised uniform syllabus for all public and private institutions, with standardized textbooks for boys and girls.[6] The six-year elementary curriculum for boys consisted of Persian (reading, writing, composition, spelling, and grammar), religious instruction, arithmetic, civics, physical education, history, and elementary Arabic (terminated in 1930 when it was added to the secondary level). The girls had a less rigorous schedule that also included sewing and drawing.[7] Furthermore, all foreign-operated schools were nationalized and required to adhere to the curriculum authorized by the Ministry.[8]

While in 1910 there were approximately 3,500 students enrolled in the country's existing schools, by 1930 there were 150,000 students in all elementary and secondary schools throughout the country, 35,000 of whom were girls.[9] Although such progress was indeed stunning, many thousands of boys and girls were not attending the new schools. For one thing, the majority of these schools were concentrated in urban areas. Lack of transportation and teacher reluctance to venture into remote regions of the country meant that students in rural areas were essentially overlooked.

As part of the country's growing need for skilled workers, the practice of sending students abroad was made possible by a government decree requiring the Ministry of Education to dispatch a minimum number of students annually to Europe and the United States. During this period, a total of 640 students, out of which 50 were young women, studied abroad. However, not one of these ladies was Muslim.[10]

Perhaps Reza Shah's most drastic measure concerning the female population—one that unintentionally impacted female education—was the abolition of the veil. In 1935, the Pahlavi government decreed that women were no longer allowed to wear the veil. With the momentous new law, Iran became the second Muslim nation, preceded only by Turkey, to officially ban this traditional female garment.[11] Girls were also banned from wearing the *chador* (an ankle-length shroud) and the head scarf in school, punishable by withholding diplomas for all pupils, while instructors who wore the head scarf or veil could lose salaries.[12] This profound departure from centuries of ingrained tradition was viewed by Reza Shah to be a fundamental prerequisite in facilitating female inclusion into modern society. He defended his controversial decision with these words:

The 1935 Abolition of the Veil

> Because of our women's custom to wear the veil, due to this igno-
> rance and illiteracy, the Europeans have always taunted and despised
> us. Discarding the veil and educating women would change that.[13]

What did this mean for girls who came from traditional religious backgrounds? Modesty and cultural prejudice prevented most conservative families from allowing their daughters to acquire an education in this newly secular atmosphere. Unaccustomed to such radical changes, the majority simply did not allow their daughters to go to school—or to appear in public—without the proper covering. And since the veil was now officially prohibited, their school-age daughters could not be part of the new educational directives. Vehemently opposed to the new unveiling law, religious families thus kept their daughters at home. Ironically, the new policies that allowed thousands of girls to get an education also resulted in keeping thousands more out of school—and behind closed doors at home.

Freeing for some and oppressive to others, the unveiling crusade (known as *Kashf-e-Hejab*) was enforced with a single-minded severity not associated with the modern notion of liberation. For example, women who wore the *hijab* were not allowed in movie theaters, and bus drivers were fined if they accepted veiled women as passengers. While the police were ordered not to resort to violence in getting women to remove their veils in public, there were occasional instances of authorities resorting to beating a woman or removing her veil by force. This typically occurred in cities; due to their remote location, rural communities were less impacted by such drastic measures.[14]

In her memoir, Reza Shah's daughter, Ashraf Pahlavi, reflects on her father's decision to ban the veil:

> [He was] determined to westernize Persia … to bring it into the twentieth century.… To do this, to make us prosperous and powerful, he could not afford to leave out women, half of Persia's population, inactive, covered.[15]

Given his groundbreaking proclamation, one would assume that Reza Shah celebrated the unveiling of his own wife and daughter. However, Ashraf Pahlavi's recollections disclose the personal struggle her father experienced. Requesting that they appear without the hijab at the 1936 graduation ceremony of the women's Teacher Training College in Tehran, Reza Shah admitted:

> This is the hardest thing I have ever had to do, but I must ask you to serve as an example for other Persian women.[16]

Historians maintain that "while reaction to the state's coercive measure differed from class to class and region to region," unveiling became "in the mind so of many Iranians, the point of women's awakening and the cause of their resentment towards Reza Shah."[17]

January 1935—Reza Shah Pahlavi and daughters leaving the Royal Palace on the day when the chador ("veil") was officially prohibited.

Ironically, this seemingly liberating measure had the opposite effect for a large segment of the female population that was unaccustomed to going out in public without the proper head covering. Stifled by this new policy, they remained in seclusion, relying instead on their fathers, husbands, and sons.

While the unveiling law resulted in many Iranian girls being kept out of school by their parents, others were able to benefit from the expanding educational opportunities afforded by the Pahlavi regime. The inauguration of new schools for girls, coeducational facilities, and the Teacher Training College, along with the extension of

In 1935, women were admitted for the first time to the University of Tehran.

primary schooling and technical and vocational institutions, were instrumental in the push toward expanding educational opportunities for women.[18] By 1935, despite unrelenting prejudice by the religious establishment, an official decree by the Ministry of Education led to the increased presence of young women in academia. Women were admitted to the University of Tehran in 1935 for the first time, and in 1936, women were admitted for the first time to the newly established Tehran Teachers' College.[19] Isa Sadiq, founding member of the University of Tehran and possibly the most influential reformer in twentieth-century Iran, declared:

> The education for girls is an important duty ("vazife") of the government, which is likely to launch Iran on the path to westernization and progress ("tarraqi").[20]

TOO MUCH, TOO SOON

Not surprisingly, there were objections from the orthodox establishment against the campaign for female literacy, prompting the Speaker of the Parliament to declare:

> Women's studies should be in line with the tasks they are supposed to perform in society. We must ask, why do we send girls to school? The answer is to enable them to take better care of their children, be better housekeepers.... Why do girls have to learn mathematics? We should teach them cooking and sewing instead.[21]

There was no denying that a majority of the traditional population, as well as the clerical establishment, resented such drastic changes. The clergy were not only deprived of their stronghold in the school system, but many of the newly established secular laws reduced their overall power in the academic sector after centuries of control.

Exacerbating matters was the introduction of legal codes based on European models. For example, the enactment of the Marriage Law (*Qanun-e Ezdevaj*) of 1931, mandating compulsory registration of marriage and divorce in state notary offices, limited jurisdiction of the clergy in judicial matters.[22] Such revolutionary measures led author Nikki Keddie to conclude, "Rapid modernization from above helped create two cultures in Iran, which became more acute in later decades."[23]

For the first time since the advent of the Safavid Dynasty in the sixteenth century, the relationship between the monarchy and the clerical establishment was strained. Once Reza Shah embarked on a more secular path, the religious echelon no longer played the lead role. Furthermore, the more conservative clergy were vehemently opposed to any and all social changes attributed to the West—considered a violation of true Islam and incompatible with the intrinsic nature of Iranian society. Religious leaders as well as a large segment of Iran's traditional population deeply resented the image of the "emancipated" Iranian woman. They were unable to accept or relate to such drastic overnight changes.

In the overall assessment of Reza Shah's sweeping changes, it is important to note that despite such reforms, he was a devoutly religious man. Nonetheless, he believed that the clergy were thwarting progress in Iran. Although I contend that he was absolutely correct, it is my belief that he should have allowed his agenda to evolve more gradually. Given the country's religious backbone and deep adherence to faith, the new Pahlavi policies were definitely a case of *too much, too soon.*

In evaluating the new direction undertaken by the monarch, historians have held diverse viewpoints, with some questioning Reza Shah's religiosity and others rationalizing his policies as simply a desire to dispense with what he believed to be an outdated system that needed to evolve. Renowned authors and historians Shireen Mahdavi and David Menashri provide additional perspectives on this subject.

Mahdavi believes that, like many enlightened intellectuals, Reza Shah envisioned the compatibility of Islam with more progressive measures, while Menashri counters that the monarch appeared "more anti-clerical than anti-Islamic, but [that] such a distinction is alien to Islam, which rejects the sacredness of the temporal and the spiritual. This [in turn] implied reducing the influence of the *ulama* (clergy) in all spheres of life and confining them to matters of faith and ritual, similar to that customary in the Christian West at the time."[24]

In fact, the following statement by Reza Shah's son and successor, Mohammad Reza Pahlavi, provides support for Menashri's assessment: "[He] never advocated a complete break with the past;

he pushed the clergy into the background because at the time many of them were hindering the country's progress."[25]

As is often the case when swift and radical change rocks the boat, not everyone wants to remain on board. Those with traditional, conservative values chose to adhere to the dictates of the clergy, as Reza Shah's transformative decrees constituted a foreign way of life for the sheltered masses. Author Eliz Sanasarian underscores the difficulty in "preaching equal rights to a female population with an illiteracy rate of 95%."[26] On the other hand, women (and men) largely from urban areas and from the upper and upper middle classes enthusiastically welcomed the progressive policies. Author Azar Tabari provides an interesting overview regarding what historians believe was a growing divide between women during the Pahlavi era.

> The professional women of the 1920s and 1930s were mostly from the upper middle class.... [They] largely accepted and adapted to the changes and the secularization imposed by Reza Shah. [They] emerged from the social layers that identified with general notions of social progress and modernization associated with European civilization and endorsed by the modernists and reformers of the Constitutionalist Movement....[27]

SPREADING THE WORD

As part of the regime's overall objective of bringing women out of centuries of seclusion and into mainstream society, formal education was essential. So was connecting with other like-minded women in a new era of expanded opportunities—and women's magazines and organizations were viewed as instrumental in this endeavor.

A number of independent women's publications flourished in the immediate aftermath of Reza Shah's rise to power. *Alam-e Nesvan* (*Women's Universe*, 1920–1934) was the frontrunner in supporting the state's female agenda. Throughout its years of publication, *Alam* profiled various professions suited to the unveiled Iranian woman, as well as European role models, lifestyles, and perspectives. A bi-monthly publication with semi-independent status, it published such impassioned editorials as this one decrying misogynistic marital practices and women's illiteracy, and endorsing the new government:

> Are we aware that whenever they want to, men can throw their wives out of the house? Are we aware that women's illiteracy, lack of knowledge, and superstitions are harmful to society, the country, and the family? Do we know that in villages people illegally marry off a ten-year-old girl to a sixty-year-old man? Today, we have a government that listens to sensible argument and protects women and children.[28]

In fact, in 1931 the new Marriage Law stipulated that the minimum marriage age would be increased from thirteen to fifteen— which may not seem wildly significant to twenty-first-century Westerners, but it signaled progress in 1930s Iran. *Alam*'s reference to illegally marrying off a child to an old man highlights the publication's support for the state's progressive agenda for women and its belief that Reza Shah's regime was proceeding in the right direction.

Alam was the longest running women's journal until it was abruptly terminated in 1934 for unspecified reasons. Over the years, there has been speculation regarding the closure of the magazine, leading to the conclusion that perhaps an article published in 1933 too ominously denounced the unveiling of women as a superficial emblem of emancipation. The author of that article spoke out:

> A group of people including myself believe that the removal of the chador [veil] will not create freedom nor will hejab [veil] prevent moral corruption....[29]

In 1935, *Kanoon-e Banovan* (Ladies Center) was established.

Once Reza Shah was firmly in power, women's independent activities were curbed and by royal command directed and regulated into a single organization. In 1935 *Kanoon-e Banovan* (Ladies Center) was established as the primary vehicle to promote the regime's preferred image of the modern Iranian woman. Two of Reza Shahs's daughters, Ashraf and Shams, were involved in the center, which additionally organized lectures, adult classes, and sports clubs for women.[30] In 1937, Sadiqeh Dowlatabadi, a leading pioneer of the early women's movement, was appointed president of the center.[31]

Paradoxically, under the regime of Reza Shah, the women's organizations and magazines that had begun to emerge in the teens and early twenties declined on many fronts, leaving room only for a women's movement dictated by the Pahlavi monarchy.

EDUCATION WILL STEER THE SHIP

Reza Shah's son and successor, Mohammad Reza Pahlavi, came to power in 1941—after the invasion of allied forces during World

War II—and continued "the vigorous reform program inaugurated by his father."[32] In reality, the monumental reforms instigated by Reza Shah had primarily impacted the urban population, and only a predominantly cultured, progressive-minded and privileged few had been able to capitalize on the new employment and educational opportunities. For example, only I percent of Iran's total school-aged population was enrolled in elementary schools upon Reza Shah's departure. Meanwhile, such developments were essentially invisible to the majority of conservative Iranians, who resented the Pahlavi regime for, in their view, obstructing the sacred codes of Islamic tradition.

In the over 50,000 villages that constituted rural Iran, a number of factors stood in the way of educational progress. Most importantly, as citizens of a primarily agricultural nation, parents did not consider education a priority; rather, they viewed their children as part of the family's workforce. Lack of transportation and modern amenities in the rural areas, a shortage of instructors, and insufficient economic resources also contributed to the challenge.

Nonetheless, Reza Shah's equally ambitious heir was committed to taking his father's reforms to the next level. The extraordinary reign of Mohammad Reza Pahlavi was characterized by rapid urbanization, banning of the Communist Tudeh Party[33] in Iran, nationalization of Iranian oil, development of a modern military, expansion of the existing educational infrastructure, and considerable reforms for women.[34]

The devastation of World War II had led the Shah to seek assistance from the United States, which as part of the allied war effort had begun to take a more active role in alleviating the ravages of a damaged nation.[35] The post-war phase additionally resulted in the temporary revival of British involvement in Iran, which had significantly subsided toward the end of Qajar rule. The assistance provided by the governments of these two countries was instrumental in alleviating Iran's faltering economy.[36] Over the following decade, U.S. involvement surpassed that of the British, as the 1941 Lend-Lease Act and the 1949 Point Four Program provided aid and technical support, mainly in agriculture, public health, and education, and primarily through contact with U.S. business and educational institutions.[37]

In subscribing to the principle that "all modernizing nations need a plan of action," the regime resorted to the services provided by American consultants in the formulation and launching of the country's First Seven-Year Plan (1948–1955).[38] The plan, which included programs in health, agriculture, education, mining, and oil production, was an instant failure due to the shortage of funds, administrative constraints, and political disruptions.

With the gradual rise in oil revenues, the government embarked on implementing the Second Seven-Year Plan (1955–1962), which once again proved ineffective due to its "vagueness" and "absence of specific time-targets."[39] In 1957, a planning unit supported by the Harvard Advisory Group was incorporated within the plan organization, leading to the country's Third National Development Plan (1962–1968). This plan combined investment programs with forecasts in the public and private sector and specific tasks for ministerial and government agencies, in addition to a twenty-year collaborative program with international experts providing specialized attention in the field of education.[40]

In the Fourth National Development Plan (1968–1972), qualitative enhancements and structural changes outlined in the "principles" and "objectives" of education specified compatibility of this infrastructure with "modern scientific and educational progress and the requirements of modern times."[41] A significant component of this agenda entailed specialized teacher training programs for girls, specifically since "the total number of girls in Iranian schools did not exceed 1/3 of the total number of pupils." It effectively led to reduced illiteracy and an increase in the number of students at the primary and secondary levels.[42]

The Pahlavi era's Fifth National Development Plan (1973–1978), was enacted during a decade when the quadrupling of oil prices enabled a widening of the scope of educational and social development, including "trained manpower, equalizing opportunities between the rich and poor, raising the levels of female education, and expanding research to eradicate illiteracy," along with a forecasted projection of a "Sixth Plan" for "increasing the country's educational system, utilizing foreign professionals and experts, expansion of educational buildings, and improvements in educational standards," which paved the way for "higher education to respond more rapidly to the country's requirements."[43]

In the art of "nation building," analysts and economists "regard education as an investment rather than a consumer item. As one of the most important sectors of social services, education is highly regarded as a long-term investment, catering to the needs of a society."[44]

Shortly after ascending the throne, the Shah declared "only education could steer the national ship (*kashti-ye vatan*) toward the shores of progress (*sahel-e tarraqi*)."[45] To that end, in 1943 the government ratified a law providing free and compulsory education for all citizens. But its enforcement was impossible given the scarcity of facilities and instructors, particularly in rural and tribal areas.[46]

In this monumental task, U.S. assistance once again proved instrumental in training Iranian educators. The Department of

Research and Curriculum Planning worked in partnership with a team of American advisors to modify all elementary and secondary programs, enabling students to learn a variety of skills in conjunction with the set curriculum.[47] Brigham Young University, Utah State Agricultural College, and the University of Nebraska developed extensive agricultural programs throughout the country and in the process created a system of movable tent schools for the nomadic tribal population. Supplementary measures carried out by the Ministry of Education and UNESCO resulted in the establishment of specialized departments to administer vocational and agricultural schools throughout the provinces.

Teaching English, an important component of the educational system, was also integrated into the curriculum by the new administration. By 1959, all 8,000 state-run primary schools and 1,100 secondary schools offered instruction in the English language.

The Shah, educated in Switzerland, and his Minister of Education, Isa Sadiq, who was educated in France and the United States, were acutely aware of the enormous benefits of modernizing the school system. In the following passage, Sadiq, one of the most influential educational reformers in twentieth-century Iran, asserts "[tradition] can be changed" in order to benefit the society:

> First, the shackles of tradition ('sonnat') and the past were removed from my hands and ankles. Before traveling to the U.S., all customs, habits, practices, laws, institutions, seemed to me unchangeable. In the U.S., I learned that traditions can be changed, and they were created in the first place for the utility and progress of society. If they do not benefit the community, it is possible to adapt them to the needs of a different time and place.[48]

American influence clearly played a role in revamping Iran's educational infrastructure. Prior to 1957, the system had been based on the French model, consisting of two cycles of six years each. In 1957, on the recommendation of U.S. consultants, secondary education was divided into two halves, making it equivalent to the American junior and senior high schools. Later, the Ministry of Education implemented a three-tiered structure consisting of five years of elementary, three years of intermediate, and four years of high school.[49]

In 1960, the Shah expressed his desire to "establish a university modeled on American lines, with a primarily American staff" which would help meet the requirements of the "thousands of young people who at present go to study abroad."[50] In order to make his vision a reality, a team of advisors from the University of Pennsylvania in cooperation with Iran's educational elite embarked on the task of developing the Pahlavi University in Shiraz.[51] Officially inaugurated in 1963, the university was largely staffed by American graduates, with English as the primary language of instruction and a curriculum based on institutions of higher education in the United States. The "Penn Team" was responsible for developing an integrated core curriculum centered on a liberal arts education, creating a faculty of arts and sciences and launching The Asia Institute to house the Iranian Studies Program.

How did these monumental changes impact women? In subscribing to his father's ideology, the Shah announced:

> I should personally like to see further advances in broadening the opportunities for our women … my aim being that our women should enjoy the same basic rights as men…. If a woman wants to become a physicist, she should have the opportunity to do so, regardless of sex….[52]

In reference to the veil, he deviated from his father's enforced mandate. In his own words, the Shah "preferred to see a more natural progression towards this endeavor."[53]

Despite the government's efforts to increase female access to educational institutions and expand schooling throughout the provinces, a disparity persisted between the rural and urban populations. According to official government statistics, during the 1950s only 17 percent of villages had schools, and out of the 10 percent of girls between the ages of twelve and eighteen attending secondary schools, the vast majority were concentrated in Tehran.[54] The Shah therefore came to the conclusion that "no basic solution to the country's educational problems was possible by ordinary methods; and [in order] to transform these circumstances, rapid and effective war on illiteracy by revolutionary and unusual means was necessary...."[55]

In 1962, the White Revolution (*Enqelab-e Sefid*) was launched. Given that name to reflect that the Shah's reform movement was bloodless, it was also known as The Revolution of the Shah and the People (*Enqelab-e Shah va Mardom*). This multidimensional package of policy guidelines, designed to facilitate the transition from an agrarian to an industrial economy, was viewed by the Shah as "essentially an Iranian revolution compatible with the spirit and tradition of the Iranian people."[56]

Although land reform was the principal objective of these new policy guidelines, a primary feature was the enfranchisement of women. The Shah believed that this decree would "free women of their age-long captivity, and put an end to a social disgrace [which is] contrary to the real spirit of Islam."[57] He justified his decision to give women the right to vote with these powerful words:

> How can a man give rights to himself yet deprive his mother and sister of the same rights? How can a man say that his mother who has given him his very life, is in the same category as lunatics? This argument is against nature, humanity and civilization.[58]

In 1963, Iranian women were given the right to vote as part of Mohammad Reza Shah's White Revolution *(Enqelab-e-Sefid)*—a multi-dimensional package of policy guidelines including the enfranchisement of woman.

LITERACY ADVOCATES

Included in the Shah's White Revolution package were free and compulsory education for children of all ages and the establishment of the Literacy, Health, and Reconstruction Development Corps, whose mission was to improve the quality of life throughout the provinces, raise productivity, eradicate illiteracy, and facilitate the transition from an outdated system to a market economy.[59] The Literacy Corps *(Sepah-e Danesh)*, designed to combat rampant illiteracy in rural areas, was composed of male urban middle class high school graduates who were given the option of serving as instructors in lieu of a two-year mandatory military service. The corpsmen's various duties were not limited to instruction, and they included health and hygiene instruction as well as large-scale development projects throughout the provinces.[60]

Established in 1968, and also part of the White Revolution, Women's Social Services (*Khadamat-e Ejtemai-ye Zanan*) led to the formation of the Female Literacy Corps. Similar to the roles performed by their male counterparts, young urban women were recruited to advise and instruct the rural female population. They wore European-style military uniforms, reinforcing a westernized outlook.

Although the Corps became instrumental in the Pahlavi regime's quest to reduce illiteracy and establish a modern nation state, it proved incapable of altering the conventional religious mind-set of a large segment of the population. Despite the fact that government statistics reflected increased educational facilities and enrollment, a considerable number of families beholden to traditional norms continued to feel that it was inappropriate to send girls over the age of ten or eleven to schools that had by then become predominantly coed-

Member of the Female Literacy Corps—c.1970.

ucational.[61] Aware of this reality, Corps members resorted to various strategies, ranging from Koranic recitations and daily prayers to the separation of boys and girls in the classroom, but to no avail.[62] During what effectively constituted an era of unprecedented transformation, the implementation of new measures increasingly provoked the wrath of the clergy who regarded such trespasses on their authority as unconstitutional and a violation of the principles of Sharia.

In direct contrast to rural areas, the impact of radical educational reform became exceedingly apparent among the urban female population, where the percentage of girls attending primary school increased from 34 percent in 1966 to 42 percent in 1977.[63]

The move toward adopting a more Western philosophy within the academic system required revisions in primary and secondary textbooks. The objective was to ensure that both text and image reflected the monarchy's vision of a modernized, predominantly secular society, with few religious features.[64]

EVERY PICTURE TELLS A STORY

Sociologists regard the early years of education, including what is communicated via elementary textbooks, as a vital component of a child's socialization. *Socialization* is a term used by sociologists, anthropologists, social psychologists and other professionals to refer to the process by which an individual learns the norms, customs, and ideologies that will provide her or him with the skills and habits necessary for participating in his or her particular society. It is widely acknowledged by child development experts that the period in a young person's life between the ages of seven and twelve is when an important phase of this process takes place and core values are instilled.

Sociologist Daniel Coleman confirms that the preadolescent years (ages seven to twelve) are when children begin to exhibit "more realistic views of life as opposed to the intense fantasy-oriented world of earliest childhood," fortified by a more mature, sensible, and realistic perception of behavioral conduct.[65] This age group is distinguished as the initial stage when a child begins to develop a pronounced sense of the future along with a more formulated moral compass.[66] The structured learning environment of elementary school is considered to be a child's earliest means of perceiving the world beyond the realm of the household.[67]

Emile Durkheim, the father of sociology and architect of modern social sciences, underscores the vital role education plays in instilling society's values. He specifically focused his studies on the socialization of the younger generation in the school system and concluded:

> Education is the action exercised by the adult generation over those that are not yet ready for social life. Its purpose is to arouse and develop in the child a certain number of intellectual and moral states which are demanded of him by both the political society as a whole and by the specific environment for which he is particularly destined.[68]

In terms of the Shah's sweeping plans for Iran, he and his education advisors recognized that one of the most effective ways of transforming a society is to instill new values in its youngest citizens. Children tend to model their behavior after their parents, but they are also introduced to role models at school—and their earliest schoolbooks are an integral part of that role-modeling process.

As one of the hallmarks of early childhood socialization, the elementary school textbooks (grades 1–5) used during the reign of Mohammad Reza Pahlavi were analyzed in order to determine the extent to which they portrayed the monarchy's gender ideology. The term *gender ideology* refers to attitudes regarding the appropriate and expected roles and obligations of men and women in a given society, which are often reflective of the doctrines of the ruling regime.[69] A "traditional" gender ideology emphasizes the distinctive roles assigned to both sexes based on presumed innate differences, with men as breadwinners and women as homemakers and principal caregivers within the family unit. In direct contrast, an "egalitarian" philosophy regarding the family endorses shared gender responsibility both in the private and public domain.[70]

Were the Shah's visions of westernized Iranian women reflected in the elementary textbooks employed during his administration? What unspoken messages were communicated in the textbook images presented to elementary school students during the Shah's tenure? How did the colorful illustrations reflect family life, work, careers, and gender roles in mid-twentieth-century Iran?

Given the agenda and the progressive ideology of the Pahlavi regime, perhaps it is no surprise that elementary school textbook illustrations portrayed a westernized lifestyle and perspective, one that the Shah hoped would spread throughout a rapidly changing Iran.

In the Farsi textbooks (grades 1–5) from the late Pahlavi period, men, women, and children are mostly presented in Western attire in a distinctly urban environment. When a classroom is shown, it is usually coeducational and presided over by both male and female teachers. Men and women are portrayed as mothers and wives, fathers and husbands, and teachers. There are occasional images related to farm labor but very few illustrations that depict men and women in either skilled or unskilled professions. Women and young girls are shown performing a variety of domestic-related chores, and in some settings both sons and daughters are shown washing dishes together in the kitchen.[71]

Family members are shown in activities such as shopping, going to the park, walking to and from school, and visiting the museum.[72] Boys and girls appear to be engaged in common activities, and only in rare instances are they playing with gender specific toys such as dolls or trucks.[73]

Illustrations that reflect a more rural or conservative population are fairly scarce. There are occasional pictures of pastoral settings that depict women in village attire, as well as some images of segregated classrooms and the occasional elderly woman wearing a head scarf.[74] But these represent only a small minority of the overall textbook graphics.

The mathematics (*Hesab va Hendeseh*), social studies (*Tarikh va Goghrafi*), and science (*Ulum*) textbooks refrain from distinguishing specific male/female domestic or professional roles. The science books in particular show images of boys and girls equally engaged in a variety of fieldwork and scientific experiments.

On balance, these illustrated textbooks for elementary school students portray a society in which girls and women participate in activities and perform jobs along with their male counterparts. For the most part, the unspoken message seems to be: females are free to have a life outside the home and to engage in pursuits equally with males.

With that said, there was a noted lack of female role models in textbooks of this era. The elementary textbooks of the Pahlavi period failed to reference women in roles other than mothers and teachers. The only female role model depicted or referenced was the *Shahbanou* (Empress) of Iran and wife of Mohammad Reza Pahlavi.[75] From a sociological perspective, this was a missed opportunity. Given that the Shah's policies favored women's access to a wide range of occupations, it would seem that educational materials published during his reign should have reflected that ideology. Drawing on the regime's progressive perspective with regard to the role of women, a more concerted effort should have been made to incorporate into elementary textbooks accomplished Western women, such as chemist Marie Curie, as role models.

Pahlavi-era elementary school textbooks.

MAJOR GAINS—AND SOME LOSSES

The Pahlavis' core objective was to modernize Iran and improve not only its economy and standing in the world but the quality of life for its citizens—including women. Education was seen as the primary means to that end. Schools, universities, textbooks, teacher training, and educational policies were brought closer in line with Western standards. The Literacy Corps sent educational emissaries to the rural areas to take a stand against illiteracy. More students, including a small percentage of women, were given the opportunity to study abroad, primarily in the United States. Clearly, thousands of females benefited from these changes. As we've seen, however, too many potential female students—those from rural communities and traditional families—could not partake of these new opportunities.

Nevertheless, political stability and improvements in education led to new possibilities for urban women. A surge in the number of women completing a higher education meant increased employment opportunities. New labor laws provided "equal pay for equal work."[76] And the percentage of employed literate women grew from 30 percent in 1966 to 65 percent in 1976, with women comprising 28 percent of civil servants, 30 percent of secondary school teachers, 54 percent of elementary teachers, and 100 percent of kindergarten teachers.[77]

There were profoundly important changes for women in other spheres of life as well. The 1967 Family Protection Act meant increased autonomy for women and the removal of restrictions in marriage, divorce, and child custody matters. In 1975 the act was augmented to provide additional social and professional benefits to women, including a complete ban on polygamy.[78]

In her memoir, *Faces in the Mirror*, the Shah's twin sister, Princess Ashraf Pahlavi, a leading advocate of women's rights in Iran, spoke of the impact of the Family Protection Act. Her book provides an enlightening narrative of the challenges entailed in transforming an entrenched way of life and the instrumental role played by the Princess in this process:

> This act gave Iran's women the most sweeping civil rights in the Islamic Middle East. It recognized a wife as an equal partner in marriage: in decision making, in planning the future of the children, in divorce, and in the matter of child custody. It limited a man to one wife (indirectly, since the Koran permits as many as four) by laying down strict conditions which virtually made it impossible for him to marry a second time: the prospective polygamist had to have his first wife agree; had to have the financial means to support equal households; had to prove that his first wife was sterile or incurably ill. The act provided that a woman could seek divorce on the same grounds open to a man (these grounds were now clearly defined), and it created a machinery whereby she could seek, and collect, alimony and child support. In the event of her husband's death, the guardianship of children would be awarded to the wife; previously all her male in-laws would have been given precedence.
>
> To get these laws passed was an uphill fight all the way. Our various committees labored for hundreds of hours to word these provisions in such a way as to minimize both secular and religious resistance. We enlisted the cooperation of various ministers, since it was obvious to me that you cannot emancipate women in a male-dominated society without the active support of at least some of those men, and we sought the endorsement of Iran's more progressive mullahs (clergy) (to whom we always prefaced our appeals with such remarks as, "Well, of course we understand that a woman's primary responsibility is to her husband and her children, but....")
>
> Of course, there were compromises at almost every step we took: For example, we wanted to put an end to the civil code provision that a woman could not hold a job without her husband's consent. "But just a moment," said one of the ministers at our meeting, "suppose my wife should decide to take a job that is not in keeping with my dignity."

"I'm afraid you'll have to give me an example," I said.

"Well, suppose she takes a job in a factory, or singing in a nightclub?"

"Are you saying these jobs are less honorable than the one you hold?"

Actually I realized while we were talking that if this fairly enlightened man was raising an objection, then certainly the less progressive gentlemen in our midst would balk at a law allowing a wife unlimited job options. So we added a clause "protecting" a man's dignity—but at the same time we insisted that the clause be reciprocal and apply equally to men's jobs and women's dignity.

When it was finished, I said to my co-workers: "Do you realize that we have won something of a victory with this compromise? This is the first time that Iranian law has even recognized that Iranian women have any dignity, let alone agreed to 'protect' it."

By the time of the revolution, we had almost complete equality with men, at least in the eyes of the law. We had even managed to allow abortion—indirectly, since our religion would not allow us to do it any other way—by decriminalizing it by setting up medical guidelines under which it could be performed.

There were more areas that still needed work: one was the law governing inheritance, the second was the law that required a wife to obtain her husband's permission whenever she wanted to travel outside of the country. Resistance to change came from a fear that we could have a rash of "runaway wives," though I argued long and hard that it was much more important to guard against "runaway husbands," who were, in most families, the major breadwinners. The final item on our agenda was the elimination of article 179 of the penal code, which allowed a man to escape punishment if he killed his wife in a situation where he believed she had been guilty of adultery. This law had been so liberally interpreted in the past, that a brother had once escaped sentencing for killing his sister—because he saw her getting into a taxi with a man.

Although implementing our reforms was by no means an easy task, we had many satisfactions. There was the day a minister friend of mine came to me and complained that women's rights had gone too far in Iran, because he was having a very hard time divorcing his wife. "I'm very sorry if anything I've done has caused you problems," I said. "But I can't really say the day is past when a man can discard a wife simply because he feels like it."[79]

This daughter of a progressive and visionary leader dared to defy centuries of tradition in order to craft laws that she and many others hoped would emancipate the women of Iran as well as change the mindset of the Iranian man. And it is interesting to note that while the Pahlavis reduced the role of the clergy, and unlike the Safavids and Qajars did not defer to them, there still was an underlying element of placating religious leaders.

The seeds of change implanted by the Pahlavi monarchy would continue to benefit Iranian women even after the Islamic Revolution. In particular, the educational foundation launched during the Shah's administration remained a surprising yet crucial legacy for Iran's religious female population. We will explore that outcome further in Chapter Four.

Irrefutably, wide-ranging, valuable gains were achieved by the Pahlavi regime, particularly for women.

And then there were the losses—namely, a curb on various women's associations and political parties that challenged the Pahlavi regime. During the initial phase of Mohammad Reza Pahlavi's rule (1941–1953), political parties and women's associations could freely espouse their views. However, the 1953 coup d'état that overthrew Dr. Mohammad Mossadegh, the democratically elected prime minister of Iran from 1951–1953, heralded an era of strict governmental control and the termination of all "oppositional and independent political parties and organizations."[80]

Mossadegh took up the cause of nationalizing Iran's oil industry (which had been under British control since 1913 through the Anglo-Persian Oil Company [APOC]) so that the country could be self-sufficient and free from foreign domination and constraints. A patriot and nationalist in the true sense of the word, Mossadegh wanted Iran to have complete control over all of its resources and not be beholden to outside powers. He was a popular figure who gained the support of the middle class and thus mobilized a mass movement for progressive social and political reform.

Mohammad Mossadegh

In pressuring the Iranian Parliament to accept his nationalization bill, Mossadegh created the National Iranian Oil Company (NIOC) and began negotiations with the Anglo-Iranian Oil Company (AIOC) for transfer of control. He also engaged in a campaign against the Shah and the British. The British retaliated by freezing Iranian assets, which resulted in a full-blown crisis. The British Secret Intelligence Service (MI6) and the American CIA organized a covert operation known as "Operation Ajax" to overthrow Mossadegh. The Shah finally agreed to Mossadegh's overthrow after Kermit Roosevelt Jr. asserted that the United States would proceed with or without him.[81] Discovering the plan, Mossadegh alerted his supporters, who took to the streets in protest. At that point, the Shah left the country, allegedly for medical reasons.[82]

In 1953, Mossadegh's government was indeed overthrown in a military coup d'état. In the immediate aftermath of the coup, the Shah amended the Iranian Constitution, giving himself the authority to appoint the prime minister.[83]

How did the Shah's systematic control impact the country's female population? The independent women's organizations that had flourished prior to the Pahlavi era were abandoned due to the strict oversight of the monarchy. Women's organizations and periodicals were now under the purview of the Pahlavi administration. By 1959, all women's associations were brought under the umbrella of the Federation of Women's Organizations (*Shoraye-ali-ye Jamiat-e Zan*), later transformed into the High Council of Iranian Women's Associations (*Shoraye Jamiat-e Zanan-e Irani*), with the Shah's twin sister, Ashraf Pahlavi, serving as honorary president. This entity, which predominantly focused on charitable functions and promoted the education of women, was replaced in 1966 by the Women's Organization of Iran (WOI) (*Sazeman-e Zanan-e Iran*). Inaugurated by Ashraf Pahlavi, who served as president, the WOI flourished with more than 400 branches and 120 centers providing literacy classes, vocational training, and legal advice. A forceful advocate for equal rights, this organization was instrumental in employing women as judges, mayors, cabinet officers, and diplomats.

As for women's publications: the two major state-sanctioned women's publications of the Pahlavi era represented the regime's vision of the westernized-emancipated Iranian woman. *Ettela'at-e Banovan* (*Ladies' Information*, 1957) and *Zan-e Ruz* (*Today's Woman*, 1964) were owned and operated by the country's largest publishing houses. Officially sanctioned by the state, both of these competing periodicals essentially avoided national politics. But there were distinct differences between the two magazines. *Zan-e Ruz* offered articles on beauty, fashion, and celebrities, whereas *Ettela'at-e Banovan* was concerned with more serious subjects affecting women.

More specifically, *Zan-e Ruz* included glamorous photographs of the latest haute couture and accessories, swimwear, lingerie, hairstyles,

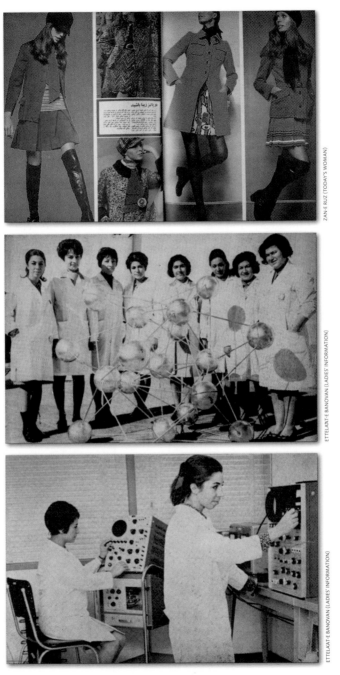

ZAN-E RUZ (TODAY'S WOMAN)

ETTELA'AT-E BANOVAN (LADIES' INFORMATION)

ETTELA'AT-E BANOVAN (LADIES' INFORMATION)

Women's publications of the Pahlavi Era.

and beauty products. Articles and exposés on Persian and European royalty, Persian and foreign celebrities, in addition to numerous "sexy" cover photos adorned the pages of the magazine. The occasional references to career, employment, and educational opportunities for women were overshadowed by emphasis on the latest plastic surgery techniques as well as seductive actresses such as Farrah Fawcett and Raquel Welch. One can only assume that such issues and images would hold minimal appeal for the traditional Iranian woman, who could not possibly understand or relate to women in a bikini or miniskirt.

In contrast, *Ettela'at-e Banovan* offered its readers articles not only about career and educational opportunities but also family law, social reforms, and accomplished women in Iran and abroad—including well-known athletes, lawyers, pilots, scientists, and physicians. The magazine's focus on significant topics was exemplified as well through its editorials, such as "Women's Rights in Iran," "The Success of Iranian Female Students in America," "Women Factory Employees," and "Women and Freedom in Iran." There were also articles that

Women's publications of the Pahlavi Era.

showcased the achievements and challenges of women in other parts of the world, including "Uganda's First Female Minister," "What Our Muslim Sisters Are Doing," and "Women Rule in the United States of America." While *Ettela'at-e Banovan* occasionally published recipes and fashion spreads, its overall content was geared toward encouraging women's participation in society at large. Unlike in *Zan-e Ruz,* the majority of women portrayed in *Ettela'at-e Banovan* were clearly Persian and conservatively dressed. Although the magazine rarely reflected the rural community, conventional attire, or Islamic designs, it acknowledged Iran's modest culture by refraining from provocative Western trends and fashions.

While both magazines were bestowed with the monarchy's seal of approval and may have appealed to a minority of educated, progressive women, one can only assume that they would be of little or no interest to the traditional female population, which had limited exposure to and/or understanding of Western-influenced culture.

Despite the demise of a number of women's independent organizations and magazines, these losses were far outweighed by the gains. The Pahlavi regime's tenacious pursuit of emancipation for women through education, career opportunities, family law, and many other areas distinctly reflects the initial stages of a feminist agenda. Although girls from traditional families were unable to take advantage of the many opportunities provided during the Pahlavi era, were it not for the monarchy's belief in increased possibilities and equality for women, liberating strides could not have been made by the thousands of Iranian women who benefited from the new policies. Clearly, this important period in Iranian history saw a flourishing of women's roles in society, and the seeds of change would continue to grow into a full-fledged women's empowerment movement in the decades to come.

Reza Shah photographed with a young Mohammad
Reza Pahlavi and his twin sister Ashraf.

Iranian schoolgirls during the reign of Reza Shah, c. 1936.

Girls' gymnastics at the *Alliance Israélite Universelle* school, Hamadan, Iran, c. 1936.

Reza Shah and Crown Prince Mohammad Reza Pahlavi visit an all-girls school, Iran, c. late 1930s.

Mohammad Reza Shah Pahlavi
(1941-1979)

Princess Ashraf Pahlavi

Farokhroo Parsa—Iran's first female minister.

Mahnaz Afkhami—Iran's second female minister.

The Female Literacy Corps.

Empress Farah Pahlavi with Gilan schoolgirls, Iran c. 1960s.

Reza Shah Kabir High School girls' basketball team, c. 1964.

The modern Iranian schoolgirl of the Pahlavi era, c. 1974.

The first graduating class of the Imperial Iranian Female Naval Officers, Tehran, c. 1973.

The emerging shadow of dichotomous trends in Iranian society, Tehran, c. 1975.

ALAIN KELER/SYGMA/CORBIS

Chapter Four

KHOMEINI'S BLUNDERS

The fervor touched everyone around me and we all looked for ways to participate.
Shirin Ebadi, Nobel Laureate, referring to her
initial support of Ayatollah Khomeini
(One of the first women to become a judge in Iran during the reign of Mohammad
Reza Shah, Ebadi nevertheless supported the revolutionaries against the Shah.
Once Khomeini was in power, she was stripped of her judgeship.)

In the midst of its groundbreaking modernization program, the Pahlavi monarchy was brazenly dismantled in 1979 by Ayatollah Ruhollah Khomeini and his many followers.

The 1979 Islamic Revolution spearheaded by Khomeini ushered in a theocracy that dismantled the progressive agenda of the Pahlavi era and instituted a constitution that stipulated governance according to the precepts of Sharia (Islamic law).

Although this radical shift had many dire consequences for women, it also had unexpected benefits for a large segment of the country's female population. An unintended consequence of Khomeini's Islamic Revolution was that many of the seemingly patriarchal mandates intended to establish a chaste atmosphere might have inadvertently empowered women. This was particularly the case for traditional women who felt alienated and disconnected from the Pahlavis' visionary yet disruptive policies that had favored the adoption of a Western lifestyle. It seems that the Khomeini regime made certain mistakes, however, in administering its "Islamized" educational policies. And these blunders resulted in female students being unintentionally influenced by Western ideology.

How could Khomeini's administration have caused such errors? What doors unexpectedly opened for so many young women when coeducation was abandoned? How did the Iran-Iraq War inadvertently lead to women's empowerment? And what were the hidden opportunities brought on by the Islamic Revolution that resulted in the women's movement taking hold in such a repressive environment? These are the key questions that we will explore in this chapter.

WHO WAS KHOMEINI?

Ruhollah Mousavi was born in 1902 into a family of Shiite scholars in the town of Khomein. Later taking his hometown as his surname, Ruhollah became known as Ruhollah Khomeini. He and his older brother, Seyed Mourteza, both attained the status of Ayatollah, which is given only to Shiite scholars of the highest knowledge.[1]

A Young Ruhollah Khomeini

Ayatollah Ruhollah Khomeini (1902–1989) emerged during the early 1960s when he voiced opposition to the Shah's White Revolution, including the emancipation of women, which he viewed as a violation of true Islam. A scholar and teacher who wrote extensively on Islamic law and philosophy, he was an advocate of strict adherence to Sharia—a position that attracted many adherents. His sermons against the Shah's westernization agenda inspired numerous demonstrations that were ultimately put down by the Pahlavi regime. Although Khomeini was exiled in 1964 to Najaf, Iraq, he continued his efforts against the Shah's government from abroad, where his rhetoric centered on the premise that the Pahlavi monarchy was a pagan institution *(Taqut)* incompatible with the true nature of Islam. He also denounced the Shah for supporting Israel against the Muslim world and for allying himself with the West.[2] Fundamentally, Khomeini and his supporters viewed the Shah as a puppet of the United States and the Western world.

Khomeini's followers continued to grow as he established himself in Iraq and devised a plan of action for launching an Islamic state. During his years in exile, he formulated his Doctrine of Clerical Rule *(Velayat-e-Faqih)*, in which he maintained justification within Islamic doctrine for creating an Islamic state in the absence of an Iman (an infallible successor to the Prophet Muhammad.)[3] By appealing to those who resented both foreign intervention in Iran and the Shah's progressive, secular agenda, Khomeini was able to expand his revolutionary movement from his temporary outpost in Iraq. Eventually, however, the Iraqi government, namely Saddam Hussein (probably at Iran's request, although this cannot be verified), pressured Khomeini to put an end to his political activities. Khomeini refused and was asked to leave Iraq.

In 1978, he went to Paris. Ironically, it was in this major Western city that Khomeini managed to consolidate his revolutionary movement, primarily due to these two factors:

1. Khomeini now had worldwide exposure, as he was able to give more than 120 interviews a day during his four months in Paris. He never had this kind of media exposure during his years in Iraq.

2. The excellent air and telecommunication links between Tehran and Paris allowed for much closer coordination and communication between Khomeini and the revolutionary movement brewing in Iran, which could not have gained this kind of momentum from Iraq.

And so it was in Paris that the groundwork for a full-blown revolution was solidified.[4] Khomeini's sermons reflecting his vision of an "Islamic utopia" and a return to cultural authenticity via Shiism had mass appeal that would ultimately overturn the Pahlavi regime.[5]

By 1979, large-scale social and political discontent brought about the dissolution of the monarchy and the institution of Ayatollah Khomeini's Islamic Republic of Iran.

February 1, 1979: The return of Ayatollah Ruhollah Khomeini to Iran.

The baffling mass participation of secular and religious women against the Shah, Tehran, c. 1978.

WHY DID WOMEN SUPPORT KHOMEINI?

Initially, Khomeini's followers constituted a somewhat diverse group, and their mobilization around a common platform ultimately ensured the revolution's victory. As for the female population, while it makes sense that those from conservative backgrounds would embrace Khomeini's sermons, how does one account for the support provided by many accomplished women who had gained substantially from reforms undertaken by the Pahlavis? What would lure those who were direct beneficiaries of the Shah's emancipatory agenda to gravitate toward the Ayatollah's populist Islamic ideology?

As mentioned previously, Nobel Laureate Shirin Ebadi, one of the first women to become a judge in Iran during the reign of Mohammad Reza Shah, nevertheless supported the revolutionary movement. In her memoir, Ebadi explains her initial attraction—and that of many other like-minded women—to Khomeini's rhetoric:

Faith occupied a central role in our middle-class lives.... Who did I have more in common with, in the end: an opposition led by the mullahs who spoke in the tones familiar to ordinary Iranians or the gilded court of the Shah, whose officials cavorted with American starlets at parties soaked in expensive French champagne? ... Most of the country identified far more with the opposition.... Among these opposition groups, the mullahs' voices were the loudest; it was the clergy whose network of mosques spread out across the country, who had standing centers from which to raise their voices and organize. It did not seem so alarming that the mullahs should take the lead.... As the days went by, the fervor touched everyone around me and we all looked for ways to participate.[6]

Whether the Shah and his officials actually cavorted with American starlets and drank expensive European champagne, Ebadi's characterization of the monarchy was one that was shared by many middle class Iranians back then, including women.

Shirin Ebadi

In fact, in her memoir published shortly after the revolution, the Shah's twin sister, Princess Ashraf Pahlavi, sheds additional light on this baffling phenomenon. A powerful advocate of women's rights in Iran, she reflected on whether this class of women could ever have identified with the newly adopted Western standards:

Persia's backward conditions were relics of social traditions ... and the women for that matter weren't ready to exchange the protection they had traditionally enjoyed for the unknowns of a new social status.[7]

In contemplating the insurmountable task of implementing such monumental changes, she candidly admits:

> It is equally obvious and it became clear … that no ruler can legislate a social revolution. He can implement the outward form of social change, but he cannot legislate change in the minds of the people. Stable and lasting change has to evolve slowly and gradually over a period of many generations.[8]
>
> What signaled the beginning of the end … was the radical modernization program, which virtually affected every aspect of Iranian life … [including] the sweeping emancipation of women, which moved as it were 13 centuries in the course of three decades.[9]

The Pahlavi regime's swift, far-reaching changes, the Princess concludes, led Iranians to see "all modernization as a sacrifice of old values in exchange for those of the decadent godless West."[10] In her final departure from Iran at the cusp of the revolutionary upheaval, the reality of such extremes unfolded before Pahlavi's eyes:

> As I flew over, I saw that one corner was completely dark. A moment later I realized this black mass was a mass of Iranian women—women who had achieved the highest levels of emancipation in the Middle East. Here they were in the mournful black chador [veil] their grandmothers had worn. My God, I thought. Is this how it ends?[11]

While the mobilization of various disgruntled groups around an anti-Shah platform ensured the revolution's victory, the mass participation of women perhaps constitutes the insurgency's most shocking aspect.[12] For Guity Nashat, professor of Islamic and Middle Eastern history at the University of Illinois at Chicago, the paradox lies in the fact that "women in general, including the most westernized individuals and groups, came out strongly against a regime that purportedly was helping free them from the bonds of oppression."[13]

Draped in the "flag of the revolution," women from diverse backgrounds contributed to a major transformation in Iran—for various reasons. Some wanted the revolution to result in national independence; others hoped it would result in a revitalized culture reflecting true Shiite values.[14]

Ali Ansari is among the distinguished group of scholars who maintain that the ambiguous nature of the revolution was instrumental in assuring its success. By appealing to disparate groups that opposed the Shah, Khomeini ultimately succeeded in reinstituting a clergy-state alliance.[15] And as for the patronage provided by women, it seems that many may have been misled by Khomeini's early pronouncements. In fact, a close examination reveals an often vague rhetoric, which could be misconstrued as egalitarian. For instance, in 1978 the Ayatollah stated the following in a message delivered to Iranian women from France:

> We are proud that our women, young and old, are active in the educational and economic field … forwarding the goals of Islam and the Holy Koran. Any nation that has women like the women of Iran will surely be victorious.[16]

And in an interview given to a German publication in that same year, he further declared:

> In an Islamic Republic, women have complete freedom in everything they do, just as men are free—in everything.[17]

In a correspondence with the *Guardian* newspaper in Paris, Khomeini again reiterated:

> Women are free in the Islamic Republic—in the selection of their activities, in their future, and their clothing … [18]

However, once in power, Ayatollah Khomeini radically shifted from his previously stated views, proclaiming to Italian journalist Orianna Fallaci:

> The women who contributed to the revolution were and are in Islamic dress, not elegant women at all, made up like you, who go around dragging behind the tail of men. Those who put on makeup and go into the street showing off their necks, their hair ... did not fight against the Shah. They never did anything good—Not those! They do not know how to be useful, neither socially, nor politically, nor professionally.[19]

In fact, *A Clarification of Questions*, Khomeini's discourse on the appropriate conduct of the devout, categorically testifies to his personal ideology regarding the position of women:

> A woman who has been contracted permanently must not leave the house without the husband's permission and must surrender herself for any pleasure that he wants.... If she obeys the husband ... the provision of her food, clothing and dwelling is obligatory for the husband. If the wife does not obey her husband ... she is a sinner and has no right to clothing, food and shelter.[20]

In retrospect, such misogynistic declarations are not surprising, as Khomeini had always subscribed to such principles, as evidenced by his opposition to women's enfranchisement and other liberating measures initiated during the Pahlavi regime. And yet his earlier statements seemed to promise an Islamic Republic in which women would "have complete freedom in everything they do." Were these pronouncements mere public relations—meant to pacify potential critics and entice women to join in his revolutionary movement? In the immediate aftermath of the revolution, it became quite obvious that the Ayatollah's assertions regarding women's promised "freedom" represented nothing more than a disingenuous platform to amass support.

In reality, it took very little time for the post-revolutionary euphoria to subside. Once Khomeini took the reins, many of his female supporters, including Shirin Ebadi, became profoundly disillusioned. Stripped of her judgeship, as Islamic law prohibits women from serving as judges, she expressed her misconceptions about the revolution she had initially supported:

> It took scarcely a month for me to realize that, in fact, I had willingly and enthusiastically participated in my own demise. I was a woman, and this revolution demanded my defeat ... My naiveté astounds me.[21]

A NEW AND VIRTUOUS ORDER

With his triumphant comeback on February 1, 1979, the Ayatollah designated himself Iran's Supreme Leader, a position incorporated into the Constitution and regarded as the highest political and religious authority of the nation. Now the country would be governed according to the principles of Islamic law, thus ushering in "a new and virtuous order" in which secular affairs would conform to divine mandates.[22] Sharia law would replace secular law in every sphere of life: political, social, judicial, and economic. A significant part of the economy would be transferred from private to government hands. And the state under the Islamic Republic would dictate the standards of morality—from attire to family life to music.[23] The regime's outlook toward the West, and America in particular, was reflected in its declarations against the "great Satan" accompanied by the slogan "death to America" (*marg bar amrika*).[24]

The initial phase of the new administration was characterized by rapid Islamization, reinforcing patriarchal mandates within a legalized framework. Unquestionably, the enormous impact of this cultural upheaval was reflected in the overall status of women, who once again were entangled in clerical doctrine that justified their second-class standing. Iran's extreme ideological shift was a backward jolt for women. While the regime hailed women as guardians of the private sphere, it simultaneously instigated decrees depriving them of the rights and opportunities they had gained during the Pahlavi era.

These decrees included the abolition of the Family Protection Laws; reduction of the minimum marriage age to thirteen (changed in 1991 to fifteen); reinstitution of Islamic Retribution Laws (*Qesas*) stipulating that the "blood money" (*diyeh*) for women is half that of men, as is their share of inheritance; and reinstitution of temporary marriage (*sigheh*).[25] The practice of temporary marriage involves a valid contract that allows a couple to get married for anywhere from a few minutes to as long as ninety-nine years. Since Islam dictates that women be virgins when they get married, temporary marriage "legally wraps premarital sex in an Islamic code.... A married man can have as many temporary wives as he wants, and up to four permanent ones, and can break the contract anytime he wants, whereas women cannot." [26]

The overall status of women was shrouded in restrictions, with patriarchal pronouncements ingrained in the Civil Code and the Constitution of the Islamic Republic. In the Preamble to the Constitution, the separateness of "male" and "female" attributes was highlighted specifically where the previous regime strove to omit such distinctions:

> The family is the fundamental unit of society and the main center for the growth and edification of human beings.... The view of

the family unit delivers women from being regarded as an object or instrument in the service of promoting consumerism and exploitation. Not only does a woman recover thereby her momentous and precious function of motherhood and rearing ideologically committed human beings, she also assumes a pioneering social role … Given the weighty responsibilities that a woman thus assumes, she is accorded in Islam great value and nobility.[27]

The Islamic regime thus meant to convey that the new constitutional decrees would liberate women from being treated as "objects"—and enable them to take on the pioneering role of raising "ideologically committed human beings." In fact, the constitution's definition of "the rights of women" is supremely ironic. Article 21 of the Islamic Constitution ensures "the rights of women in all aspects, in conformity with Islamic criteria," implying that the laws applicable to the female population are subject to religious interpretation. In other words, women are ensured their rights, as long as those rights conform to the dictates of the patriarchal religious establishment.

And what are some of these dictates? Article 105 specifies that "in a relationship between a man and a woman, the man is responsible as head of the family." Article 1117 of the Civil Code incorporates stipulations such as "a husband may ban his wife from any technical profession that conflicts with family life or her character."[28] Article 907 of the Civil Code stipulates that when a father dies, his son(s) are entitled to twice as much as his daughter(s).[29] And Article 1108 states: "If the wife refuses to fulfill the duties of a wife without a legitimate excuse, she will not be entitled to *nafaqa* (maintenance)." "Maintenance" refers to the husband's duty to financially support his wife. Among the wife's "duties" are sexual submission and obedience (*tamkin*).[30]

Further sealing the fate of the female population were laws prohibiting women from the presidency and judgeships, along with compulsory veiling and gender segregation in communal arenas.

All of these laws were instigated for the purpose of redirecting women into what the clerical establishment saw as a female's "primary role in society: domestic responsibility."[31]

THE INHIBITING/LIBERATING VEIL

The most visible change initiated in the immediate aftermath of the revolution was that all women were now required to wear the veil (*hijab* or head covering) in public. How women felt about this requirement depended on their background and their own personal ideological disposition.

Assumed by some to be synonymous with an inferior status, the veil is, for many outsiders, symbolic of the radical gender policies of Iran's revolutionary leaders. However, the issue of this mysterious black garment needs to be framed within the context of a fundamentally conservative society beholden to religious customs.

In his pursuit of a progressive agenda, Reza Shah had enacted a strict policy prohibiting the veil. Although his son abandoned the enforcement of this law, a majority of the country's conservative population continued to be resentful of the trend toward a westernized dress code during the Pahlavi era. While restoration of the veil under the Islamic regime was shunned as an emblem of servitude by secular women, it was initially enthusiastically embraced by a large segment of women from traditional backgrounds.

The Islamic Republic's veiling decree did not automatically lead to compliance by all women, nor did it inhibit some from articulating their contempt against a burdensome custom. And yet mandatory veiling was welcomed by millions of women who appreciated the integrity and modesty symbolized by, in their view, a liberating milestone. Ironically, they were now emancipated to a degree they had not previously enjoyed. Since they were now required to wear the veil in public, they felt comfortable leaving the confines of their homes, whether to go to school or the workplace. In other words, girls and adult women could now venture into territory they had previously avoided. Reinforcement of the veil thus legitimized their entry into the public domain.

Shirin Ebadi vividly recalls:

Girls went to class in their hejabs—Rehabilitated! Healthy! ... A generation of women whose mothers had been tethered to the house found themselves in cities, reading books.... There was no pretext left for the patriarchs to keep their daughters out of school. Slowly, it became fashionable for the daughters of traditional families to attend college.[32]

Ebadi goes on to explain the manner in which imposition of this decree paradoxically empowered women who, despite rampant discrimination, became more active in public life:

The Islamic Republic had inadvertently championed traditional women.... For they had been given a new awareness of their rights, but only crude tools to advance them.[33]

For the conservative segment of the female population, the veil did not signify either confinement or a repressive ideology; rather, it was an empowering garment that enabled them to break through previously impermeable boundaries.

Still, the veil continued to fuel conflict between the voices of tradition and modernity. Academy Award–nominated director and author Marjaneh Satrapi's internationally bestselling graphic memoir, *Persepolis: the Story of a Childhood*, offers a compelling yet humorous depiction of opposing attitudes pertaining to the veil. In one panel of her book, women on the left side shout *"The veil! The veil! The veil!"* as those on the right chant *"Freedom! Freedom! Freedom!"* Satrapi's caption reads: *"Everywhere in the streets there were demonstrations for and against the veil!* [34]

Although many progressive-minded women elected to leave the country during the initial phase of the revolutionary transition, those who reluctantly remained did not isolate themselves based on this decree. One secular woman who radically opposed the veil recalls grudgingly conceding to cover herself. In her critically acclaimed bestseller, *Reading Lolita in Tehran: A Memoir in Books,* Dr. Azar Nafisi writes of returning to work as a university professor in the years following the revolution and resenting the loss of integrity that the veil represented:

> It was not that piece of cloth that I rejected.... It was the transformation being imposed upon me that made me look in the mirror and hate the stranger I had become...that my integrity as a teacher and a woman was being compromised by its insistence that I wear the veil under false pretenses....[35]

While the modern woman felt demeaned and restricted by her inability to choose her own attire, the conservative woman, who had felt vulnerable leaving her home unveiled during the Pahlavi era, now felt protected.

In the three-and-a-half decades since the revolution, re-veiling initially proved to be the ultimate salvation for a vast majority of the female population, allowing them to take advantage of a westernized educational infrastructure instituted by the monarchy. Therefore, in many ways, the unanticipated consequence of the veil was that it "empowered those it was meant to restrain."[36]

ISLAMIZING EDUCATION

The Islamic Republic inherited the monarchy's system of education and almost immediately embarked on the task of purifying the embedded infrastructure in order to foster a solid Islamic identity. In fact, in its quest to Islamize the nation, one of the Republic's highest priorities was transformation of Iran's westernized education system. Shortly after the revolution's victory, Khomeini declared:

> Our universities are westoxicated.... Many of our universities are at the service of the West. They brainwash our youth.[37]

The term "westoxication" derives from the title of a well-known book written in the early 1960s by Iranian intellectual and author Jalal Al-i Ahmad entitled *Occidentosis: A Plague from the West*. Renowned for coining the term *gharbzadegi* (westoxication), the author critiqued the West, stressing the loss of cultural identity and the contradictions arising from rapid westernization in Iranian society. Al-i Ahmad maintained that this foreign intrusion would transform Iranians into "aliens with unfamiliar customs" and contended that the westernized vision of the "emancipated" Iranian woman would lead to "swelling an army of lipstick and powder aficionados."[38]

As part of Khomeini's new directive, it was stipulated that education at all levels must "reflect the independent nature of Islamic thought, and cleanse itself from all western values and influence," as the previous leadership was "contaminated and controlled by the superpowers...."[39] In accordance with this mandate, the Constitution specified providing all citizens with "free education through secondary school and expanding higher education to the extent required by the country for attaining self-sufficiency."[40]

Accordingly, the official launch of the Cultural Revolution (*Enqelab-e Farhangi*, 1980–1984) engaged in a systematic cleansing (*paksazi*) of every facet of Iranian life, including its educational landscape.[41] In 1980, the Council for Cultural Revolution, a seven-member task force selected by the Ayatollah, began dismissing all "non-believers," including professionals, administrators, students, professors, and supporters of the *ancien regime*. All universities were shut down for a period of four years (1980 through 1983) in order to formulate the foundations of an Islamic education. During this time, the Center for Textbooks, composed mainly of clerics, produced some 3,000 college-level textbooks in conformity with "Islamic criteria."[42]

When the universities reopened, they had been purged of all dissident faculty and pupils with a revised rule mandating "ideological testing" for recruitment and admission. This so-called "purification" procedure resulted in the departure of the country's most educated citizens, which struck "a major blow to Iran's intellectual life and achievement...job skills and capital."[43] What was Khomeini's response to the escalating brain drain? These are his words:

> They say there is a brain drain. Let these decaying brains flee and be replaced by more appropriate brains. These brains are of no use to us. If you know this is not the place for you, you should flee.[44]

Given the regime's aversion to a foreign ideology, the practice of study abroad, which had significantly climbed during the previous era, was almost entirely eliminated. According to statistics from the U.S. Bureau of Educational and Cultural Affairs, while in 1978/1979 there were some 50,000 Iranian students matriculated in institutions all over the United States, the numbers drastically diminished to 14,000 in 1985 and to barely 4,900 in 1992. Furthermore, as part of a fervent quest to dismantle all remnants of Western influence, a number of well-known modern schools of the Pahlavi period were renamed to reflect the sacred climate of the era. Religious practices were initiated, including daily prayers and Koranic studies, and a moral education teacher (*morrabi-ye tarbiat*), well-versed in Islam, presided over all religious functions. Persian became the primary language of instruction, and while English and other foreign languages were initially banned, they were allowed in later years.[45]

The new regime was additionally committed to allocating substantial funds toward the expansion of education and the extension of urban amenities to rural areas.[46] In this process, the Literacy Movement Organization (LMO) replaced the Literacy Corps of the Pahlavi era, tackling illiteracy and the training of qualified personnel committed to Khomeini's Doctrine of Clerical Rule (*Velayat-e Faqih*).[47] The First Republican Plan (1983–1988), presented under the banner of "changed priorities" and "new policies," underscored the importance of education within an Islamic framework in its opening statement:

> In Islam, education is a form of worship and the search for knowledge a jihad for Allah. Education is not just a social necessity, but a Holy Duty.[48]

By 1984, the Council for the Cultural Revolution, renamed the Supreme Council for the Cultural Revolution (SCCR, *Shoray-e Enqelab-e Farhangi*) and described as "the highest body for making policies and decisions in connection with all cultural, educational, and research activities within the framework of the general policies of the system," had evolved to having seventeen members with over twenty satellite institutions.[49] Headed by the country's president and accountable only to the Supreme Leader, this entity was composed of high-ranking Shiite clerics and powerful government figures, as well as the Women's Social and Cultural Council (WSCC), the Republic's first organization on women's affairs, established in 1988 within the SCCR to ensure conformity with Islamic principles for the female population at large.[50] In compliance with the regime's mandates, the council guaranteed "gender appropriateness" within academia by prohibiting married women from studying abroad unless accompanied by their husbands and restricting their enrollment in a variety of typically male-oriented disciplines, including mining, technology, animal husbandry, and agriculture.[51]

These restrictions adhered to the guidelines for gender instruction prescribed in the Principles of the System of Education decreed by the Ministry of Education, placing "education for girls and women" within the framework of "recognizing the identity of women and their roles within the family and society on the basis of Islam" and "planning for the content and method of her schooling accordingly."[52]

The plan additionally stipulated that the

educational guidance of girls should be based on their capabilities and interests, and their vocational guidance should take into consideration the kind of occupations needed by and best fulfilled by women given their role and responsibility within the family ... with curriculum development emphasizing the sanctity and stability of the family by introducing the different role of men and women in marital life.[53]

The educational ideology of the Republic stood in stark contrast to that of the Pahlavi regime, wherein educational objectives avoided gender-specific formulations and were stipulated in the context of "providing equal opportunity for all Iranian men and women, in all classes of the population, urban or rural."[54] The moral educational goals were additionally specified within the framework of cultivating "human qualities and virtues inspired by spiritual principles, while making judicious use of social rights ... [as] members of a free and progressive society."[55] A delineation of religious instruction was noticeably absent within the defined objectives and ethos of the Pahlavi educational establishment.

Khomeini's aim was to dismantle the Shah's educational system and infuse Islamic ideology into every aspect of Iran's academic environment. Given the Islamic Republic's preeminent objective, logic dictates that the strategy would be to revert back to the traditional *maktab* school system. What is puzzling here is that for unspecified reasons, the state chose to retain the infrastructure created by the Pahlavi regime—one that was facilitated by a team of Western advisers.

In referring to this miscalculation, author David Menashri estimates that this unusual course of action indicates that the Republic had "inherited a working institution ... which was readily available for [its] use."[56] An alternate explanation for this significant oversight could simply be a lack of expertise in the art of nation-building by the architects of a newly conceived Islamic empire.

In the aftermath of the revolution, Khomeini continued his gender-biased sermons, which combined with the already enumerated directives concerning the female population at large, point to his overriding conviction that female education must be compatible with women's "role" and "responsibility" within the family. With that said, it is important to note that although women were not prohibited from pursuing a career, the plethora of patriarchal edicts handicapped their autonomy in society. Author Parvin Paidar concludes that the regime was confident that their traditional gender policies would work to consolidate women's continuous support.[57]

There is no doubt that Ayatollah Khomeini regarded education as means to cultivate the ideal person (*ensanha-ye nemuneh*), and that this would be accomplished through transformation of the educational system into "training" (*tarbiyyat*) institutions.[58] It was his intention that female education instill in future mothers the proper knowledge to raise children according to the ideals of the ruling authority. Given these objectives, however, one is left with these questions: Did Ayatollah Khomeini really execute radically new educational policies? Or did he inadvertently maintain much of the monarchy's curriculum? Were the elementary school textbooks inherited from the Pahlavi era unintentionally left largely intact—and is it therefore possible that the Islamic regime merely imported westernized educational materials from the Shah's administration—only superficially instilling them with religious dogma?

DID KHOMEINI FORGET TO DE-WESTERNIZE THE SCHOOL BOOKS?

The clue to one of Khomeini's biggest blunders lies in the illustrated pages of Iran's post-revolutionary elementary school textbooks. The regime meant to "cleanse" all educational content of its "westoxicated" ideology, but did they overlook an important building block of the educational infrastructure? To what extent did these seemingly innocent curriculum materials adhere to or deviate from the gender ideology of Islamic lawmakers? In order to answer these questions, it is necessary to ascertain whether Iranian schoolgirls were exposed to images and ideology that conflicted with the government's desired role for women in an Islamic Republic—that of wife and mother.

As discussed in Chapter Three, child development experts affirm that the pre-adolescent years (ages seven to twelve) are when core values are instilled. Given the relevance of what sociologists regard as the "impressionable" pre-adolescent phase, it is essential to examine elementary school textbooks as a crucial component of the socialization mechanism and determine whether or not they achieve socially defined gender roles.[59]

Textbooks at this particular level are considered to be one of the major tools communicating relevant information regarding ethics, codes of conduct, and behavioral guidelines by the ruling entity. And textbook content is an important indicator of gender socialization among the younger generation, who are future participants in the society at large.[60] Renowned sociologists Jerome Karabel and A. H. Halsey maintain that "revolutions do not merely make educational change possible, they require it...."[61]

Given this all-important distinction, the academic arena requires transformation in order to sufficiently reflect the ideological tenets of the regime. Failure to undertake such changes may undermine the revolution, "for it is the education system that is responsible for the molding of future generations...."[62] And the purpose of education, as sociologist Emile Durkheim concluded in his studies on the socialization of young children within the school system,

> is to arouse and develop in the child a certain number of intellectual and moral states which are demanded of him by both the political society as a whole and by the specific environment for which he is particularly destined.[63]

Therefore, the possibility that the "intellectual and moral states" of elementary schoolgirls may have inadvertently been impacted and developed by the relatively liberal imagery and text included in the Pahlavi era textbooks is profoundly consequential.

Although the few studies done on post-revolutionary elementary textbooks have noted the insertion of religious content, research concerning identity formation by way of a revised elementary curriculum remained relatively unexplored, specifically where it applied to long-term implications for the female population at large.

Therefore, this research study was undertaken. In examining both text and illustrations in the elementary textbooks (grades 1–5) of the Republican era, specific attention was given to *gender ideology*—a term referring to attitudes regarding the appropriate, expected roles and obligations of men and women in a given society.[64] A "traditional" gender ideology emphasizes the distinctive roles assigned to both sexes based on presumed differences, with men fulfilling their primary duty as breadwinners, and women as homemakers and principal caregivers within the family unit. In direct contrast, an "egalitarian" ideology regarding the family unit endorses the shared responsibility of both men and women in the private and public sphere.[65]

Textbook topics, themes, and storylines were assessed for gender visibility, professional and domestic undertakings, and performance of stereotypical and nonstereotypical tasks, in order to determine the overall message internalized by young minds regarding the "appropriate" male and female roles in an Islamic society and the degree to which the curriculum mirrored the gender ideology of the ruling entity.

The study's findings are as follows:

In the *Reading and Writing Farsi (Khandan va Neveshtan-e Farsi)* textbooks (grades 1–5) of the Islamic Republic:

- Men, women, and children are cloaked in somber attire, with the female population conforming to the veiling laws of the regime.
- Women are portrayed as mothers, wives, teachers, and physicians.[66]

- Women are also shown undertaking numerous rural tasks and engaging in various professional occupations in the urban community at large.[67]
- There are relatively few passages and illustrations presenting women in typically "blue-collar" occupations. Those cited and/or exhibited include "factory worker" and "seamstress."[68]
- Men are depicted as fathers, husbands, soldiers, pilots, farmers, physicians, and teachers.[69] Moreover, they are pictured in diversified blue-collar occupations, including construction worker, mailman, grocer, and cobbler.[70]
- Aside from their portrayal in the medical, education, and aviation industries, the male population is conspicuously nonexistent in excerpts and images representing them in any other occupational capacity.
- The absence of women from manual and technical labor is countered by their presence in an array of white-collar vocations exemplified by their portrayal in medical and healthcare facilities and an assortment of professional office settings.[71]
- The lack of women in the specified unskilled trades is not highly unusual, in view of the fact that until fairly recently, the delineated tasks tended to be performed by men in most traditional and Western societies.
- Contrary to strict Islamic ideology, public segregation of men and women is portrayed only in classroom settings and mosque prayer scenes.[72] Female instructors are shown teaching girls, and male instructors are exclusively situated in the boys classroom,[73] but in every other public or private environment, integration of the sexes is shown, with boys and girls frequently portrayed together in various leisurely activities.
- Mothers, fathers, and children are seen interacting as a family unit, both within the household and in the community at large.

Post-revolutionary elementary school textbooks.

♦ The following textbook passages and illustrations reflect scenes highlighting public and private interaction with the opposite sex, in addition to a shared responsibility in performing domestic chores and parental cooperation in child rearing:

▶ Men, women, and children engaged in farm labor[74]

▶ Kitchen scene:
  • Young girl fills the sugar bowl
  • Mother washes the spoons and plates
  • Father carries the serving tray of teapot and teacups[75]

▶ Mothers and fathers shopping with their children in the bazaars[76]

▶ Boys and girls walking together to and from school, sharing picture books, playing in the snow, and building a snowman (see below)[77]

▶ Narrative of a young girl simultaneously comforted by her father and mother[78]

Post-revolutionary elementary school textbooks.

▶ Passage about a father tenderly and lovingly dispensing advice to his daughter[79]

In the social studies (*Taalimat-e Ejtemai*), mathematics (*Riazi*), and science (*Ulum-e Tajrobi*) textbooks of the Islamic Republic:

- There is no evidence relating to stereotypical chores performed by the female population. The social studies books are essentially constituted by geography lessons and extensive narratives on revered Islamic figures and ancient Persian rulers. Except for classroom scenes, men, women, and children continue to be shown in "mixed" settings, participating in a variety of indoor and outdoor activities.

- The mathematics and science books substantially replicate those from the late Pahlavi period, with an overall balanced depiction of boys and girls engaged in coloring activities, laboratory experiments, and field assignments.

- Both sexes adorn the pages of most textbooks and are likewise illustrated in a multitude of coeducational settings in the scientific arena.[80]

- Men and women continue to be engaged in a variety of leisurely activities and continue to be shown as mothers, fathers, instructors, and physicians.

- In a photograph of children playing in the park, some of the girls are surprisingly shown without their headscarves (next page).[81] This may have been a snapshot inadvertently incorporated from the Pahlavi period, but an obvious faux pas by the architects of the post-revolutionary educational system.

In the second grade religious manual introduced by the Islamic Republic, entitled *Gifts from Heaven* (*Hediye-hay-e Asemani*):

- God's illustrious attributes and His venerated gifts to humankind are enumerated.

- There is extensive coverage of sacred Islamic customs and time-honored celebrations, narratives about the Prophet Muhammad and members of his immediate family, and descriptions of major world religions.

Post-revolutionary elementary school textbooks.

♦ With regard to the manner in which males and females are depicted, only three sections in the entire *Gifts from Heaven* series describe the role and responsibility of men and women in the family. The following passages highlight the importance of marital partnership in an Islamic community:

1. Mr. Mahmoud Hashemi (husband/father) works in the post office, and Tahereh Khanum (wife/mother) is a homemaker. In this family everyone is obligated to help one another. When Mr. Hashemi leaves work, he shops for the family on his way home. In addition to housework, Tahereh Kanum works as a seamstress so that she is able to contribute to the household expenses with the money she earns.[82]

2. We are all members of the same family. Mothers and fathers provide us with food, clothing, and shelter. They take care of us and when we are sick they take us to the doctor. Mothers and fathers are kind and they make sacrifices for our comfort.[83]

3. Every member of the family has a responsibility. Usually the father works outside of the house. In some families, the mother works outside of the house as well. In villages, women work in agriculture and carpet weaving. In cities, some women work in schools, hospitals, factories, and offices.[84]

It is important to note that these excerpts are not altogether indicative of a traditional division of labor, nor do they exclusively delegate domestic and childcare responsibilities to the female head of the household. They neither reflect the myriad gender-biased declarations of Islamic leaders, nor endorse many of the laws designed to redirect women into the private sphere.

In the *Koranic Studies* (*Amuzesh-e Koran*) textbooks of the Islamic Republic:

- Strictly based on religious guidance and discipline, the content and images are comparable to the *Reading and Writing Farsi* textbooks in their depiction of gender roles in the household and community at large.
- Segregation of boys and girls is found only in the depiction of prayer sessions in mosques and all instructional spaces.
- On the other hand, families are shown in a number of outdoor recreational activities, with a noticeable absence of specific references to male/female functions and any citations of religious justifications for gender stereotyping.

TEXTBOOK STUDY CONCLUSIONS

The secular curriculum of the monarchy was indeed transformed as part of the Islamic Republic's overriding mission to cultivate and nurture the ideal citizen, with the overall aim being to blend Islamic principles into the educational system. However, with the exception of classroom and prayer scenes, the integration of the sexes is clearly apparent in the schoolbooks' depiction of leisure activities. These graphics neither endorse nor reflect the Republic's mandate for the public segregation of men and women outside of the private sphere. But somehow they were not edited out of the Republic's educational materials.

Additionally, secular role models featured in post-revolutionary textbooks are virtually identical to those of the Pahlavi era. For example, the celebrated physicians Muhammad Zakariya Razi (AD 864–930) and Avicenna (c. 980–1037), representing the Golden Age of Persia, are acknowledged for their humanitarian contributions, and ancient Persian dynasties and their rulers are eulogized for their conquests. Renowned Persian poets Hafez, Saadi, and Ferdowsi are praised for their classical prose, and noteworthy inventions of the late nineteenth and early twentieth centuries by Alexander Graham Bell, the Wright brothers, and Thomas Edison are extolled.

It must be stated that during the monarchy, female role models were generally nonexistent in elementary texts, other than mothers, teachers, and the *Shahbanou* (Empress) of Iran and wife of Moham-mad Reza Pahlavi.[85] The recurring theme of motherhood, however, is one that is highlighted in numerous passages in the Farsi text-books of both the Pahlavi and Khomeini eras. Women as mothers are uniformly exalted in poems such as "Kinder than Mother" and "Mother"—commemorative tributes to a mother's nurturance, em-pathy, and devotion to the younger generation.[86]

It can be argued that both regimes fundamentally presented the world from an overtly male perspective: both failed to mention wor-thy contributions made by women in various fields.

The overarching question is this: Did the gender ideology con-veyed in the "Islamized" curriculum differ substantially from that found in Pahlavi era textbooks? This study concluded that it did not. In fact, it may surprise many to learn that the books utilized in post-revolutionary elementary schools often praise, acknowledge, and are appreciative of contributions made by all family members, and do not typically portray a society that discriminates against women. Aside from being shown wearing the veil and being segre-gated in the classroom, girls and women are presented as autono-mous beings, relatively unburdened by household tasks. The Islamic era schoolbooks do not reflect an aversion to women's employment, nor do they appear to view women's economic activities as secondary to domestic and maternal obligations.

Given such evidence, it is possible to conclude that a distinctly inadequate effort was made to socialize female students so that they would be induced to conform to the Republic's vision of the ideal Islamic woman.

With that said, it is important to acknowledge that the elementary curriculum in both the Pahlavi and Khomeini periods may not have been entirely successful in systematically and sufficiently socializing young women to embrace the respective gender ideologies of either the monarchical or the Islamic prototype. Interestingly, while textbooks from the Khomeini era depict a wide array of professions for both women and men, books from the reign of Mohammad Reza Pahlavi underscore household and teaching roles for women but fail to include potential occupations available to females in a progressive society.

While the Republic intended to indoctrinate young minds with its patriarchal dogma, it proved inadequate in socializing the pre-adolescent female population. The "revised" post-revolutionary—era elementary textbooks *did not* differ substantially from those of the Pahlavi regime because the Khomeini regime neglected to make significant changes when they adapted the schoolbooks from the previous government. This meant that the books distributed at the newly Islamized schools were insufficiently revised versions of those from the secular, westernized Pahlavi period.

The significance of this major oversight is that girls from traditional backgrounds were exposed to a world beyond their formerly sheltered lives. It is especially relevant that young girls' exposure to images and ideology that did not reflect the preferred female role in an Islamic society—that of wife and mother—occurred during the impressionable pre-adolescent years—a crucial time when culturally and socially defined gender roles are acquired.[87]

How did this happen? How did Islamic officials in charge of educational policies fail to notice that these textbooks contained images and text that clearly reflected Western values?

When the Islamic Republic undertook its Cultural Revolution to Islamize the nation, the logical course of action with regard to education would have been to completely dismantle the westernized school system put in place by the Pahlavis and replace it with the *maktab* structure that existed prior to the monarchy. Islamist officials also would have rewritten all the textbooks to accurately reflect the state's preferred role for women. But by neglecting to make these changes, the Khomeini administration left the door open for schoolgirls to learn a way of life that was essentially incompatible with conservative Islamic values. And this fundamental blunder partially accounts for the failed gender ideology of the Islamic Republic.

In addition, since the coeducational schools ushered in during the Pahlavi era were now transformed into same-sex institutions, girls from conservative families who had previously been kept at home could now go to school in the newly chaste environment. Unbeknownst to the architects of post-revolutionary educational policy, Iran's same-sex classrooms also opened a new door to female empowerment.

GIRLS ONLY! — SINGLE-SEX EDUCATION

In the aftermath of the revolution, the Islamic Republic under Khomeini instituted policies segregating the sexes in order to reinstate a culture of modesty and conservatism. Soon after the collapse of the Pahlavi monarchy, the Ministry of Education banned coeducation in academia as part of the measures initiated to "bring back a glorious tradition of what was perceived to be 'true' Islam."[88] By 1982, all levels except for higher education were transformed into single-sex institutions, expediting the entry of the traditional female population into the educational arena.

Coeducation instituted by the Pahlavi monarchy had been one of the numerous measures that was largely unfamiliar—and in some cases even viewed as offensive—to conservative families who for centuries adhered to the cultural notion that women should be separated from men. Therefore, it was not surprising that many of these families kept their girls from attending the coed schools of the Pahlavi era. Although the Literacy Corps during the Shah's regime had adopted strategies intended to attract conservative families, such as Koran recitations to the separation of boys and girls within the classroom, the inability of the conservative population to adjust to the monarchy's policies prohibited them from participating in the new educational program.

The eradication of coeducation, seen as incompatible with the intrinsic nature of Iranian society, likely contributed to the liberation of many traditional young women by inadvertently providing them with an enhanced learning environment. In fact, perhaps the Republic's greatest triumph in instituting same-sex education was an influx of rural women into the classroom.[89] According to the 1976 census, a mere 10 percent of all women residing in provincial regions were literate. In 1986, this figure stood at 37 percent. In 1996 it was 78 percent, and by 2006 it had increased to well over 90 percent.[90] (Although this remarkable occurrence reflects the power of Islam for traditional families, it is important to note that while during the late Pahlavi period over half of Iran's population lived in the provinces, by 1996, over 60 percent had migrated to urban areas.)[91]

How did same-sex education, ushered in with the Islamic Revolution, benefit girls from the conservative families who made up a majority of the Iranian population? Was the Islamic Republic's decree for separating the sexes a blessing in disguise for future generations of Iranian women?

The previous section on post-revolutionary elementary textbooks revealed how the Islamic regime failed to adequately communicate to the younger generation of females the image of the time-honored Muslim woman—an unintended consequence of utilizing minimally revised Pahlavi-era educational materials. Same-sex classrooms also represent an unintended consequence in that young women became more empowered as a result of being educated in a segregated (female only) environment.

The government's decree mandating gender segregation in Iran's schools has been broadly cited by historians as responsible for luring young women from modest families into the educational arena. However, the social and academic advantages of same-sex education have been inadequately addressed in terms of providing for Iranian girls an avenue away from "traditional" life and toward female self-determination.

A number of analyses since the early 1990s among Western nations testify to the benefits associated with adolescent young women acquiring an education in single-sex schools. These studies may help to explain not only the advances in Iranian women's achievements, despite the patriarchal decrees, but the seismic shift in their perspective on women's role in society and their determination to overcome a subordinate status.

Research applicable to Iranian women and their experience in single-sex institutions is virtually nonexistent, as no studies have considered its potential benefits as a means for counteracting the dictates of a patriarchal society. This investigation is therefore focused on Western research—specifically that pertaining to pre-adolescent and adolescent girls.

For the purpose of this book, it was important to consider the impact on pre-adolescent and adolescent girls. As renoun social psychologist Erik Erikson (1902–1994) points out, this is a crucial time for identity formation and gender-role socialization. Erikson is best known for coining the term "identity crisis," and while he acknowledged that identity issues occur throughout an individual's lifetime, dilemmas associated with its formation are more intense as children transition into adolescence.[92] Psychologists elaborate on this theory by confirming that during the pre-teenage and teenage years, males and females are especially cautious to ensure gender-role conformity.

While early adolescence represents a difficult milestone for both sexes, it is considered to be an especially challenging juncture for girls.[93] The transformation of a young girl into a young woman is complex, as it entails meeting the unique demands of society, which at times assigns females roles that are clearly less valued than those allocated to men. Studies have reported a substantial deterioration in the self-esteem and confidence levels of adolescent girls, which often occurs at the expense of academic achievement.[94] The conflicted view of the self during those years is supported by research showing that girls need to be actively encouraged to participate in class and therefore require additional nurturing and teacher time.[95]

Could single-sex schools be the answer? The value of acquiring an education in single-sex schools, especially for girls, has become the subject of an ongoing debate in the United States and other Western countries over the last two decades.

The origins of coeducation in the United States date back to the mid-nineteenth century, when women initially demanded access to education as part of the early efforts spearheaded by equal rights activists, whose leaders maintained that "mixed" learning environments were an essential prerequisite of emancipating women from their "separate sphere."[96]

During this period, select communities in Massachusetts began to experiment with the "radical" concept of a high school education for girls, and the coeducational "common school system" pioneered by education reformer Horace Mann came to be seen as "America's great equalizer."[97] The impact of this revolutionary new concept varied considerably among different groups, with adversaries becoming increasingly concerned about the sexual consequences of a mixed learning environment, as well as the necessity for boys and girls to be educated separately for their "distinct life paths."[98] Advocates of coeducation countered that it gave girls access to better educational opportunities, while their presence in class would placate the rambunctious nature of boys. This contentious debate was eventually resolved on the basis that separate schools for girls and boys ultimately required higher taxes and consequently should be viewed as an economically unviable and unfeasible option.[99]

In 1961, sociologist and author James Coleman questioned the social climate of coeducational institutions in the United States, concluding that the prevailing youth culture, which interfered with academic performance and underscored popularity, proved especially damaging for girls, who became consumed with a self-imposed mission to render themselves "desirable objects for boys."[100]

It took another two decades for additional studies to confirm Coleman's earlier findings and to draw attention to ongoing sexism in coeducational schools. By the early 1990s, a number of new studies began to report that girls were in fact not receiving the same quality of education as boys, due primarily to male disciplinary problems demanding additional teacher time and attention.[101] Nationally acclaimed reports claimed an unconscious gender bias in coeducational classrooms that significantly shortchanges young women both so-cially and academically.[102]

The publication of these studies offered a new message: "Schools without boys seem to be good for girls."[103]

Among the most relevant findings:

- ◆ Noted psychologist Carol Gilligan refers to the adolescent years as a "watershed in female development, a time when girls are in danger of drowning or disappearing."[104] She maintains that girls often lose their "authentic voice" during adolescence as they become overwhelmed by the patriarchy of their daily surroundings.[105] In contrast to boys, Gilligan contends, girls tend to be "passive players" and consequently require additional encouragement in a coeducational classroom setting in order to overcome their reluctance to speak up.[106]
- ◆ Professors of Education Myra and David Sadker documented the challenges faced by adolescent girls stemming from gender bias in the school system.[107] In their 1994 book, *Failing at Fairness: How Our Schools Cheat Girls,* the Sadkers reported that boys dominated classroom discussions while girls reluctantly became *"passive participants."*[108] Teachers, the authors report, unintentionally spend the majority of their attention either praising, criticizing, correcting or assisting boys rather than girls.[109] The Sadkers argued that an "uneven distribution of teacher time" takes its toll on girls, often impacting their self-esteem and academic achievement and ultimately escalating into a "silent erosion of female potential."[110,111]

The Sadkers found that in single-sex schools, girls spoke their minds with ease, asked more questions, openly admitted to their confusion with confidence and determination to master the subject at hand, and were more successful in their studies.[112] The authors revealed that girls in single-sex schools have a stronger sense of identity, display more interest in the nontraditional subjects such as math and physical sciences, and find more positive role models and mentors.[113]

- The Wellesley College Center for Research on Women assessed the collective studies of adolescent girls' learning experiences,[114] surveying more than 1,300 studies. Documenting a shortfall for adolescent girls in receiving equitable amounts of teacher time, it cautioned that America might in fact be responsible for nurturing a generation of women with low self-esteem.[115]
- Dr. Rosemary Salomone, Associate Dean and Director of the Center for Law and Public Policy at St. John's University, published findings that support and corroborate those of earlier studies regarding the benefits of single-sex schools for adolescent young women.
- In 1990, Dr. Cornelius Riordan, Professor of Sociology at Providence College, released the first of many publications arguing that all-girls schools consistently provided a more effective educational atmosphere over coed schools.[116] In 2008, he published the results of a three-year study commissioned by the U.S. Department of Education, confirming the innate biological differences in the learning styles of boys and girls, overall positive student/teacher interaction, decreased distractions, and teacher testimonials for less serious behavioral problems in single-sex schools.[117]

While the very notion of separating boys and girls in the twenty-first century is considered by some to be an outdated approach, the extensive research exposing the natural learning differences between males and females has led many educators to view the single-sex model as creating more positive and equitable outcomes. Indeed, the benefits of a segregated learning environment tend to be especially pronounced for adolescent girls, frequently resulting in increased confidence, academic engagement, and achievement.[118]

How do these Western findings pertain to traditional schoolgirls of post-revolutionary Iran? Since single-sex schooling is inherently compatible with the underlying culture of modesty in Iranian society, girls have no choice but to learn within a segregated environment. And the benefits described in the Western studies apply to female Iranian students as well. The eradication of coeducation at the elementary and secondary levels may have proved to be blessing for Iranian girls, as it led to the avoidance of the obstacles affiliated with co-ed classrooms—difficulties that the studies have shown to interfere with women reaching their full potential. Furthermore, for young women born and raised in a patriarchal society, the benefits associated with a single-sex learning environment are priceless. The "girls-only" classroom becomes a haven, a place where female students can feel empowered.

The fact is that the so-called Islamization of education has proven to be responsible for generating unprecedented educational gains for the vast majority of the female population. The mandate for single-sex schools by the Islamic Republic created an atmosphere in which adolescent girls are allowed to have a voice without the constraints of a coeducational learning environment and consequently are given a platform to excel.

Single-sex education has dramatically contributed to providing Iranian girls with the social and psychological capacity to challenge the misogyny of the regime—and we will explore this further in the following chapter on the current women's movement in Iran.

FEMALE LITERACY SURGE

In the three-and-a-half decades since the Islamic Revolution, there has been an unprecedented surge in female literacy in Iran. On the eve of the revolution, the overall literacy rate for the country's female population stood at 35.5 percent. In 2007, it was an astonishing 80.34 percent.[119] Today, Iran exhibits one of the highest female-to-male ratios at the primary level among all sovereign nations. In 2006 the gender gap in Iran's universities closed, reflecting a 50/50 ratio, and by the 2007/2008 academic year it had shifted in favor of women.[120] The trend towards the "feminization" of higher education continues as women have begun to outnumber men at the post-graduate level by a ratio of 127/100.[121] A 2006 BBC article poignantly captures the obvious surplus of women in higher education:

> Twenty post-graduate students are sitting in a plush classroom listening to a lecture on environmental management at the Islamic Azad University—a private institution with 1.6 million students across Iran. Three quarters of the students in the classroom are women. The five men in the class are huddled together in a corner.[122]

This unique and unprecedented trend has been distinguished as a major stimulus fueling women's empowerment to resist and combat their mandated subordinate status. In this process, Iranian women are in effect obstructing the regime's envisioned objective of giving rise to the "ideal Muslim woman."[123] One is thus compelled to reflect on this irony: a nation that has legally handicapped half of its population has nonetheless systematically spawned a society noted for its surge in female literacy. Author Hamideh Sedghi points out that with their presence in the educational arena, "women have begun to pose indirect challenges to the political and social taboos that uphold womanhood and wifehood as a woman's primary responsibility."[124]

Iranian schoolgirls in post-revolutionary Iran.

Women in Iran continue to outnumber men in higher education.

PERSIAN "ROSIE THE RIVETERS"

Based on a popular song from 1943, "Rosie the Riveter" was not a real person. She symbolized the thousands of American women who joined the workforce during World War II in order to fill positions vacated by male workers who had been sent to war. Many of these women worked in munitions factories and at other jobs traditionally considered unsuitable for women.

During the Iran-Iraq War (1980–1988), Iranian women were similarly called upon to take on positions outside the home during this time of crisis.

The Iran-Iraq War began when Iraq invaded Iran in 1980, following a long history of border disputes. Partially motivated by fears that the 1979 Iranian Revolution would inspire insurgency among Iraq's Shiia majority, Iraq hoped to take advantage of the revolutionary chaos in Iran and attacked without formal warning. The war was costly for Iran, both in terms of lives lost and economic damages. But there was an unintended—and liberating—consequence for women.

Women during the Iran-Iraq War (1980-1988).

When Ayatollah Khomeini referred to the war as "a blessing" and called on women to assist in the war effort, he underestimated how women's participation would challenge the ideology of women's role in a patriarchal society.[125]

Initially paralyzed during the war by the absence of fathers and husbands, and burdened by their dual roles as providers and caregivers, women nevertheless responded with valor and conviction to the requirements of a daunting task. Women's rights activist, Azam Taleghani, recalls the nature of cooperation among women at large during this challenging time:

> During the war we joined the Sisters Mobilization Organization. We worked in the mosques, prepared food, blankets and medicines for the men at the war front.... In the war zone areas, women were involved in the distribution of arms amongst the population and the soldiers. In other areas, women set up mobile hospitals and looked after the injured. As the war continued, women had to return to their homes, but they still continued their voluntary work, and had to organize their time in a way that would allow them to do their housework and their voluntary work in order to keep their family members happy.[126]

Iranian women were mobilized in both urban and rural areas to cook, provide medical assistance, and seek employment to support their families—much in the same manner as World War II had compelled many women to do so. Women from traditional backgrounds, most of whom had not participated in mainstream society during the Pahlavi era, were now inspired to do so due to the exigencies of war. Reinstated Islamized dress codes meant they felt comfortable enough to emerge from their homes in order to earn an income and contribute to the war effort.

Author and researcher Dr. Elahe Rostami-Povey writes that the war reduced the supply of male labor and increased the number of women seeking work. Despite the "rigidities in the system, determined by the ideology of a gendered division of labor," the demand for workers meant that women filled positions in a number of fields previously deemed improper for females:

> The demand for female teachers and nurses increased, despite the initial attempt to stop women tending to male patients and teaching male students. Also, a significant number of women were employed, and even occupied important positions for the first time.[127]
>
> They worked at home, producing handbags, blankets, sheets, etc ... They sold them to the co-operatives, neighbors and local shops. Some worked as cab drivers. Their income was essential to cope with inflation, paid for their families' debt and mortgage, etc.... Furthermore, no one ever asked them what they did, and they thought if they were asked for statistical purposes, they would call themselves housewives, because they produced the commodities while they were doing the housework.[128]

Rostami-Povey reports that women also worked for small businesses that paid them less than the minimum wage. By not reporting these workers, employers avoided paying taxes to the state and benefits to the workers. This lack of recordkeeping also accounts for the fact that there are no statistics regarding how many women were employed during the war years. (By contrast, figures pertaining to the American workforce during World War II reveal that between 1940 and 1945, the percentage of women in the U.S. workforce increased from 27 percent to nearly 37 percent, and by 1945 nearly one out of every four married women worked outside the home.)[129]

Unfortunately, Iranian women's expanded roles during the eight-year war did little to alter the legal barriers erected by the Khomeini regime that barred them from their inherent rights in the family and in society at large. War widows, in particular, were outraged when Sharia-based laws assigned guardianship of minors and childcare payments from the Martyrs Foundation (*Bonyad-e Shahid*) to the child's paternal grandfather.[130] In 1985, as a result of vehement protests and petitions, the parliament approved a bill granting custody of children whose fathers had been killed in the war to their mothers.[131] Sporadic concessions such as this one signaled the state's need to rely on women in a calamitous time. Rising to the occasion, Iranian women took pride in their wartime resilience and self-sufficiency in the absence of men.

Author Louise Halper believes that as difficult as those years may have been, they were instrumental in "altering the consciousness of many women, particularly popular class[132] women [who] not only felt empowered, but [also] obliged to discuss their status and establish the continuity of their participation in public life."[133] And legal anthropologist Ziba Mir-Hosseini asserts that in light of women's wartime efforts, "a door from within was opened that could no longer be closed."[134]

In other words, having worked outside the home during the war, Iranian women proved to themselves and others that they could play an important role in the survival of their families and in the society at large.

ENVISIONING OPPORTUNITY

Certainly Khomeini did not intend for women to become empowered when he consolidated his rule. But as we have learned in this chapter, due to several of the policies he put into place—namely, single-sex schools and compulsory veiling—a majority of pre-adolescent and adolescent girls were able to glimpse the expanded opportunities that might await them. Many attended school for the first time, and through Western-influenced textbooks from the Pahlavi regime that had barely been altered, these girls learned about a way of life that fostered more self-determination and equality for women.

I believe that this unintended exposure likely accounts, at least in part, for why a new generation of women in Iran do not subscribe to the gender ideology of the Islamic Republic. I also contend that the quasi-westernized education that these girls received in single-sex schools is one of the underlying reasons that a women's movement has developed in post-revolutionary Iran.

I often get asked: *How is it that Iran is experiencing a feminist movement within a patriarchal Islamic climate? Why don't women who were born and raised in Iran after the revolution subscribe to the Islamic Republic's gender ideology? And what is fueling Iranian women's quest for empowerment despite continuous obstacles?* My briefest answer is this: even within a repressive environment, girls who are exposed to empowered female role models through books and a decent education—and who are free to learn and express themselves in a girls-only classroom—have a fighting chance.

In the next chapter we will discover how the schoolgirls of the Khomeini era grew up to participate in an unexpected yet fervent women's movement and are being joined by thousands of others, both secular and religious.

Chapter Five

A RELIGIOUS/SECULAR SISTERHOOD

Old enemies may turn into new political allies when it comes to resisting the onslaught of male supremacy.[1]
Parvin Paidar, author

We know that secular women do not share our convictions, but this does not give us any problems, since we are all working to promote the status of women.
Mahboubeh Abbasgholizadeh (aka Zahra Ommi), women's rights activist and editor in chief of *Farzaneh*, a post-revolutionary women's journal

If religion goes against freedom, it will lose.
Mohammad Khatami, former president of Iran (1997–2005)

With Ayatollah Khomeini's death in 1989, his successor, Ayatollah Ali Hosseini Khamenei, who served as Iran's president from 1981–1989, continued to uphold the sacredness of divine authority and supreme leadership of the nation. The gender-bias disposition of the ruling establishment continued, with Khamenei's numerous pronouncements, including:

The real value of a woman is measured by how much she makes her family environment for her husband and children like a paradise ....and the fundamental job assigned to a woman is marriage and motherhood.[2]

While the war years had been marked by ideological stability, the presidency of Akbar Hashemi Rafsanjani (1989–1997), following Iran's cease-fire with Iraq, marked the emerging stages of a more tolerant atmosphere. Although patriarchy continued to be the dominant force, the moderate changes instigated by Rafsanjani spread the seeds of a more lenient atmosphere for women in Iran. This new trend further gained momentum during the presidency of Mohammad Khatami (1997–2005), whose more progressive reforms, including those advancing women's rights, briefly displaced the conservative restrictions, facilitating the country's passage into what one journalist referred to as a "thrilling Tehran spring."[3]

In this chapter we will explore the post-revolutionary climate that inadvertently led to an unlikely sisterhood and a flourishing women's rights movement. Refusing to succumb to the demands of an ongoing misogynistic ideology, religious and secular women found common ground in challenging their subordinate status. Despite the fact that the majority of religious women seek reform within a non-Western, indigenous, or Koranic framework, and their secular sisters subscribe to a separation between "church and state" (and to the egalitarian principles enshrined in the 1979 Convention on the Elimination of All Forms of Discrimination Against Women), Iranian women disregarded their personal differences and gave precedence to eradicating an inferior existence.[4]

To provide a context in which to understand how Iranian women from such disparate factions became united in their goal to expand their rights and opportunities, we will examine the shifting political tides after Khomeini—from the reconstruction period of President Akbar Hashemi Rafsanjani through the reformist era of President Mohammad Khatami.

We will also survey the wide range of women's publications from this era that reveal female commitment to free expression and political struggle. And we will listen to the remarkable voices that gave birth to religious-secular solidarity—and what is referred to by some as Islamic feminism.

Ayatollah Ali Hosseini Khamenei

A DRIVING FORCE OF MODERATION

Following Ayatollah Khomeini's death, Aytatollah Ali Hosseini Khamenei was appointed as Iran's Supreme Leader and Ayatollah Hashemi Rafsanjani, an influential Shiite cleric, was elected as the fourth president of the Islamic Republic.

In the late 1950s, Ayatollah Rafsanjani had been a pupil and disciple of Ayatollah Khomeini at the Qom Theological Seminary, the largest center for Shiite scholarship in the world and a major pilgrimage destination. During the 1960s, Rafsanjani was imprisoned for organizing anti-Shah riots and for his political activities promoting Islamic resurgence. With the victory of the revolutionaries in 1979, he was elected Chairman of the Iranian Parliament and served as de facto commander in chief of the Iranian army during the Iran-Iraq War.

During Rafsanjani's presidency, Iran embarked on a period of reconstruction following the devastation of the war years. As a moderate facing serious challenges and a declining economy, he advocated a free market economy and favored privatization of state-owned industries.[5] He chose to have a cabinet of predomi-

President Ali Akbar Hashemi Rafsanjani (1989-1997)

nantly "well-educated technocrats rather than revolutionary ideologues," declaring that he wished for a "government of experts, not politicians … as is needed in the period of construction."[6] Criticized for having a significant number of "Western-educated" ministers, he responded by stating that "studying in American universities was not and is not a negative point."[7] Furthermore, he declared: "Iran cannot live in today's world without the material capabilities and the advancement of science and technology,"[8] an attitude that was in direct contrast to Khomeini's ideological disposition and cultural revolution.

Rafsanjani's shift in gender principles became apparent with his removal of quotas for women in fields of higher education and the launching of a nationwide campaign to stabilize the massive population growth.[9] His government reversed the Republic's opposition to family planning, and the Ministry of Health authorized clinics throughout the country to promote and dispense contraceptives as part of its family planning services, resulting in a dramatic reduction in population growth from 3.2 percent in 1986 to 1.5 percent by 1996.[10] According to the United Nations Population Fund

(UNFPA), Iran experienced one of the fastest-known reductions in fertility, with the most significant decreases occurring in rural areas.[11]

While minor criticism of the state was tolerated during Rafsanjani's tenure, demonstrations against the government in the early 1990s were severely repressed.[12] And yet opposition to the official ideology mounted. The moderate changes initiated under Rafsanjani were not sufficient to assuage the dissatisfaction with the new Islamic Republic among a number of factions. In the decade following the revolution, rising social tensions and criticism of the Islamic regime stimulated a rudimentary alliance between disillusioned supporters of the revolution and marginalized secular and religious women.[13] The interconnection between church and state that had been the dominant order for centuries—with only a brief interruption during the Pahlavi regime—was being challenged once again.

KHATAMI'S REFORMS

Disparity between the progressive and conservative visions of an Islamic state that surfaced during Rasfanjani's term continued to give rise to ideological conflict. Reform-minded constituencies opposed to traditionalist policies led to the ascendency of Mohammad Khatami, who served as Iran's president from 1997 to 2005. A moderate cleric whose reformist policies would displace the previous conservative agenda, Khatami had

President Mohammad Khatami (1997–2005).

~ 133

served as Iran's Minister of Culture and Islamic Guidance (1982-1986 and 1989-1992).

The reform movement ushered in by Khatami resulted in the modification of numerous patriarchal decrees, thereby diminishing repressive measures, including those pertaining to family law, education, and employment.[14] Not only were a number of reformist politicians and Islamist women appointed to positions of authority, but the Center for Women's Participation (*Markaz-e Mosharekat-e Zanan*) was created as an extension of the president's office in order to raise awareness and improve women's rights.

Among the accomplished women appointed to office were Zahra Shojaie as Advisor on Women's Affairs, Massomeh Ebtekar as Head of the Environmental Protection Organization, Dr. Jamileh Kadivar as Special Advisor on Press Affairs, Dr. Zahra Rahnavard as Chancellor of Al Zahra University, and Khatami's wife, Zohreh Sadeghi, as head of a newly-conceived committee for addressing the deficient conditions of rural women.[15]

The appointment of Dr. Ata'llah Mohajerani, husband of Dr. Jamileh Kadivar, as Minister of Culture and Islamic Guidance, fostered greater autonomy in the media and the arts, substantially accelerating the dissemination of controversial literary and cinematic works. Previously affiliated with Rafsanjani's Construction Party, Dr. Mohajerani's official liberal stance of "tolerance and laxity" (*tasahol va tasameh*) was the basis for a directive that sustained a dynamic women's press, already set in motion by Khatami in his capacity as Minister of Culture and Islamic Guidance under Rafsanjani.[16]

Avant-garde filmmakers, including Tahmineh Milani (*Two Women*, 1999), Rakhshan Bani Etemad (*The May Lady*, 1997), and Samira Makhmalbaf (*The Apple*, 1998), along with progressive female journalists at various women's publications, reflected the growing artistic and social forces challenging Iran's suffocating patriarchal atmosphere.[17]

New organizations and publications employed a more tolerant rhetoric, asserting the need for a "radical re-thinking of law, policy, and constitution." The formation of more than six hundred nongovernmental organizations (NGOs) contributed to the integration of women from divergent backgrounds,[18] and this ambitious undertaking elevated the consciousness of the female population, who began to participate in a variety of reformist groups engaging in gender debate and resolution.[19]

Although these forms of expression began to penetrate Iranian society, persistent interventions by the Council of Guardians and the Supreme Leader disrupted the progressive platform, which as early as 1998 was threatened with laws forbidding the use of non-Sharia standards for advocating women's rights.[20]

By April of 2000, such assaults, symbolic of the ongoing political schism, led to the closure of over thirty reformist publications and the arrest and imprisonment of numerous defiant journalists. The attempt to repeal such severe rulings by a parliament controlled by reformists merely exacerbated tensions, prompting Ayatollah Khamenei to release the following statement:

> If the enemies infiltrate our press, this will be a big danger to the country's security and the people's religious beliefs. I do not deem it right to keep silent.... There are 10 to 15 papers writing as if they are from one center, undermining Islamic and revolutionary principles, insulting constitutional bodies, creating tension and discord in society.... Unfortunately, the same enemy who wants to overthrow the regime has found a base in the country.[21]

In the same year, the coerced resignation of Minister of Culture Mohajerani amidst allegations of a "permissive stance" further solidified the crackdown.[22] These attacks were especially disconcerting for Khatami's female constituency, who, along with the country's youth, had been drawn into a pledge of "religious democracy."[23] Furthermore, except for Zahra Shojaie, who held cabinet rank as the president's advisor, the obvious absence of women in ministerial positions after Khatami had vowed "he would make no distinction between men and women when it came to assigning [cabinet] posts" only appeared to validate claims of the Islamic Republic's deceptions.[24]

Although for many, Khatami's election may have culminated in unrealized promises, his more lenient and unconventional policies were incompatible with the antiquated ideology of a conservative leadership. Despite Khatami's popularity and his landslide victory, he was routinely handicapped by the power elite, whose members denounced his constituency as "diseased people."[25] For example, when Khatami initiated the adoption of the Convention on the Elimination of All Forms of Discrimination Against Women (CEDAW), which was approved by a parliamentary majority, it was overruled by the Council of Guardians on the grounds that it "conflicted with several principles of the Constitution, including inheritance and divorce laws, the veil, and polygamy."[26] Given the severity of such impediments, it is likely that Khatami felt it necessary to proceed with caution, despite his campaign assurances, rather than take the risks inherent in making full-blown concessions to a "radical" agenda.

Nonetheless, Khatami's numerous moderate reforms partially account for an invigorated social platform whose influence continues to reverberate in Iran today. And historians acknowledge that by accepting the election of Khatami, Iran's conservative leadership "miscalculated the potential for the reform movement to garner popular support."[27] Author Ali Ansari estimates that "much to everyone's astonishment, the appeal of the modest intellectual proved infectious," while sociologist Asef Bayat confirms that "Khatami's discourse of civil society, democracy, transparency, and rule of law, which were quite absent in the 1980s, became the dominant concept."[28]

For women in particular, Khatami's moderate yet enlightened perspective was indeed inspiring. Encouraged by the more open political climate, many were empowered to actively strive for and advocate a more liberated existence. The Khatami administration's "move to allow greater freedom of expression to the press changed the face of media in Iran," effectively throwing open the floodgates for a thriving women's rights movement that to this day refuses to surrender, despite the barricades erected by powerful patriarchal forces.[29]

A UNIQUE BRAND OF FEMINISM

The seeds of a women's liberation crusade sown over a century ago in Iran blossomed into a unique brand of feminism during a most unexpected era. As the reformist platform gained increasing support during the Khatami era, a distinctive feminist movement was born. Energized by a new spirit of tolerance within the country and by an eclectic variety of post-revolutionary women's publications, women began to identify with a growing movement that defined itself under the banner of various labels, including "women's rights advocacy," "Islamic feminism," "secular feminism," and "indigenous feminism."[30]

In its broadest definition, feminism refers to the array of movements and ideologies "advocating women's rights on the grounds of sexual equality,"[31] and it has come to be regarded by many scholars as harmonious with an interpretation enabling "women to maintain their religious beliefs while promoting a more egalitarian Islam."[32]

Today, "Islamic feminism," a term initiated by female expatriates, flourishes as the predominant paradigm within Iran among both devout and secular women who seek equality within the bounds of religious scriptures.[33] Islamic feminism aims to dismantle the dominant gender precepts—that is, those passages in the Koran that justify the denigration of Iranian women and are then objectified in divine law.[34]

Scholars have debated the compatibility of the essentially Western ideology known as *feminism* with the formulation of an indigenous definition that is based only partially on that ideology. This new brand of feminism, which seeks to break the bonds of tradition through reinterpretation of Koranic passages, has been both simultaneously praised and criticized by scholars in Iran and abroad. Writers including Nayereh Tohidi, Afsaneh Najmabadi, Haleh Afshar, Valentine Moghadam, and Ziba Mir-Hosseini support the objective of Islamic feminism: the alteration of misogynist formulations within sacred manuscripts. They applaud this new directive for "expanding legal, literary and gender consciousness," thus authorizing a woman's right to *ijtihad* (independent reasoning) with respect to religious interpretation.[35] For women to actively pursue the authority to alter what has historically been regarded as divinely ordained in the Koran is extremely significant, particularly for religious women. Endorsement by prominent female writers of a revisionist approach to religious scripture not only aims to diminish clerical authority but "to recapture both the purity and vitality of Islam that existed at its inception."[36]

At the opposite end of the ideological spectrum are scholars Haideh Moghissi, Hammed Shahidian, and Sharzad Mojab, who assert that Islamic feminism is essentially "a compromise with patriarchy."[37] This group believes that a "religion based on hierarchy" is insufficient, particularly in its neglect of broader social issues, including sexuality and personal autonomy.[38] For example, Shahidian maintains:

> If feminism is a movement to abolish patriarchy, to protect human beings from being prisoners of fixed identities, to contribute towards a society in which individuals can fashion their lives free from economic, political, social and cultural constraints, then Islamic feminism proves considerably inadequate.[39]

Nonetheless, other historians assessing "women's responses to patriarchy" acknowledge that educated Muslim women, along with their secular counterparts and enlightened intellectuals, have been a significant force in constructing many of the early arguments concerning Islam, gender, and equality.[40] The rise of this new discourse has been instrumental in emphasizing that there is "no inherent or logical link between patriarchy and Islamic ideals."[41] Over the last two decades, the many voices in the vanguard of Iran's Islamic feminist movement have included the following women:

- ◆ **Zahra Rahnavard:** Former Chancellor of Al Zahra University; wife of former reformist prime minister and presidential candidate Mir Hossein Mousavi:

  > "Getting rid of discrimination and demanding equal rights with men is the number one priority for women in Tehran."[42]

- ◆ **Dr. Jamileh Kadivar:** Professor and founding member of the Association of Iranian Female Journalists:

  > "The interpretation of Islamic laws and regulations by the members of the Council of Guardians and some Islamic jurists has in practice disqualified women from running for presidential elections. Similar interpretations have been used to argue against women becoming deputy presidents, cabinet ministers

and local governors. I argue that some male conservative institutions have taken on the role of the official interpreters of the constitution and the shariah; however, these interpretations are being contested by women and through the changing political environment in Iran."[43]

◆ **Parvin Ardalan:** Journalist and cofounder of the One Million Signatures Campaign:

"Islamic laws are not fixed. Since the revolution, some articles have been changed; it is possible. Many laws are political rather than religious and it is up to the government if they want to change them...."[44]

◆ **Faezeh Hashemi:** Founder of the magazine *Zan (Woman)*; former member of parliament and head of the Women's Sports Federation; daughter of former President Rafsanjani:

"Some customs in our society have been imposed, and an imposed custom is without value and cannot persist. Therefore, when I do not believe in that custom and I do not believe them to be logical or I do not value them to be beneficial to society, especially to girls and women, I do not see it necessary to follow them."[45]

◆ **Azam Taleghani:** Former member of parliament; founder of the publication *Payam-e Hajar (Hajar's Message)*; daughter of Ayatollah Mahmoud Taleghani:

"People are united in wanting to keep an Islamic Republic, but if the Islamic Republic doesn't evolve and does not give priority to the will of the people, what remains of [the republic] to be kept?"[46]

◆ **Mehrangiz Kar:** Attorney and human rights activist:

"Today both religious and nonreligious women are bent on regaining their individual identity and freedom. Those who adhere to the principle of a religious government are striving to unearth feminist concepts in Islamic texts. And those who are advocates of the separation of religion and state parade their feminine identity using Western symbols and social attitudes. They also tirelessly fight to keep their lives private and out of sight of governmental agents. Overall, these two groups of women have inched closer to their ultimate goals throughout the years. They criticize the current situation and claim their rights."[47]

♦ **Shahla Lahiji:** Founder of Roshangaran Press:

"I can remember a book published by Roshangaran entitled *Women in Pursuit of Emancipation* for which I had to modify the introduction six times to obtain paper from the ministry [Ministry of Culture and Islamic Guidance], which had its reservations about the book. It would give me the paper [to print and publish the book] only if I changed some points in the book that it had not agreed with. Over one long year we published only one book. It was a difficult beginning. What encouraged me to continue was my belief that a principal duty of a publisher was to discover young voices that expressed what was new in society."[48]

♦ **Shirin Ebadi:** Nobel Laureate and prominent attorney:

"Getting to understand Islam well and encouraging women to learn different interpretations of Islam is important. So when governments tell women "this is Islam," they will be well-equipped to counter their arguments."[49]

♦ **Shahla Sherkat:** Founder and editor in chief of *Zanan:*

"I do not believe in the division of women. Calling this reformist, and that secular and this religious or conservative, for example, does not help. We have complex and interrelated problems and it is best for us that no divisions are made. We are all trying to focus on the goals that aim towards consolidating women's rights. In the future when we resolve these problems we will have enough time to divide ourselves into numerous groups. I think the reason behind our strength and the fact that our movement is effective and has a bigger impact is because we have a variety of different views without being divided."[50]

And there have been a number of influential male supporters of this new movement as well, including Abdolkarim Soroush, Professor and nonclerical religious intellectual, about whom we will learn more in the following chapter:

"Our comprehension of religion is scientifically, socially, and culturally constructed, and hence open to interpretation."[51]

These powerful voices are blending with those of many like-minded women and men to express a new truth: the antidote to the poison of patriarchy and factionalism lies in a humane, moderate Islam that can evolve and adapt to a changing world. Proponents of Iran's new indigenous feminism are demanding that ambiguous Koranic passages are no longer to be misconstrued in order to define and constrain women as subordinate and inferior.

A theology-based rejection of unequal status according to gender came to the forefront during Khatami's presidency and continues to challenge institutionalized codes of conduct in contemporary Islamic society. And as we will discover, a range of post-revolutionary women's publications, from the distinctly conservative to the strikingly progressive, reflect the nuances of this unique brand of feminism.[52]

WOMEN'S MAGAZINES OF THE POST-REVOLUTIONARY ERA

Among the well-known women's publications of this era, a select few upheld the sanctity of immutable religious laws, while the majority became forceful advocates for change. Studies of women's magazines from this period reveal various approaches to both promoting and denouncing the patriarchal status quo within Iran. The publications advocating for women's rights represent an intellectual tour de force, disseminating a woman-centered discourse grounded in the moral and spiritual dimensions of divine doctrine.[53]

Feminist scholar Valentine Moghadam believes that "women's continuous exposure to ideological challenges undermined efforts to redomesticate and privatize them, and because these women were ideologically correct, they could not be accused of *gharbzadegi* (westoxication)."[54]

The ideological challenges to which Moghadam refers are reflected in the following magazines: *Payam-e Hajar (Hajar's Message)*, *Hoquq-e Zanan (Women's Rights)*, *Jens-e Dovom (The Second Sex)*, *Zan (Woman)*, *Farzaneh (Wise)*, and *Zanan (Women)*. These groundbreaking publications embarked on a campaign to conceptualize alternative interpretations of Iran's enforced religious dogma.

Payam-e Hajar (Hajar's Message)

The weekly *Payam-e Hajar* (1980–2000), named after the Prophet Abraham's wife and launched by Azam Taleghani, became a success virtually overnight by adopting a moderate position—denouncing both the "westoxicated" woman and the traditional Muslim woman of the official ideology.[55] A political prisoner during the reign of Mohammad Reza Pahlavi for her anti-regime activities, and a member of the first revolutionary parliament, Taleghani was among the initial wave of disenchanted Islamist women who began advocating equal rights by challenging the outdated scriptures.[56]

As the official journal of the Islamic Women's Institution (*Mo'assesseh-ye Eslami-ye Zanan-e Irani*), for which Taleghani served as director, *Payam-e Hajar* openly contested the premise of many patriarchal laws in Iranian society. In one of her editorials, Taleghani argued that while the law recognizes a man's right to "take up to four wives as long as he is able to treat them all equally, the very fact that the infallible Prophet Muhammad was in principle unable to perform this task would make it highly inconceivable for the ordinary man to do so either."[57] In 2000, *Payam-e Hajar* was officially shut down for unspecified reasons.[58]

Farzaneh (Wise)

Farzaneh (1993–2009), a prominent, independent academic journal of women's studies published in both English and Farsi by the Center for Women's Studies and Research, served predominantly as a theological and theoretical campaigning medium among academics, scholars, and policymakers in Iran and abroad.[59]

Its licensee, Massoumeh Ebtekar, served in Khatami's administration, and its editor in chief, Mahboubeh Abbasgholizadeh, was a well-known women's rights activist, whose numerous public demonstrations culminated in her arrest and imprisonment in 2010.[60]

Farzaneh's exceedingly unbiased viewpoint may best be exemplified in the philosophy of Abbasgholizadeh:

> We know that secular women do not share our convictions, but this does not give us any problems, since we are all working to promote the status of women. We Islamists have abandoned the idea that we are the sole heirs to the revolution. We realize that our sectarianism during the early years led to the isolation of many competent women and this was detrimental to women in general. We want to make up for our mistakes.[61]

Despite a progressive vision and the use of a dual language reflecting the desire to engage with professional women abroad, the editorial board of *Farzaneh* avoided making any use of "feminist" terminology, simply referring to their team as *karshenas* (experts).[62]

Over the years, *Farzaneh* appeared sporadically, and while the journal never officially ceased publication, it has not been seen on newsstands since 2009.[63]

Hoquq-e Zanan (Women's Rights)

Hoquq-e Zanan (1998–1999), launched by Ashraf Geramizadegan, made a brief appearance on the media horizon. Geramizadegan focused exclusively on debating gender issues from a legal perspective in *Hoquq-e Zanan*—with an emphasis on violence against women.[64] When asked by author Ziba Mir-Hosseini why she avoided the term feminism in her editorials, Geramizadegan replied:

> Our problem with this term is that it is associated with radical and extreme expressions of feminism; that is, it has not been understood as women's social movement for equal rights and justice. Feminism is seen as a negative force and its positive contributions have been ignored. We consider ourselves to be advocates of women's rights, and if they call this feminism, then I must say we are feminist, but not in the radical meaning that they say. When we see inequality, we want to change it in line with our culture and tradition.[65]

Mir-Hosseini indicates that *Hoquq-e Zanan* argued for "attaining justice and women's equality within the norms of the Sharia, as well as Iranian mores and culture."[66]

Jens-e Dovom (The Second Sex)

Jens-e Dovom (1998–2000) was launched by Noushin Ahmadi Khorasani, who was among the first women to procure a publishing license. She often collaborated with women's rights activists in exile to gain additional insight on international women's issues.[67] *Jens-e Dovom* reported on women workers and writers, domestic violence, as well as the lives of Iranian families living outside Iran. Forced by authorities to cease publication in 2001, Khorasani launched a quarterly journal, *Fasl-e Zanan (Women's Season)* in 2002.[68]

Zan (Woman)

Zan (1998–1999), the infamously controversial publication founded by Faezeh Hashemi, the rebellious daughter of Iran's former president, Hashemi Rafsanjani, was the Republic's first women's daily newspaper. Increasingly frustrated by the condition of women in Iran, Faezeh Hashemi, who served as a member of the fifth parliament (1996–2000), was a vocal critic of the state's discriminatory practices. Her candid interviews, speeches, and editorials—a constant source of outrage for the conservative coalition—made her extremely popular among women and youth.[69] Hashemi routinely advocated that women should engage in athletics and stand as candidates for the Assembly of Experts *(Majlis-e Khobregan)*.[70] Not one to shy away from confrontation, she was notorious for her brash statements, including that "if men are our problem, then we should get them to read these issues."[71]

The paper's demise in its first year stemmed from two specific features: an interview conducted with Iran's former Empress, Farah Pahlavi, on the eve of the Persian New Year—a controversial act given that anyone from the monarchy was considered taboo; and a satirical cartoon aimed at the Islamic Retribution Law *(Qesas)*, in which the husband of a couple held at gunpoint beckons the criminal to shoot his wife: "Kill her—She is cheaper!"[72]

Hashemi's defiant nature has continuously been the subject of media coverage and ultimately not without consequence. In 2012, she was sentenced to six months in prison for "making propaganda against the ruling system" and prohibited from participating in all cultural, political, and media activities for a period of five years.[73] Throughout all of her trials and tribulations, Hashemi has always maintained that "it is not Islam which forbids women from attaining office, but the interpretation of its teachings by the clerics."[74]

Zanan (Women)

Known for its modern perspective on gender issues related to religion, law, culture, and education, Zanan (1992–2008) was launched in February 1992. This independent reformist publication was instantly classified as a "sophisticated literary magazine with an overtly feminist agenda."[75] Under the brilliant leadership of Shahla Sherkat, the monthly Zanan astutely articulated the suffering of women that had been imposed by custodians of a misogynist ideology.

We will explore in depth the story of Shahla Sherkat and Zanan magazine in the following chapter.

With regard to women's magazines upholding the Islamic Republic's patriarchal stance on gender issues, the following are major publications sanctioned by the state:

Payam-e Zan (Woman's Message)

Inaugurated in 1992, Payam-e Zan is the official journal of the Qom Theological Seminary. Written and edited by men on the grounds that women are not permitted at the seminary, the magazine denounced gender parity as a Western concept with no place in

Islam. Under the editorship of cleric Seyyed Zia Mortazavi, this entity held the "pronounced patriarchal biases of Sharia legal rulings to be immutable."[76]

Over the years, *Payam-e Zan* has vociferously denounced the equality premise in scriptures and even gone so far as to buttress its refutations by publishing a series of one hundred interviews with well-known professional Muslim women who adhere to the principles of sacred authority. In reviewing their dialogue, author Janet Afary has concluded that while these women are ideologically sanctioned by the traditional order and work in close proximity with various government officials, "not one appears to be a conventional wife and mother."[77]

Rah-ye Zeynab (Zeynab's Path) and Zan-e Ruz (Today's Woman)

The two women's publications employed during the Pahlavi regime to propagate a Western lifestyle were relaunched after the revolution as a powerful "arm of activism" on behalf of the reigning orthodoxy.[78]

The bright, colorful pages of *Ettela'at-e Banovan (Ladies' Information)* and *Zan-e Ruz (Today's Woman)* were replaced with somber graphics and text endorsing the official creed of a religious empire. *Ettela'at-e Banovan* was taken over by the Islamic Republican Party and renamed *Rah-ye Zeynab (Zeynab's Path)* after Prophet Mohammad's granddaughter, while *Zan-e Ruz* retained its original name and operated under Dr. Zahra Rahnavard and the editorship of Shahla Sherkat.[79]

Neda (Proclamation)

The conservative journal *Neda (Proclamation)* was dedicated to a traditional Islamic agenda, supporting privileges for women solely within the boundaries of a repressed atmosphere. Launched in

1990, the quarterly journal of the Women's Association of the Islamic Republic of Iran (or Women's Society of the IRI, *Jami'at-e Zanan-e Jomhuriy-ye Islami*), a state-sponsored organization headed by Khomeini's daughter, Zahra Mostafavi, appeared at irregular intervals under the editorship of Khomeini's granddaughter, Fereshteh A'arabi. Given its limited circulation and general lack of appeal, the journal was mainly employed for governmental and institutional research purposes.[80]

FROM ANTI-FEMINIST TO ISLAMIC FEMINIST

Given the fact that various Islamic precepts impede female equality, some scholars question the validity of Islamic feminism. However, it is possible to consider this unique brand of feminism as a viable movement—and a crucial first step toward gaining emancipation from outdated patriarchal doctrine. It is important to acknowledge that many devout women initially refrained from any association with the word "feminist." Feminism was perceived as Western terminology fundamentally incompatible with, and irrelevant to Iranian women's demands. Instead, religious women who sought change chose to employ more generic labels, such as "women's rights activist" or "women's rights advocate."

By the mid-1990s, however, as a result of the government's relentless discriminatory practices, a specifically feminist consciousness had gathered momentum. Among the many spokeswomen articulating a new spirit of righteous advocacy were:

♦ **Mahboubeh Abbasgholizadeh,** who wrote many articles for *Zan-e Ruz* during the early 1980s rejecting the term "feminism," shifted her stance during the 1990s. As the editor of *Farzaneh,* she argued that "women's issues and feminism must be studied systematically" and she aimed to "put pressure on the Islamic state by emphasizing that inequalities between men and women do not originate in the Quran but rather in the interpretation by religious authorities of the divine laws."[81]

◆ **Zahra Rahnavard,** in a 1999 interview with *Zanan,* expressed disappointment in the state's treatment of women, using the term "the second sex," the title of Simone de Beauvoir's famous feminist manifesto.[82]

◆ **Noushin Ahmadi Khorasani**, founder and director of Nashr-e Towseh Publishing House; founder of the feminist publication Jens-e Do*vom (The Second Sex)*

> For me the struggle for women's rights is life itself. So, like many other women's rights activists, abstaining from such endeavors is basically impossible for me. While my fellow countrywomen suffer from discrimination and prejudice, my fight against such inequity is among the pillars of my life.[83]

◆ **Faezeh Hashemi** who, during the early revolutionary years was adamant that the hijab was "an indisputable symbol for Muslim women" presented a far different picture in 1997, when author Jane Howard was introduced to her at a state dinner given by Khatami's wife, Zohreh Sadeghi:

> She was tall, leggy, with blond hair. She was wearing a long black velvet gown covered in sequins and split up thigh high.... Hers was the daring outfit of the evening.[84]

It is reasonable to assume that some female Muslim loyalists would adopt a discreet approach to women's rights advocacy, rightfully fearing that moving too fast would obstruct the future of the movement. In fact, by avoiding Western terminology, these women were able to successfully renegotiate and even reverse some of the initial discriminatory laws and policies regarding employment and education, including permission for unmarried women to study abroad and to serve as "investigative" and "research" judges.[85] And in 2010, when Zahra Rahnavard publicly denounced the state's initiative to reintroduce a bill granting men the right to polygamy without the consent of their wives, she diplomatically employed the following rationale to demand that "experts and progressive-minded individuals" reassess the issue:

> Calling off the bill from the Parliament's agenda is not a feminist demand, but rather a symbol of the national demand for the prosperity of the Iranian nation and the stability of the Iranian families.[86]

Forged out of a common commitment to women's rights, a united force has emerged between secular and religious women. The experience of women from traditional backgrounds was different from that of their mothers and grandmothers. Educated in a school system unintentionally influenced by a Western infrastructure, they had been exposed to a certain degree of modern ideology with regard to women's roles. Their textbooks revealed a world in which women and men often shared the same activities and responsibilities. And their single-sex education motivated them to thrive in the classroom, resulting in a sense of self-determination and empowerment. Those who took on responsibilities outside the home during the Iran-Iraq War were further detached from the idealized version of the Muslim woman. And finally, having been inspired by many of the women's publications that had begun advocating a more equitable role for females—including religious females—these women were ready for change.

While their political stance regarding women's rights was not identical to that of their secular sisters, it was closer than it had ever been. Disappointed in the unfulfilled promises made to women during the pre-revolution fervor, Islamic women were on a new path, one that ran parallel to their nonreligious counterparts.

In assessing the burgeoning women's rights movement in post-revolutionary Iran, it is important to understand that Islamic women's commitment to reinterpreting religious texts is not only a significant means of liberation but also a strategic and exhilarating "opening act."

As women's rights advocates in Iran continue to bridge the gap between religious and secular perspectives, they are proving that a women's movement based upon the shared goals of gender equality, female empowerment, reinterpretation of the Koran, and the eradication of misogynist policies is not only possible but inevitable.

In the following chapter, the history of *Zanan* magazine—Iran's leading post-revolutionary women's publication—will serve to illuminate the future of this movement.

Chapter Six

ZANAN MAGAZINE

It takes artfulness to address taboo issues.... Doing journalism in countries like ours—where ... the system thinks if you say anything it's going to fall apart—it's like being a trapeze artist.[1]
Shahla Sherkat, award-winning journalist, founder and editor in chief of the feminist magazine *Zanan (Women)*

[Zanan was shut down for] endangering the spiritual, mental and intellectual health of its readers, and threatening psychological security by deliberately offering a dark picture of the Islamic Republic.[2]
Press Supervisory Board of Iran, backed by the Ministry of Culture

The men who try to stifle her or others similar to her should really keep in mind that these are demands and issues that their family members, their wives, their mothers, their sisters, and their daughters are dealing with, and just suppressing them is not going to make them go away.[3]
Susan Tahmasebi, women's rights activist, regarding Shahla Sherkat's relaunching of *Zanan-e Emruz* in 2014

As we discovered in the previous chapter, the post-revolutionary era in Iran engendered an unexpected sisterhood of religious and secular women. The flourishing of publications that catered to a broad female readership played a key role in solidifying this unlikely union. Although the word *feminist* was rarely used, a number of women's magazines were committed to the free expression of ideas that challenged Iran's patriarchal status quo. The publication having the greatest impact on Iranian women during this time was very likely *Zanan* (1992–2008).

Launched in February 1992 by Shahla Sherkat, *Zanan* was independent and reformist—and instantly classified as "a sophisticated literary magazine with an overtly feminist agenda."[4] The exceptional contribution of this leading feminist publication has been applauded for its daring ventures, including a predilection toward a modernist interpretation of gender issues in the areas of religion, law, culture, and education.[5] Fiercely committed to women's rights, deeply respectful of both religious and secular women, and unreservedly bold in its ideological objectives, *Zanan*, from its inception, offered its readers incisive articles and editorials that did not equivocate in confronting the male-controlled clerical establishment. In fact, in its very first editorial, the magazine challenged the reigning Islamic order with a pointedly progressive, feminist perspective:

> It is time now for the sage and the intellectuals caring for religion, in their contemplation of fiq'h[6] and its edicts, to think more seriously about issues related to women, so that after centuries of the decline of Islam, the Muslim woman can rid herself of disorientation, distraction, and multiplicity of orientation [chandgunegi] toward her religion and at times even her God. This is to uncover the kind, rational, and progressive vision of religion in the tired souls of women, thereby substituting love for force, respect for fear, prayer for hypocrisy, and tranquility for anxiety.[7]

This chapter will explore *Zanan*'s profound impact on the women of Iran, in spite of ongoing political challenges. We will learn how the magazine managed to impart a radically reformist ideology that represented a potent response to the critics of Islamic feminism in Iran. In considering its endurance and popularity, it will also be apparent why *Zanan* became a crucial part of consciousness-raising for adolescent females in Iran. Its pioneering and provocative articles revealed to readers that they shared a common cause, not only with women in their own country, but with all women seeking to overcome patriarchal oppression. It was in this very personal yet fundamental way that *Zanan* helped forge a global sisterhood linking Iran to the West.

A NEW DAWN

Throughout *Zanan's* years in operation, Shahla Sherkat managed it with a small staff, mostly women, who labored tirelessly under extremely modest conditions in order to expose the oppression of women under the Islamic regime.[8] As the country's most popular and influential women's journal, with an approximate circulation of 40,000 per month, *Zanan* signified a new dawn through its fearless coverage of forbidden topics and its brazen, alternative analysis—a much-needed antidote to the prevailing mind-set.[9] *Zanan* made an indelible impression at home and abroad as its articles and editorials boldly traversed uncharted territory with a calculated, cutting-edge philosophy and the participation of a diverse group of contributing writers.[10] Its credibility and influence among women was unprecedented, specifically when its endorsement and coverage of Khatami's bid for the presidency were credited with mobilizing the support of this constituency for the reformist candidate.[11]

Passionate, inspiring editorials written by an array of enlightened intellectuals filled the pages of Sherkat's magazine, communicating the harsh realities of everyday life for Iranian women. Coverage of reformist politicians, women's rights activists, and renowned Western feminists was both innovative and stylish. The journal's "round-table" deliberations on women's issues provided a comprehensive road map for women handicapped by societal constraints.

Under the astute leadership of its award-winning editor in chief, *Zanan* was distinguished as a "major voice of reform," "challenging the foundations of the dominant forms of Shi'ite jurisprudence" by demonstrating the multiple ambiguities in Koranic verses.[12] Afsaneh Najmabadi, Professor of History and of Studies of Women, Gender, and Sexuality at Harvard University, contended that, "At the center of *Zanan's* revisionist approach is a radical decentering of the clergy from the domain of interpretation ... which challenges the foundational concept [of] deference to the rulership of the ... *velayat-e faqih* [guardianship of the jurist]."[13]

Zanan's deliberate departure from the status quo has been widely applauded for inaugurating a "new chapter," influencing "the evolution of ideas ... and the progression toward a Sharia-based feminist discourse."[14] In communicating with her readers, Sherkat employed a diversified approach to her magazine, in which unorthodox opinions suggested the fluidity of women's prerogatives in Islam. Her broad-minded journalistic style was reinforced by a group of progressive clerics and intellectual dissidents, who "called for modern interpretations of classical traditions."[15]

In an assessment of all 152 issues of *Zanan* (from February 1992 to January 2008), the magazine's penchant for confronting the disturbing and controversial realities facing Iranian women is immediately apparent. The publication's front-page features, part of *Zanan's* enduring legacy, include the following articles on these important topics:

- ◆ Domestic violence
  - ▶ "Sir, Have You Ever Physically Assaulted Your Wife?"
  - ▶ "The Beating of a Woman Is One of the Areas of a Man's Authority"
- ◆ Gender discrimination
  - ▶ "Female Students behind Invisible Fences"
  - ▶ "Why Don't Women Get Paid as Much as Men?"
  - ▶ "Women's Issues Do Not Have Priority"
  - ▶ "Once Again—Limitations on Young Women Entering Universities"
- ◆ Biases found in the Islamic Constitution
  - ▶ "Article 1133 of the Constitution: A Man Can Divorce His Wife Anytime He Wants"
- ◆ Patriarchal laws
  - ▶ "Man: Partner or Boss?"[16]

Provocative features also focused on such taboo subjects as "The Arrival of the New IUD" and "This Is Forbidden Love Street," which dealt with the state's infringement on the natural sexual desires of adolescent boys and girls.[17]

Zanan's monthly "roundtable" discussions provided insightful discussions by men and women from various intellectual fields on relevant topics, including "What Are the Most Important Issues Facing Women?" Their dialogue on such issues as "the necessity for women to develop themselves in all areas," "the division of labor in the household" and "the state's exaggeration of the importance of motherhood"[18] provided a multidimensional overview of prevailing inequalities.

Appearing in the magazine as well were numerous translated features on parenting and childrearing practices in Western nations, celebrating the virtues of the career-oriented wife and mother while chronicling the physical and emotional ramifications of confinement to the domestic sphere. Articles such as "Working Mothers and Feelings of Guilt," "We Should Not Be Slaves to Our Children," "Do I Have the Right to Enjoy My Job?" and "Mother, Why Do You Work?" exposed the personal and professional benefits of working women and the "normal" feelings of separation anxiety associated with this lifestyle.[19]

The following excerpts from *Zanan* articles dealing with the challenge of balancing family and work enumerate the merits of finding fulfillment outside of the household and the importance of communicating this message to one's children:

- Do you always feel that all your time is at the service of your children and that you neglect yourself most of the time? Just because you are a mother does not mean that you have to sacrifice your entire life.... Your child needs to slowly take other matters into consideration, to be respectful towards your feelings and your right to accomplish what you want.[20]

- For every moment that I feel good about my career, I have moments where I feel guilty.... But, in fact, the time that I spend at work provides me with the strength to perform household work. If I were to spend all of my time with my children, I would not appreciate them as much.[21]

- The children of working mothers are more successful in the community as well as in group work. They are also better students in school.[22]

- Your conversations about your profession with your children will help them feel proud of a mother who works. The working woman can be a role model for her child, in that she takes pleasure from both her family and her job.[23]

Such articles originating from the West advocated the notion of personal fulfillment and were emblematic of a deliberate attempt to counter the antiquated gender ideology of the reigning conservative leadership.

Zanan also featured the writing of internationally recognized Western feminists—a defiant and audacious undertaking for a publication in a post-revolutionary climate. In presenting her readers with a collection of translated feminist writing, bringing to their attention the powerful voices of historically disempowered women in Western nations, Sherkat connected Iranian women to a liberation movement that stood in stark contrast to the Islamic Republic's ideology.

Excerpts from Western feminist classics that poignantly articulated women's struggles in Europe and the United States in many ways echoed the predicament of women in post-revolutionary Iran. Among the revered writers whose work was featured in *Zanan:*

◆ British novelist **Mary Wollstonecraft** (1759–1797), whose *A Vindication of the Rights of Woman* (1792) disclosed the manner in which "religion" and "the language of men" have devalued women and deprived them of their "natural prerogatives in life." Wollstonecraft addressed the "pernicious effects arising from unnatural distinctions established in societies," and how "man" has manipulated the system in order to impose "an unconditional obedience," reducing a woman to "a slave in every situation."

◆ American novelist **Kate Chopin** (1851–1904), whose short story "The Story of an Hour," published in 1894, covers one hour in the life of Louise Millard, who appears to be in a distressed state upon hearing the news of her husband's sudden death. The reader learns, however, that Louise is in fact invigorated at the thought of regaining her freedom: "FREE, FREE, FREE! ..." Her euphoric episode is short-lived, as she abruptly has a heart attack and dies upon being informed that Mr. Millard is in fact sill alive. The story of this despondent housewife held captive by social norms symbolizes that the only way for a woman to hold on to her newly-found freedom would be through death.

◆ British novelist **Virginia Woolf** (1882–1941), whose acclaimed 1929 essay, "A Room of One's Own," included her bold declaration: "Lock up your libraries if you like, but there is no gate, no lock, no bolt that you can set upon the freedom of the mind."

◆ American feminist **Charlotte Perkins Gilman** (1860–1935), who wrote *The Home* (1903), *The Man-Made World: Or, Our Androcentric Culture* (1911) and *Herland* (1915) as a response to the male-centered ideology of divine scriptures, declaring that there is "no female mind, as the brain is not an organ of sex." Perkins advanced the notion that "a normal feminine influence in recasting religious assumptions will do more than any other thing to improve the world."

◆ French feminist and author **Simone de Beauvoir** (1908–1986), whose revolutionary treatise *The Second Sex* (1949) significantly contributed to feminist rhetoric by challenging a woman's "assigned" role as "the second sex." Critical to her argument is her infamous adage, "One is not born, but rather becomes, woman" (*On ne naît pas femme, on le devient*). The author contends that women have the ability to destroy the fabricated social distinctions between the sexes: "When we abolish the slavery of half of humanity, together with the whole system of hypocrisy it implies, then the 'division' of humanity will reveal its genuine significance and the human couple will find its true form."

◆ American writer **Judy Syfers**, whose essay "Why I Want a Wife" appeared in the inaugural issue of *Ms.* magazine in 1972.[24] In her sarcastic monologue, Syfers enumerates the enormous benefits of being a married man: "It suddenly occurred to me that I, too, would like to have a wife. Why do I want a wife? I would like to go back to school, so that I can become economically independent, and support myself.... And while I am going to school, I want a wife to take care of my children.... I want a wife who will take care of my physical needs.... I want a wife who cooks the meals.... I want a wife who will not bother me with rambling complaints.... I want a wife who is sensitive to my sexual needs.... My God, who wouldn't want a wife?" With her sardonic wit, Syfers shrewdly communicates the slave-like existence of the average American housewife and mother.

◆ African American author **Alice Walker**, whose *In Search of Our Mother's Garden* (1983), a collection of thirty-six essays, presents a gripping portrayal of survival and women's solidarity amidst unimaginable injustice—the degrading, inhumane treatment of the enslaved woman and the multiple burdens of racial and gender oppression.

These and countless other feminist articles, excerpts, and essays published in *Zanan* revealed a forbidden ideology and language in which "prescribed social roles based on biological identity are replaced by representations of 'real' women as they actually are or can be."[25] For a generation deprived of access to many facets of Western culture, these published accounts by Western women revealed the universality of women's struggle to overcome male dominance.

It is also quite likely that *Zanan* played a significant role in the social awareness and identity formation of its younger readers.[26] Social psychologists have long confirmed that adolescents often acquire the ideals of womanhood from a variety of women's publications. Beauty and fashion magazines are implicated for propagating an unrealistic feminine ideal during a vulnerable phase when young women may be conflicted by contradictory information concerning their role as women in society.[27] However, the opposite can also be argued; that is, the messages conveyed by more serious women's publications, such as *Zanan*, may have the ability to diminish the impact of "unhealthy societal messages."[28] Mary Pipher, clinical psychologist and bestselling author of *Reviving Ophelia*, validates that exposure to strong female role models in cultures where women are expected to "sacrifice" and "relinquish" their "true selves" can profoundly alleviate many of the anxieties associated with a subordinate existence.[29] Developmental psychologist Jean Piaget's theory of cognitive development attests to this as well. He emphasizes the value of acquired knowledge in the development of "morally autonomous" individuals and the formation of their capacity to emerge as agents of social change in societies that devalue and degrade freedom.[30]

Adolescent girls (and women) were introduced to the "voices, visions, and lived experiences" of women through articles in *Zanan* that chronicled female oppression, and such content was potentially a potent means of consciousness-raising. Just as we learned of the liberating impact of single-sex education on female adolescents, the ideas expressed in *Zanan* can be considered an empowering influence as well. The magazine's pervasive feminist content has likely been part of the socialization journey of countless adolescent females in Iran. By presenting articles to a generation of women fascinated by Western culture, yet for the most part deprived of access to it due to censorship, *Zanan* has introduced its readers to a prohibited ideology of enhanced freedom and infinite possibilities.

In publishing the writings of esteemed female authors, *Zanan* highlighted in a poignant and powerful way the common concerns of Western and Iranian women. Given Iran's extremely youthful population, this powerful and credible discourse in the nation's foremost women's publication has most likely had an extraordinary impact over a period of nearly two decades.

Having been exposed to feminist articles and literary excerpts in *Zanan,* young Iranian women raised in an intolerant environment had the opportunity to engage in a powerful learning experience through which they might understand the similarities between their own struggles and those of women from other cultures. Introduced to the experiences, challenges, thoughts, and opinions of renowned female writers from Europe and the United States, they were exposed to an illuminating and liberating gender ideology.

First issue of *Zanan*
Magazine, February 1992.

Zanan Magazine endorses
Mahmoud Khatami's
presidential bid.

One of *Zanan's* infamous cover photos.

Another of *Zanan's* infamous cover photos.

IS ISLAM OPEN TO RE-INTERPRETATION?

Zanan magazine had a major role in advancing a new interpretation of Islam—one that eschewed patriarchal and misogynistic beliefs. Laying the foundation for this liberating theological perspective were a number of influential thinkers.

Abdolkarim Soroush, Hujat ul-Islam Muhammad Shabestari, Seyyed Mohsen Saidzadeh, and Hujat ul-Islam Mohsen Kadivar were among the architects of theological theory expressing "equality and empowerment in Islam's true spirit."[31] These and other individuals, referred to as "neo-religious thinkers" (*no-andishan-e dini*), elucidate a more tolerant and liberal Islam by arguing "that the Qur'an and hadith are part of divine and eternal religion," and therefore "the interpretation of these texts is a matter of human and religious knowledge and is thus open to debate."[32]

Abdolkarim Soroush, a professor and nonclerical religious intellectual, who was chosen by *Time* magazine in 2005 as one of the 100 most influential people in the world, is possibly the leading "intellectual force behind the Islamic Republic's pro-democracy movement."[33] Drawing from both Western and Islamic sources, Soroush laid the foundations for "Islamic pluralism" by challenging Ayatollah Khomeini's concept of the guardianship of the jurist. One of the leading ideologues of the Islamic Republic, he was one of the original seven members of the Council for Cultural Revolution assigned to Islamize all universities in the aftermath of the revolution.[34]

Soroush, born Hossein Dabbagh in 1945, was raised in a religious household and pursued higher education in both Iran and England, where he studied the history and philosophy of science after earning degrees in pharmacology and analytical chemistry.[35]

In his monthly publication *Kiyan* (1991), Soroush began to revise and reinterpret Islamic theology, based on his extensive knowledge of philosophers such as Hegel and Fromm, without sacrificing the essence and sanctity of divine principles.[36] Greatly admired by women and youth, Soroush's argument that "our comprehension of religion is scientifically, socially, and culturally constructed, and hence open to interpretation," supports a rapprochement between Islam and democracy, and accordingly facilitates the disclosure of feminist ideals in religious dogma.[37]

In a 2000 interview with *Zanan*, Soroush articulated his belief that "God manifests himself in each historical period according to the understanding of the people of the era," and thus justified Islam's harmony with modern conceptions of scientific knowledge, human rights, and democracy.[38] Anthropologist and author Ziba Mir-Hosseini confirms that "Soroush's approach to sacred texts has not only enabled women in *Zanan* to frame their demands within an Islamic framework, but also encouraged clerics for whom gender has become a 'problem' to address it from within a '*fiq'h*' framework."[39]

Like many of his progressive-minded counterparts, Abdolkarim Soroush eventually fell victim to the tide of conservative backlash. His liberal sermons were often disrupted, and he was persistently harassed and eventually forbidden to teach. Since 2000, he has continued his new age discourse as a visiting scholar and lecturer at Harvard, Princeton, and Yale, where he remains an icon of enlightened religious theory.[40]

High-ranking Shiite clerics Mohsen Kadivar and Hujat ul-Islam Muhammad Shabestari undertook paths similar to that of Soroush and disputed the absolute authority of the clerical establishment. In a 2008 interview in the German online publication for dialogue with the Muslim world, *Qantara*, Shabestari stated that "Islam is a religion in every sense, not a political agenda.... The first priority for the

Islamic world today is that it should become aware of the present state of humanity."[41]

In 2004, Mohsen Kadivar, the brother of former parliament member Jamileh Kadivar and brother-in-law of politician Ata'ollah Mohajerani, declared:

> Every member of society and every member of government is sub-ject to the law. No one can be above it. Everyone has the same rights, yet the root of the *faqih* is inequality. He assumes he is above it.... It is time for the Supreme Leader to be subject to the Consti-tution too. After all, the Supreme Leader doesn't come from God![42]

In 1999, Kadivar was tried and sentenced to eighteen months in prison for challenging the doctrine of clerical rule. Today, he resides in the United States, where he is a visiting professor in the Depart-ment of Religion at Duke University.[43]

A CLERICAL-SECULAR COLLABORATION

The wisdom and insight of these thinkers validated *Zanan*'s objec-tives, as did the collaboration between a young, mid-ranking cleric well-versed in juridical protocol and a secular attorney with legal expertise. Regular features by Seyyed Mohsen Saidzadeh and attor-ney Mehrangiz Kar, "one a male religious scholar and one a female intellectual—side by side—pursued discussions regarding women's related jurisprudence and law."[44]

Saidzadeh, possibly the most "radical ... and vocal proponent of gender equality" and one of the earliest advocates of Islam and feminism in post-revolutionary Iran, was born and raised in the small town of Qaen in the province of South Khorasan.[45] A graduate of the Qom Theological Seminary (*Madrese-ye-Ali-ye Qazai'i-ye-Qom*), he resigned soon after earning his judgeship in 1983 to embark on a personal exploration of religious issues relating to women. Saidzadeh began writing in May 1992, when his first series of articles appeared in *Zanan* under the name of his wife, Mina Yadegar Azadi, an unknown secondary school teacher.[46] His editorials examining Islamic law within the family, the capacity of women to serve as judges (*mujtahid'n*), and women in the penal system (*qesas*) "showed with certainty that there is no unanimity regarding women-related religious commands, and, secondly, that these directives must change on the basis of the requirements of the time."[47] In later years, when his authorship was uncovered, Saidzadeh explained that the pretense was solely for the purpose of providing his wife with entry into the field of journalism. However, given the controversial nature of these pieces and fearing the loss of her employment, Azadi denied any connection with the articles.

In the aftermath, Saidzadeh continued to write, establishing the need for women's roles to be "regulated by familial and social circumstances ... as opposed to natural or divine will."[48] Saidzadeh, like Soroush, considered the traditional religious approach applied in modern-day society as "the lowest-ranking religious science" and maintained that a reformulation of the body of Islamic laws within the "new political context" would enable women to engage in advancing their own needs.[49]

Saidzadeh's moderate clerical philosophy corresponded to the secular views of human rights activist and lawyer Mehrangiz Kar. Born in 1944, Kar was raised by a "veiled yet Western-oriented" mother. In the aftermath of the 1979 revolution, she had only recently passed the bar. Like all other female lawyers, she was not prevented from practicing law but could not hold certain positions and instead was confined to a more bureaucratic position. Eventually, however, she managed to represent women in divorce, adultery, and child custody cases. Adhering to the new Islamic laws in order to protect herself from being banned from working as a lawyer, she reluctantly gave in to the dress codes and worked within the boundaries of the system, while at the same time citing modernist Islamic thinkers in her defenses.[50]

Drawn into collaborating with her Islamic counterparts, Kar joined the reformist movement in the early 1990s. She was initially skeptical about meeting with Shahla Sherkat, as she was hesitant about a religion dismissive of the inequality between men and women.[51] However, her cynicism was almost immediately dispelled. She recalls her astonishment upon visiting the offices of *Zanan* in 1992:

> Something is happening which is no lesser in significance than the Islamic Revolution. Cultural and intellectual forces were openly engaged in a challenge with those forces of the regime…. It was becoming obvious to me that a split had begun to take place within the ideologues and cultural forces of the ruling system. A new force emerging from within had begun to challenge the status quo.[52]

Kar, who had never resorted to religious criteria in her writings, and whose work prior to 1979 focused primarily on social reform, agreed to work for *Zanan* as she was convinced "that this was a historic occasion—one that she knew would benefit women and the women's movement."[53]

In 1993, with Kar's permission, Saidzadeh modified her written work as a precautionary measure aimed at preventing the magazine from "being charged with

Mehrangiz Kar

blasphemy."[54] Her inaugural article titled "Women's Position in Iran's Penal Law," published in the summer of 1993, was a critique of the Retribution Law in a manner reflecting the necessity for "universal human rights to be the basis of all legislation."[55] Kar's articles, which appeared in *Zanan* at regular intervals, revealed her knowledge of the judicial process, while Saidzadeh's "mastery of the Sharia ensured that the debates remained within the acceptable boundaries of religious dogma."[56]

In 1998, this unusual collaboration ended with the abrupt demise of Saidzadeh's career, after he published an article in the daily newspaper *Jame'eh* (*Society*) comparing the discriminatory policies of the state to those of the Taliban in Afghanistan:

> Based on these traditional texts, they should follow the same route as the Taliban have, and some in Iran have actually done so. One example is the story of some fanatics in Iran who have tried to prevent women from biking, which is in the same tradition as that of the Taliban's prevention of women from riding horses.[57]

As a consequence, Saidzadeh was excommunicated, imprisoned, and forbidden to publish.[58] Nevertheless, Saidzadeh continues to maintain the validity of feminism in Iran as a viable "social movement," which, through emphasizing the common humanity of the sexes, endeavors to free women "from an unwanted subordination imposed by [an] androcentric society."[59]

DISCORD BETWEEN FEMINIST ALLIES

Mehrangiz Kar remained with *Zanan* until her arrest in April 2000, after she and sixteen other reformist women, including Shahla Sherkat, attended the Berlin Conference on "The Future of Reform in Iran."[60] In the aftermath of this meeting, the groundbreaking reconciliation between secular and religious women was momentarily brought to a halt when Kar was sentenced behind closed doors to four years' imprisonment for her criticism of the Islamic Constitution, while Sherkat was tried, fined, and released in an open court for questioning the religious dress code.[61] Kar was bitterly dismayed at Sherkat for not coming to her defense and for choosing to protect her magazine over her relationship:

> We always sensed that there was a gap. It simply became clear after Berlin that the reformists would never take any risks for us, or defend us....[62]

Kar was diagnosed with cancer after spending two months in prison. Under pressure from the European Union, Khatami officials intervened, allowing her to leave for treatment in the U.S.[63]

Over the years the rift between the two women has been attributed to Kar's secularism versus Sherkat's religious identity, and there has been a range of speculation including Sherkat's alleged fear of "possible retaliation by the system, loss of employment and imprisonment."[64] Although such conclusions are entirely plausible, the decisive issue for Sherkat may have been neither one of those considerations. For sixteen years, she routinely faced legal action for allegations regarding her magazine's controversial articles.[65] But it is important to consider the factor of *Zanan*'s solvency. Far from being a lucrative enterprise, *Zanan* was continuously under financial strain. In a 2007 interview, Sherkat described the extent of her burden:

> In terms of financial obstacles, Zanan is under tremendous pressure. No one backs us financially. Day after day wages rise, the price of paper increases by double or more and the office rent is climbing. All this puts us in an incredibly compromising situation. I have had to sell my mobile phone and car to cover the expenses. I have also had to sell my house.[66]

Despite the difficulties of keeping *Zanan* afloat, it appears that the determining factor for Sherkat was to forge ahead with an arduous undertaking and her altruistic mission, believing that "nothing is impossible."[67] Therefore, the alleged act of betrayal of her colleague Mehrangiz Kar is in all likelihood attributable not to differences in personal ideology but to Sherkat's commitment to advancing the women's movement in Iran by making certain that *Zanan* endured.

HOW DID *ZANAN* MANAGE TO SURVIVE?

During a period in which reformist publications were regularly shut down for the slightest deviation from state ideology, it is a bit of a mystery how *Zanan* managed to survive for almost two decades. *Zanan* endured despite its articles that portrayed the bitter realities of daily life for Iranian women and contested the premise of the country's patriarchal laws. Why was the magazine allowed to publish such "inflammatory" material, such as that excerpted from prominent Western feminist writers?

Did Sherkat's affiliation with Mohammad Khatami, dating back to their time at the Keyhan Institute and *Zan-e Ruz* in the 1980s, play a role in *Zanan's* longevity, allowing Sherkat to remain below the radar and evade drastic penalties despite her blatant ideological transgressions? Her connection to Khatami—as evidenced by his approval of Sherkat's license to publish in 1991 and the magazine's endorsement of his presidential bid—cannot be denied.

While Sherkat's passion, determination, and dedication are obvious, and her skill in presenting controversial topics is no small achievement, the magazine's staying power is baffling given that its content is far more radical than that of other similar publications. Although it has published numerous articles reflecting Western ideology, as well as countless articles that were overtly critical of the regime's blatant discriminatory laws and practices, *Zanan* has endured while other magazines have been systematically terminated for the slightest infraction, including "collusion and conspiracy with the West."[68] Although Sherkat's travails were by no means without complications, she was consistently exonerated of all accusations.[69] Authors Elaine Sciolino and Ida Lichter, who have both remarked on the magazine's survival, are equally perplexed.

During her many trips to Iran, Sciolino, a correspondent for *Newsweek* and the *New York Times,* often contemplated this unusual fact: "Sometimes I could not figure out why *Zanan* had not been shut down."[70] In her extensive documentation of women in the Muslim world, Ida Lichter considers the same question: "It is remarkable that *Zanan* has survived for sixteen years in a country that Reporters Without Borders has called the biggest prison for journalists in the Middle East."[71]

In April 1997, Khatami acknowledged in an interview with Sherkat that "the culture of patriarchy is one of the most important impediments to women in Iran, and ... the laws pertaining to gender equality will benefit civil society."[72] Mir-Hosseini observes that, although Khatami's pledge for freedom was not entirely fulfilled, "reformist efforts to reconcile Islam, democracy and human rights brought to the surface many of the inherent contradictions between the Constitution and gender rights in Sharia law and democratic ideals."[73] In many ways, Sherkat's role as a "persistent trespasser" has been indisputable in this regard.[74]

While Khatami was unable to prevent the closure of numerous reformist publications, he may have traveled the extra mile for *Zanan.* Unfortunately, the magazine finally fell victim to the conservative climate of the Ahmadinejad era (2005–2013). On January 28, 2008, the Press Supervisory Board of Iran, backed by the

Ministry of Culture, announced the revocation of *Zanan's* license for "endangering the spiritual, mental and intellectual health of its readers, and threatening psychological security by deliberately offering a dark picture of the Islamic Republic." Although no specific article or articles were named in this accusation, there was speculation that an investigative piece on the martyrdom movement entitled "Dying in Order to Kill" triggered the shutdown. This contention stems from the charges accusing Sherkat of "breaking the law and defaming military and revolutionary institutions."[75]

Zanan's demise resonated in Iran and around the world, as activists and supporters petitioned the Iranian government to reinstate the journal's license.[76] Sherkat's legal advisor stated that the manner in which the magazine was shut down may have violated official standard procedure:

> Events that have taken place since the license revocation suggest that the decision was motivated more by personal and ideological animosity of a few individual members and not the whole Press Supervisory Board which presumably ordered the license revocation.[77]

After the closure of *Zanan,* Sherkat—who was honored in 2004 with the Courage in Journalism Award by the International Women's Media Foundation for her "dangerous and challenging work" and in 2005 with the Louis M. Lyons Award for Conscience and Integrity in Journalism from the Neiman Foundation for Journalism at Harvard University—accepted a management position in an arts and cultural institute. In 2010, this divorced mother of two described her anguish over the loss of *Zanan:*

> Every day I arrive at work but a piece of the puzzle of my being has been lost. It has been two years since they have taken from our family our 16-year-old daughter *Zanan.* I have walked up and down

many stairs and corridors to find my lost one. But have not had any success.[78]

THE WOMAN WHO GAVE BIRTH TO *ZANAN*

Zanan's story began with Shahla Sherkat, a passionate, unwavering activist who defied the established boundaries of a coercive regime. Her impartial, tolerant outlook, as reflected in her groundbreaking magazine, quite likely derived from her personal history. Born in 1956 to a devout family in the city of Isfahan, Sherkat's upbringing was unlike that of many conservative households that remained apprehensive about the westernized climate of the Pahlavi era. Her parents, a housewife and a civil servant, remained comfortable in a secular atmosphere despite their own religious convictions, and this laid the groundwork for their daughter's outlook.

Annette Bening presents Shahla Sherkat with the Courage in Journalism Award in Beverly Hills, California, 2005.

In an interview with BBC correspondent Jane Howard, Sherkat recalled attending elementary school in this dual atmosphere:

> He [her father] was very particular about the hijab and we even wore our headscarf to school and sometimes the chador too.... At the time I went to school, there would be girls sitting next to me with miniskirts, but I was never made to feel uncomfortable.[79]

In later years, at her mother's insistence, the family moved to Tehran, where Sherkat earned her undergraduate degree in psychology from Tehran University.

Shahla's initial journalistic venture coincided with the collapse of the Pahlavi monarchy. As a revolutionary enthusiast, she found employment at *Rah-ye Zaynab* (*Zaynab's Path*), formerly *Ettela'at-e Banovan* (*Ladies Information*). In 1982, she was approached by Zahra Rahnavard to "revitalize" *Zan-e Ruz* (*Today's Woman*).[80] Mohammad Khatami was serving at that time as supervisor for the Keyhan Institute, the publishing house that owned *Zan-e Ruz*. Sherkat's indomitable spirit was immediately apparent when, much to the dismay of the editorial board, she elected to enrich the publication's content with hardcore analysis of women's issues in a post-revolutionary climate. Here is what she had to say about *Zan-e Ruz*:

> My main difficulty with them was that they wanted to portray an image of women being in the house, putting on their make-up when their husbands came home. The beds are made, the table is set.... It got to a point where I said no more.[81]

In 1991, Sherkat departed from *Zan-e Ruz* amid a dispute over the publication of an essay by renowned filmmaker Mohsen Makhmalbaf, in which he harshly reacted to criticism of one of his movies by state officials. During this period, Khatami, who was serving as Minister of Culture and Islamic Guidance, came to her defense by supporting Makhmalbaf's right to rejoinder. While this dispute caused Khatami to resign, it nevertheless placed him in good standing with Sherkat, who later endorsed his candidacy.

In 1992, Shahla, who had obtained a publication license from none other than Khatami before her departure from *Zan-e Ruz*, started *Zanan* (*Women*) and embarked on her journalistic crusade.[82]

This association represented an interlude in which Western ideas infiltrated a restrictive climate, allowing the ideals of a religious woman who was "neither apologetic nor defensive about Islam and openly associated herself with feminism," to converge with the unconventional wisdom of a devout cleric, who subscribed to and stressed the importance of "incorporating the West into one's values and life."[83]

ZANAN'S COMEBACK

On May 29, 2014, Shahla Sherkat's "daughter"—beloved not only by her but also by thousands of readers during the magazine's previous sixteen-year run—was relaunched under the banner *Zanan-e Emruz* (*Today's Women*). Available in print and online, the new version of the periodical continues to reflect Sherkat's passion and altruistic mission for advancing the rights of Iranian women. Its pages include hard-hitting, inspiring pieces, such as "Why Are Men Unaware of Their Violence and Aggression toward Women?" and "The Injustice Faced by Female Factory Workers in Iran." Articles often focus on the harrowing circumstances women face when handicapped by legal restraints, and the magazine also includes candid interviews with well-known women's rights activists in Iran, as well as coverage of international women's issues.

While the future of Iran remains hidden in a convoluted landscape, what appears certain is that despite the obstacles, women's activism is surging. Shahla Sherkat has valiantly proven that neither she nor those who believe in securing women's rights in Iran will be silenced.

In the following chapter we will examine evidence of the Islamic Republic's failed gender ideology and highlight the efforts Iranian women are making in order to answer this ongoing and provocative question: *can women in Iran ever be equal?*

Chapter Seven

CAN WOMEN IN IRAN BE EQUAL?

---

*The previous disconnect between Iranian women has transformed
into a collective movement which will not be silenced.*[1]
Delaram Ali, twenty-four-year-old sociology student arrested
and sentenced to two-and-a-half years in prison for her
participation in the Haft-e Tir Square protests in 2006

*The only way the women's movement, as a new social movement in Iran, can
move their rights forward is through a change in the laws ... Women citizens
have the right to object to discriminatory legislation. Officials should be
responsive and listen to these demands, so that this deadlock is resolved and can
help provide a peaceful, civilized life for all citizens, particularly for women.*[2]
Mansoureh Shojaee, leading Iranian women's rights activist and founding
member of the 2006 One Million Signatures Campaign for Equality

*Everything that is banned by the government is
being practiced but behind closed doors.*[3]
Kiana Hayeri, documentary photographer whose 2012
project "Your Veil Is a Battleground" captures the dual
lives of a new generation of young women in Iran

I am sorry that the chador [veil] was forced on women. [Today] people
have just lost their respect for it. We only have ourselves to blame.
People are not happy and the chador has become its symbol.[4]
Zahra Eshraghi, granddaughter of the late Ayatollah Khomeini

For over thirty years, thousands of courageous Iranian women have raised their voices in protest and solidarity, steadfast in their resolve and determination to win their rights. The heroic and resilient participants in Iran's growing women's movement have relentlessly demonstrated that they will not be deterred in their pursuit of gender equality

In post-revolutionary Iran, the obstacles have been daunting, as the theocracy presently led by Supreme Leader Ayatollah Ali Khamenei (1989–present) continues to erect barriers to women's emancipation. The most recent presidential administrations have brought both increased repression (under former president Mahmoud Ahmadinejad, 2005–2013) and renewed hope (under current president Hassan Rouhani, 2013–present). Although clerical and political leaders have significantly influenced policies affecting women's lives over the past decade, the women of Iran have been relentless in their struggle toward equal rights and self-determination.

President Mahmoud Ahmadinejad's biased interpretation of religious teachings had severe repercussions with regard to women's rights. Writing in the *Guardian* on September 19, 2013, journalist Gareth Smyth noted that

> within months of Ahmadinejad's election win in 2005, Khatami warned of a "fanatical" interpretation of Islam. The blacksmith's son was adept in addressing poorer Iranians—and had a better

understanding of them than Khatami did—but his fiery rhetoric and undiluted evocations of the 12th Imam quickly alienated the US, Europe and the Arab Sunni establishment.[5]

In 2010, Ahmadinejad called on women to have larger families and to "perform their most important duty: raising the next generation!"[6] To encourage this new directive, the Iranian government implemented a policy whereby it would pay families a sum of $950 for every newborn, with an additional $95 annually until the child reached eighteen years of age.[7] In addition, authorities became more aggressive in

Mahmud Ahmadinejad (2005-2013)

apprehending women for dress-code violations, and, as referenced in the previous chapter, the government shut down *Zanan*, the country's leading feminist magazine.

When Ahmadinejad ran against opposition candidates in 2009, tens of thousands of women from various social classes supported the two reformist candidates who advocated for greater women's rights. Although Ahmadinejad was declared to have won the election in a landslide, protests mounted amidst allegations of fraudulent votes. Nearly three million peaceful demonstrators turned out on the streets of Tehran, voicing their slogan *"Where is my vote?"* and the Iranian Green Movement was born.

Despite the nonviolent actions of the demonstrators, there were many instances in which authorities resorted to violence. In 2009, the world watched in horror the video of twenty-six-year-old Neda

The 2009 Green Movement.

Neda Agha Soltan (1983-2009)

Agha Soltan's shooting death during demonstrations rejecting the outcome of the presidential election, which was repeatedly aired in the media.[8]

Iranian-American historian, author, and director of Iranian Studies at Stanford University Abbas Milani asserted:

> The movement was widely seen as a new non-violent, non-utopian and populist paradigm of revolution that infused twenty-first-century Internet technology with people street power. In turn, the regime's facade as a populist theocracy, led by a divinely sanctioned "guardian" and supported by a deeply pious nation, was torn asunder.[9]

Women's activist Parvin Ardalan gave this first-person account:

There were so many women in the streets. It was the first time that women and men walked side by side in protest. I will never forget it. What started as a protest against the election became a general protest for human rights. All the social and political movements were there: women, students and different ethnic groups.[10]

In the aftermath of the election, Ahmadinejad lost the support of many conservative women due to atrocities committed by his security forces against protesters. Turning a blind eye toward mistreatment and harsh sentencing of women protesters, Ahmadinejad also ignored allegations of rape and torture of detainees.[11]

Hassan Rouhani, a critic of Ahmadinejad, ran for president in 2013 using the campaign slogan "Moderation and Wisdom." He called for increased engagement with the outside world and initiation of talks with the West. Women hoped that his more progressive stance would bring changes in the realm of gender equality. Although Rouhani seems committed to women's issues, and some reforms have been initiated during his tenure thus far, his views often starkly conflict with the policies and directives of the Supreme Leader, who holds the ultimate power. During a recent Women's Day speech, Rouhani criticized "those who consider women's presence in society as a threat" and said Iran still had "a long way to go" to ensure gender equality. He went on to state that "we will not accept the culture of sexual discrimination" and "women must enjoy equal opportunity, equal protection and equal social rights." Ayatollah Khamenei could not find a single phrase in Rouhani's speech to agree with; rather, he proclaimed that gender equality is "one of the biggest mistakes of Western thought."

Against this political backdrop, this chapter will investigate the many ways in which twenty-first-century Iranian women are fighting for equality with courage and resourcefulness—and how far they have come in their quest to gain their long overdue human rights.

THE ONE MILLION SIGNATURES CAMPAIGN

In 2006, a group of Iranian women's rights activists, including Parvin Ardalan and Shirin Ebadi, started the One Million Signatures Campaign *(Yek Milyun Emza bara-ye Laghv-e Qavanin-e Tab'iz Amiz)*— aimed at achieving equality for women by demanding the repeal of discriminatory laws.

Shirin Ebadi spoke eloquently of the urgent need for change:

> Is it right in the 21st century to use lashing as a form of punishment? For years, this and hundreds of similar questions have preoccupied the minds of many Iranian women. They have used various means to express their opposition to discriminatory laws, and have used every opportunity to speak of equality and justice. Whether they were arguing for the legal rights and protection of girls, opposing stoning and early marriages, or protesting against gendered discrimination in family laws, Iranian women have been voicing their opposition. And underlying all these protests was that single pressing demand: Equality of rights between women and men in the laws of Iran.
>
> Now, Iranian women are spelling out this demand. A campaign to reform discriminatory laws has begun. This campaign will collect one million signatures from Iranian women and men to protest against this legal degradation. The feminist movement has taken another step forward by demanding the elimination of ALL legal inequalities against women.[12]

The campaign gathered support across the country, expanding from Tehran to Tabriz, Esfahan, Hamedan, Gorgan, Zanjan, Karaj, Yazd, and Kermanshah. Women from all walks of life became involved in raising awareness of the need for more equitable policies. While many of the campaign's demands were unmet, the movement

The women of the One Million Signatures Campaign.

achieved tangible results. It successfully pressured parliament to amend the inheritance law in 2008, giving women the right to inherit their husband's property. Also in 2008, "women were granted the right to equal blood money in accidents covered by insurance companies, and parliament prevented passage of Articles 23 and 25 of the Family Protection bill proposed by the Ahmadinejad government in 2007, which would have enabled men to take additional wives without their first wife's consent and would have mandated that women pay a tax on their fiance's *mehrieh* (dowry gift)."[13]

The organizers of the One Million Signatures Campaign developed strength in numbers by going door-to-door in their outreach to Iranian women of varied backgrounds. Sussan Tahmasebi, Director of Middle East and North Africa (MENA) Programs at the International Civil Society Action Network for Women's Rights, Peace and Security concluded:

We managed to create a discourse on women's rights at the highest levels of government and in the public.... Even the most conservative groups we talked to agreed that our demands were just and explained that they would not accept anything less for their own daughters! ... We will continue to push for women's equality, including under the law, until it is achieved. The lesson from the [Million Signatures] Campaign is that the independent women's movement gets its strength from its ability to engage with the public and so it should continue to talk to citizens on the streets and in the public sphere and wherever else they can be found.[14]

ADVOCATING FOR EQUALITY ONLINE

In the aftermath of Khatami's presidency and the elimination of a multitude of reformist organizations, women began using the Internet to sustain and propagate women's consciousness.[15] In 2001, when the Iranian government initially launched its Internet program, access to unconventional material was tenuous at best.[16] Gradual improvements led to an increase in the number of journalists and activists launching locally-produced feminist sites.[17]

Parvin Ardalan is one of the many activists who resorted to cyberspace to generate discussions about women's rights. As founder and editor in chief of *Zanestan*, Iran's premier online women's magazine, launched in 2005, Ardalan was instrumental in organizing mass rallies and meetings throughout the country.[18]

The website *Kanoun-e Zanan-e Irani* (*Iranian Women's Rights*) was managed by award-winning freelance journalist and editor in chief Jila Baniyaghoub. An excerpt from a 2006 article entitled "Women driven out of social life in southern port city" testifies to the important issues covered by the online magazine.

Soaring unemployment among educated women in the city of Dayyer in Bushehr province (southern Iran) has worried the women.

Robabeh Amini, advisor to the deputy governor, says, "Up until 1985, there was only one woman in Dayyer with a diploma. But now that the number of educated women has increased, none of them have jobs. About 500 female university graduates in Dayyer are unemployed.

Amini added, "Even the seashore here has turned into a men's area. Women do not have the right to walk on the beach."[19]

Baniyaghoub's 2007 and 2009 coverage of gender-related protests in Iran led to her imprisonment and thirty-year ban from journalistic activities. She believes "security forces have become more and more aggressive, even as women's actions have become more peaceful over time."[20] Nonetheless, Baniyaghoub ended a letter to her husband, written from prison, on an optimistic note:

We are 33 women with a variety of opinions and at times opposing points of views at Evin's women's ward. Some prisoners are supporters of the Green Movement, others are Baha'i, Born Again Christians or members of the Mojahedin Khalgh. My dearest Bahman, what I find most attractive about this prison is that individuals with a variety of backgrounds and opposing points of view are coexisting peacefully. We sit together, share meals, have discussions and arguments. I find this peaceful coexistence extremely gratifying. My experience here behind bars has made me hopeful that I may someday witness a similar model implemented across our society at large. I look forward to the day when men and women with a variety of political and religious beliefs live together without the need to eliminate one another, or become enemies as a result of their differences of opinion, religion or political ideologies.

If such a coexistence is possible behind bars, why should it not be possible across our beloved land? I am hopeful that someday we will witness such a society in Iran and know that better days lie ahead.[21]

Access to online articles like those published in *Kanoun-e Zanan-e Irani* and *Zanestan*, as well as other feminist-oriented Internet sites, are an invaluable outreach and networking tool. For young Iranian women in particular, social media provides a venue where they can share their frustrations over discriminatory policies and their hopes for relevant change. The following anonymous testimonials confirm the relevance of shared experiences provided by "the borderless nature of the Internet":

- ◆ "Cyberspace has been a liberating territory—a place to resist a traditionally imposed identity...."
- ◆ "The Internet is a new sphere of possibilities ... to build up a connection with physically removed persons."
- ◆ "We are like scattered bits and pieces coming together."[22]

It was not long, however, before the blogosphere drew the attention of the repressive authorities. With the influx of female bloggers, the government felt obliged to formulate new Internet policies regulating the expansion of weblogs. In 2006, the Supreme Council of the Cultural Revolution (SCCR) issued the Cyber Crime Bill, providing guidelines and penalties under the guise of "safeguarding individual rights as well as Islamic, national, and cultural values."[23]

While human rights defender, legal scholar, and feminist activist Mehrangiz Kar is discouraged by these policies and views them as another attempt to "stop the trend towards liberalization and to curtail the freedoms gained during the reform era," journalist and women's rights activist Noushin Ahmadi Khorasani remains hopeful: "We are linked together indirectly through theoretical and practical work. We work systematically; therefore, we operate like a chain."[24]

Extreme measures by the authorities to curtail the women's rights movement have indeed been debilitating for activists, and yet the Internet continues to be an alluring phenomenon for the nation's youth. The closure of thousands of websites has only intensified the determined resourcefulness of a youthful population, which has begun to resort to workarounds such as proxy servers, allowing the user to be redirected in disguise to the desired destination.[25]

A recent study conducted by the United States Institute of Peace estimates that there are 60,000 to 110,000 active blogs in Iran today, reflecting not only the strong desire of young people to be part of the international community, but also that "as the most restive segment, Iranian youth represent one of the long-term threats to the current form of theocratic rule."[26]

Today, 70 percent of Iran's population under the age of thirty adheres to a philosophical outlook that identifies with the ideals implanted during the reformist Khatami era.[27] Their continued nonconformity with official values indicates that nominal concessions are no longer sufficient to hold their allegiance. Increased urbanization, high literacy rates, and rising unemployment have combined with exposure to satellite television and the Internet to accelerate the pace of social change among a nonconformist youth.[28]

The adolescent population in Iran persists in expressing their thoughts and ideas online, despite two words that routinely appear on their screens: *access denied.* The following statements in the 2008 documentary *Generation Tehran* indicate that "despite restrictions in every aspect of their lives, Iranian youth exhibit progressive aspirations":

- ◆ "Our freedom should neither violate the rights of others, nor should it be confined to boundaries that limit us from improving ourselves."
- ◆ "Over here only your thoughts are allowed to be free."
- ◆ "You will never be able to successfully define people by a piece of land."

Interviews and footage from Internet blogs and cell phone videos amplify the voices of dissent and disillusion in the 2010 documentary *The Green Wave*. Director Ali Samadi Ahmadi captures the depth of anguish among the youth who envision "endurance" as their only source of salvation. The words of young bloggers are emblematic of the rise of a fearless generation that, above all else, has come to value "transparency, cultural openness, democracy, respect for Iran's cultural diversity, respect for the rights of women, and retrieving their lost humanity."[29]

One particularly valuable website for Iranian women and youth, *Tavaana,* was launched in 2010. It offers educational material, podcasts and video lectures, online courses, and webinars on pertinent Iranian human rights topics, including women's rights. Its mission statement reads:

> Tavaana E-Learning Institute for Iranian Civil Society is Iran's pioneer e-learning institute. Tavaana—meaning "empowered" and "capable" in Persian—was launched on May 17, 2010, with a mission to support active citizenship and civic leadership in Iran through a multi-platform civic education and civil society capacity building program. Tavaana holds a vision for a free and open Iranian society, one in which each and every Iranian enjoys equality, justice and the full spectrum of civil and political liberties.[30]

Tavaana's online courses, which are provided "on a secure, anonymous platform," include an eight-session class taught by Mehrangiz Kar, entitled "Protecting Women's Rights in Iran" that covers the Constitution's view toward women, a woman's right to her body, freedom of movement, rights in marriage and divorce, protecting wives' rights in marriage contracts, gender discrimination in criminal law, and women's access to leadership and decision-making positions.

Despite women's commitment to advocate for their rights online, the *International Business Times* recently reported that Iran's crackdown on Internet activists, human-rights groups, and cyber-dissidents "reveals a split at the top between moderate President Hassan Rouhani and hardliners associated with Supreme Leader Ayatollah Ali Khamenei." The author of the article, Erin Banco, related:

> Access to the Internet...is the latest battleground in the fight between the two camps. Leading human-rights advocates say there has been a clear increase in the number of activists arrested, detained and tortured because of their activity on social media, particularly on Facebook, since Rouhani took office in August 2013. The detentions come as Iran's hardliners struggle to keep tabs on a growing population that wants greater freedom of speech, a right Rouhani promised he would fight for when he was elected.[31]

PAYING A PRICE FOR PURSUING FREEDOM

The likelihood of being arrested and serving time in prison has not been a deterrent for many reformist women. Many who have been imprisoned remain committed to the struggle within Iran once they are freed; some leave the country in order to advocate for change from abroad.

Perhaps the government's failed ideology has been most obvious to a defiant female population that continues to boldly protest their enforced status of inferiority. In a country where freedom of expression is rarely afforded, women of all ages and from all walks of life relentlessly pursue equal rights, despite the fact that their earlier hopes have been shattered. Their resolve remains strong even though some 4,000 students, women's rights activists, and journalists continue to be detained in Iranian prisons.[32] Among those paying a high price for speaking out in favor of women's rights:

- In 2006, Noushin Ahmadi Khorasani and Parvin Ardalan were part of a large contingent of peaceful protestors at Haft-e Tir Square who were arrested, tried, and sentenced on various fraudulent charges.[33]
- In 2007, Parvin Ardalan was awarded the Olof Palme Prize for courage in Stockholm, Sweden, and although she was banned from leaving the country to accept the honor in person, the recognition itself was sufficient validation.
- In 2008, Ardalan was arrested along with thirty-two other women's rights activists, receiving a two-year suspended sentenced for organizing a peaceful protest at Haft-e Tir Square in Tehran. She was charged with the intent of "endangering national security" and "propaganda against the state." As with many of her predecessors, when Ardalan eventually fell prey to the Iranian authorities, it did not go unnoticed among Western nations.[34]
- In 2011, Maryam Majd, twenty-five, one of only a handful of Iran's female sports photographers, and filmmaker Mahnaz Mohammadi, thirty-seven, were arrested for "unspecified reasons." Mohammadi understood her detention in this way: "I am both a woman and a filmmaker—sufficient to be arrested."[35]
- Controversial screenwriter Tahmineh Milani, fifty-one, who has endured numerous arrests for her fearless on-screen portrayals since her career began in 1989, is adamant "that a society which reduces women to mere sexual objects would have a high price to pay."[36]
- Faezeh Rafsanjani, journalist, founder of the magazine *Zan (Woman)*, women's rights activist, former member of Iranian Parliament, and daughter of former president Akbar Hashemi Rafsanjani, recently served a six-month prison sentence for her relentless criticism of the regime's discriminatory practices. Asked by a reporter from reformist newspaper *Etemaad* about her protests against certain enforced customs, she stated:

Some customs in our society have been imposed, and an imposed custom is without value and cannot persist. Therefore, when I do not believe in that custom and I do not believe them to be logical or I do not value them to be beneficial to society, especially to girls and women, I do not see it necessary to follow them.[37]

♦ Jila Baniyaghoub, the award-winning freelance journalist mentioned earlier, served a one-year prison sentence and wrote about her experiences in her book, *Women of Evin: Ward 209.* According to Baniyaghoub, she was initially "blindfolded, and.... interrogated."[38] However, she is unshaken when recalling her interrogation session and the manner in which she boldly stood up for and defended her actions throughout the one-and-a-half hour process:

You call a peaceful protest radical? In your opinion, I'm a radical because I came out to cover a peaceful protest as a journalist? ... Does the fact that women are demanding legal equality endanger national security? What's your definition of security anyway?"[39]

RESTRICTED BUT PERSISTENT

Regardless of perilous consequences, Iranian women continue to pursue their rights. It would appear the tides of change, so desperately anticipated, cannot be stemmed.

Activist and journalist Shahla Lahiji estimates that despite the fact that female publishers and journalists continue to be handicapped by conservative restrictions,[40] there are still more than 400 female publishers in Iran today who are "younger and better educated than their predecessors."[41] The percentage of female journalists in Iran has increased from 2.5 percent in 1971, to 10 percent in 1997, to 22 percent by 2006.[42]

In 2012, reports appeared signaling the reimposition of restrictions by thirty-six public universities across the country, banning female enrollment in seventy-seven academic fields, including mathematics, engineering, and accounting.[43] Kamran Daneshjoo, the Republic's Minister of Science and Technology since 2009, justifies this drastic policy as a measure for safeguarding adherence to "Islamic values and principles" decreed in 1987 by the SCCR (Supreme Council of the Cultural Revolution).[44] The Iranian Parliament has accordingly voiced concern over the "destructive consequences of female matriculation on family life—such as employment and delays in marriage and motherhood."[45]

The investigations of Janet Afary and Pardis Mahdavi on gender and sexuality among Iran's "dissident youth" testify that this reformist younger generation remains resolute in the face of adversity.[46] Their documentation of Iran's sexual revolution as a "source of freedom and an act of rebellion," indicates a penchant for "living unrestrained sexual lives behind closed doors."[47] Afary notes that, although these women have learned to accept the presence of religion as part of an everyday reality, the introduction to a liberal Islam has significantly contributed to "closing the gaps that separate Iran and western countries."[48]

An eighty-two-page document on sexuality issued by Iran's parliamentary research department, highlighted in a 2014 article in *The Economist* entitled "Throwing off the Covers," confirms the fact that sexuality behind closed doors is clearly at odds with governmental directives. The report found that, "Not only are young adults sexually active, with 80% of unmarried females having boyfriends, but secondary school pupils are, too. Illicit unions are not just between girls and boys; 17% of the 142,000 students who were surveyed said that they were homosexual."[49] Quoted in the article, a thirty-two-year-old woman frankly expresses her opinion that the government has no right to oversee her sexual behavior. She adds, "I have one life and though I love my country, I cannot wait for its leaders to grow up."

The atrocious punishments inflicted on the LGBT community were revealed in a recent *Guardian* article, which detailed the lifestyles of the lesbian, gay, bisexual, and transgender population in Iran.[50] A study conducted by Small Media, a nonprofit group based in London, provides hundreds of direct testimonials through a clandestine online forum, revealing that

> the bastions of the Islamic Republic of Iran fully recognize an established (albeit secretive) LGBT [lesbian/gay/bisexual/transgender] community exists beneath the folds of fundamentalism in the country.... But figuratively speaking, the Iranian government is doing its utmost to sweep this community under a densely woven Persian rug.[51]

Despite the barriers to women's rights in the realms of sexuality, academia, free speech, family life, and employment, women (and men) continue to defy the powers-that-be in Iran. Although the government in Iran persists in reverting to "the failed policies of the past," Haleh Esfandiari, Director of the Middle East Program at the Woodrow Wilson International Center for Scholars, is confident that an outdated ideology will be ineffectual in decelerating the momentum of a feminist generation, as "Iranian women have again and again shown that they can come up with new ways of pursuing their goals."[52]

CAN RELIGION EVOLVE?

If centuries-old religious tradition is the greatest obstacle to women's liberation in Iran, then the crucial question is this: can religion evolve? In considering whether reformists in Iran can succeed in modernizing religious ideology, historians have compared that possibility to theological reform in Western nations. Perhaps the individual most responsible for religious reform in the West is the German priest Martin Luther (1483–1546). Luther's bold criticism of abuses by the Catholic Church in his *Ninety-Five Theses* is a testament to people's ongoing quest to decipher the word of God.[53] His revolutionary document protesting nepotism, usury, and the sale of indulgences brought about the Protestant Reformation.

Is there a Martin Luther in Iran, an individual who could modify the teachings of Islam to the extent that women would be freed from repressive ideology? In fact, reformer Abdolkarim Soroush has been referred to as "the Martin Luther of Islam."[54] In a recent writing, Soroush sets forth his "alternate belief" that the Koran was a "prophetic experience," relegating compilation of the sacred text to a mortal seen as both "the subject and object of revelation":

Women in present-day Iran.

When you read the Koran you feel that a human being is speaking to you—the words, images, rules and regulations and the like are all coming from the human mind.[55]

Such a credo frees man from strictly adhering to that which is traditionally considered to be an eternal covenant and the finite word of God. Like many radical theologians, Souoush insightfully challenges the ancient character of traditional dogma, referred to by his fellow activist and cleric, Mohsen Kadivar, as "the reign of political charlatanism in the name of Islam."[56]

While on one level the particular journey toward religious reformation is unique to Iranian society, other historical events in which atrocities committed under the alleged guidance of the Almighty have prompted reformers to alter the established conceptions of deity. One stunning example is that of Friedrich Nietzsche's (1844–1900) contentious proclamation that "God is dead."[57] His impassioned polemic shook traditional society to the core and left an enduring legacy. Although the death of God was not implied in the literal sense, Nietzsche's philosophy fundamentally symbolized liberation from whatever fetters the mind and the spirit, much in the same manner that Christian reformists were able to "find new destiny by destroying the old faith."[58] Professor Rex Welshon explains that inherent in Nietzsche's "God is dead" philosophy is that religious human beings "killed" God through their hypocrisy and lack of morality: "God has lost whatever function he once had because of the actions taken by those who believe in him."[59] In fact, Nietzsche's proclamation of God's "death" denotes a renewed sense of purpose:

God is dead. God remains dead. And we have killed him. Yet his shadow still looms. How shall we comfort ourselves, the murderers of all murderers? What was holiest and mightiest of all that the world has yet owned has bled to death under our knives: Who will wipe this blood off us?[60]

Nietzche's philosophy was resurrected by leading theologians during the 1960s' Death of God movement. Death of God theologians Paul van Buren and William Hamilton "agreed that the concept of divine transcendence had lost any meaningful place in modern thought."[61] They offered "the option of Jesus as the model human who acted in love. Thus, even though the transcendent God was no longer relevant or 'alive,' the immanent God could be experienced through the love of Jesus, as experienced in the Christian church." [62]

How does the philosophical reassessment of Christianity apply to the potential reform of Islamic ideology? Applying Nietzsche's seemingly blasphemous proclamation to religious practice in today's Islamic Republic is not intended to denigrate Islam but rather to honor the benevolent Creator and preserve a path toward spiritual redemption. Rather than exploiting the sanctity of the Creator for the purpose of instilling a draconian ideology, Iran might choose to follow a path set by Iranian reformers toward a "responsible theology" and "a radical questioning of tradition, not [as a form of] negative rebellion, but [as part of that which] contains the seeds of affirmation of the esoteric tradition."[63]

Former president of Iran Mohammad Khatami asserted that Islam suffers from a "vacuum social theory,"[64] and while he accepts that "a Godless life is dark and narrow," he also recognizes that "the limitations and relativity of all perspectives" is an important indication that "old interpretations do not suffice anymore."[65]

Mehrangiz Kar is confident "that the new generation raised by cooperating religious and nonsectarian women will be able to dismiss the superstitions and patriarchal traditions ... and not bend to the regime's restrictions against individual freedom."[66] The emerging belief among Iranian women that they have the right to determine how to live their lives is signaling the need for a new religious philosophy, one that prohibits patriarchy and oppression.

The following statement by Abdolkarim Soroush testifies to the shift in religious consciousness within Iran:

> The very fact that it is now accepted that a woman's presence in society doesn't violate her womanhood and Muslimhood is due to the immense changes that have occurred in the realms of thought and practice; these have also found their way into our religious consciousness and our society. Women's presence in society is now as natural and logical as their absence once was. This tells us the extent to which, in our understanding and practice of religion, we act unconsciously and involuntarily; this isn't to be taken negatively but in the sense that we are guided by elements that aren't in our control. They do work, shape our lives, our mind, our language.[67]

As a reformist who believes in pursuing a renewal of Islam, Mohammad Khatami provides us with a succinct yet profound message:

> If religion goes against freedom, it will lose.[68]

Through their advocacy, commitment, and sacrifice, countless Iranian women (and men) continue to demonstrate why religion must evolve—and dispense with its absolutist tendencies—if it is to exemplify moral validity.

CAN WOMEN IN IRAN BE EQUAL?

Nearly a century ago, an enlightened avant-garde planted the seeds of a feminist agenda by protesting the archaic mores that had resulted in the deplorable status of women. The Pahlavi monarchy instigated progressive policy changes, opening the door to women's rights and opportunities, but with the dramatic 1979 Islamic Revolution and the theocracy of Ayatollah Khomeini, reinforcement of patriarchal policies took hold. Thus, the abolition of the monarchy precipitated the regression of a nation perched on the threshold of modernization, extinguishing a multitude of initiatives of which a fundamental component entailed the emancipation of the Iranian woman. In Khomeini's "Islamic Government," a misogynistic regimen became embedded in a constitution reinforcing the primacy of the Sharia (Islamic law) over civil law and the absolute leadership of a Shiite jurist over popular sovereignty.

Three-and-a-half decades of the Islamic Republic's concerted effort to indoctrinate the Iranian population with an antiquated model of the Muslim woman has yielded results antithetical to the regime's envisioned objective: there has been an unprecedented surge in female literacy, and a burgeoning feminist movement has developed in opposition to the established order. Prominent author Haideh Moghissi believes that while social and cultural obstacles continue to prevail, women have become increasingly skillful in maximizing certain opportunities enhanced by the unexpected interplay of traditional and progressive policies. Moghissi states that a popular theme in the aftermath of the revolution has been the "observation that the Islamic Republic has not opened the gates ... but that women are jumping over the fences."[69]

What has become surprisingly apparent in post-revolutionary Iran is that women have benefited from their education in ways that were not anticipated by the traditional establishment. Despite its best-laid plans, the Republic's cultivation of an "Islamized" version of the Pahlavi regime's Western education system has empowered a new generation of women to strategically challenge an inferior status supposedly ordained by Allah. On the one hand, women are indebted to the momentum ushered in by the initial wave of Islamization of

Iranian society in the aftermath of the revolution, yet they are simultaneously nourished by the social trends instigated by an abandoned Pahlavi ideology.

While Khomeini's coming to power resulted in the overnight transformation of Iranian society—including a profound loss of women's rights—the consequences of the war with Iraq (which enabled women to perform roles outside the home) and single-sex education (which enabled rural and religious girls to attend school and thrive) produced a shift in gender consciousness. Young women who had previously been confined to their homes experienced a degree of freedom and self-determination that would prove life-changing for many. Stimulated by an elementary education that was based on the remnants of a fundamentally "Western" framework, and exposed to the progressive vision of the reformist women's magazines and online networks and publications, traditional women drew closer ideologically to their secular counterparts. Although some women may avoid the word "feminist," a unique ideological model has evolved: indigenous or Islamic feminism.

An unexpected consequence of the last thirty years of Iranian history is that women from all walks of life have come together to advocate for their freedom. While they may not see eye to eye on every issue, those who identify with the more "westernized" Iranian woman ushered in by the Pahlavi monarchy and those who represent the more traditional Muslim woman of the Islamic Republic era have forged a common commitment to democracy and human rights. The emergence of an unwavering feminist movement is due in large part to the fusion of these secular and religious factions.

In an article written for *The Daily Beast,* I posed the question, "Can religion evolve?" To some, merely asking this question is blasphemous. But its answer is crucial to addressing the critical question explored throughout this book: can women in Iran be equal? The constant tension defining life in Iran is inherent in these two questions, as are two recent statements by Iranian leaders.

Elected in 2013, President Hassan Rouhani made campaign pledges of increased social freedoms. Not long ago he stated, "Women should enjoy equal opportunities, security, and social rights." Yet there have been few gains for the women of Iran because pulling in the opposite direction is Supreme Leader Ayatollah Ali Khamenei, who holds that the notion of gender equality is one of the West's biggest mistakes. In fact, the current political climate in Iran does not appear to be encouraging for reformists. The *Guardian* recently reported that the media in Iran "has been banned from publishing the name or images of Mohammad Khatami, the country's reformist former president."[70] Since it seems that the majority of Iran's population identifies with the ideals implanted during the Khatami era, it becomes somewhat obvious that Khatami is perceived as a threat to the regime's stability. In fact, the prohibition against referring to Khatami in the press underscores the failed ideology of the conservative ruling establishment.

Iran's patriarchal society embraces a traditional interpretation of the Koran, which can be read as having a male-centric God who endorses the subjugation of women. Yet feminist activists are seeking new interpretations of the holy texts, embracing a more progressive Allah and a living Koran that may become the means for liberation. Hoping to reinvent the system from within, reformists are reassessing the passages used to oppress women and seeking to elucidate sacred writings in a new light. They believe that the only way women will achieve true reform is through an ideological leap of faith, an evolution of religious scripture. These acts of reinterpretation are nothing short of courageous.

One person leading the way toward this reformation happens to be a man, Abdolkarim Soroush, who was referenced earlier. A force behind Iran's pro-democracy movement, Soroush's reinterpretation of Islamic theology makes room for feminist ideals in religious tenets. According to Soroush, "God manifests himself in each historical period according to the understanding of the people of the era." He believes the Koran is a human phenomenon, which opens the text for interpretation. This isn't the first time such a radical redefinition of the Koran has been proposed; more than a century ago, Bibi Khanum Astarbabdi (1858–1921), one of the earliest pioneers of the women's movement in Iran, questioned the lesser status of Iran's women, asking "Is this God's compassionate decree?"

Women have challenged the doctrine of clerical rule during an era in which religion no longer constitutes the "opiate of the masses."[71] Islam is in transition and religiosity as a moral compass is eroding. While Iranian women were profoundly influential in bringing about the victory of the Islamic Republic, it now appears likely that they, along with Iran's youth, could be an instrumental force in effecting its dissolution.

What will it take to make today's religious leaders embrace spiritual evolution and gender equality? Is it just a matter of time, a question of the world evolving toward equality to the point where Iran's leaders will have to relent? It is my belief that once the Koran is liberated from the chains of dogma, women's freedom can follow. An evolved interpretation of religious teaching will allow God to be integral to the liberation of women rather than partner to their oppression.

In a country ruled by a theocracy, women continue to boldly pursue liberation despite an imposed, antiquated gender ideology. Contrary to all expectations, an unprecedented surge in female literacy persists; women now constitute 60 percent of all university students, and a flourishing feminist movement remains on the horizon. The beauty in this uniquely Iranian movement derives from the fact that it is fueled by women of all social and religious backgrounds. Theirs is a passionate and common cause—a woman's right to self-determination—and they will not rest until they are granted the divine compassion they deserve.

Epilogue

EXEMPLARY WOMEN FROM IRAN
(in alphabetical order)

The following are Iranian women whom I highlighted on my Facebook page from March 2014 to May 2015. I would like to acknowledge and celebrate them for their outstanding accomplishments and advocacy on behalf of women's empowerment.

Hamideh Abbasali

In 2014, **Abbasali** became the first Iranian to win a medal at the World Karate Championships.

Mahnaz Afkhami

Iran's second female minister, **Afkhami** served as Minister for Women's Affairs (1975–1978) during the reign of Mohammad Reza Shah Pahlavi.

"Don't let anyone define who you are or what you should be."

—NINA ANSARY

Epilogue

Haleh Afshar

First Iranian woman awarded the OBE (Order of the British Empire) and First Iranian woman formally introduced into the British House of Lords.

Lily Afshar

World-renowned, award-winning Iranian classical guitarist and the first woman ever to earn a Doctorate of Music in Guitar Performance.

Nazanin Afshin-Jam

A notable public speaker and human-rights activist. In 2007, Afshin-Jam received the Global Citizenship Award from the University of British Columbia, and in 2009 she was honored with the Human Rights Hero Award from UN Watch in Geneva, Switzerland.

Nazanin Aghakhani

First female orchestra conductor in Iran.

Shohreh Aghdashloo

A prominent stage and screen actress. In 2003, Aghdashloo became the first Iranian woman to be nominated for an Academy Award, and in 2009 she hit another cultural milestone by becoming the first Iranian to win an Emmy from the Academy of Television Arts and Sciences.

Shiva Nazar Ahari

Notable Iranian journalist, award-winning human-rights activist, and founding member of the Committee of Human Rights Reporters (CHRR). "When your heart trembles for the right of another human.... that is when you become the accused."

Haideh (Aida) Ahmadzadeh

Iran's first prima ballerina.

Qurrat al-'ayn (aka Tahirah)

Tahirah (1817–1852), considered the first suffrage martyr in Iran, was imprisoned for courageously defying societal customs by appearing unveiled in public. Her pioneering spirit is hauntingly captured in a final rendition prior to her strangulation with a silk scarf. "You can kill me as soon as you like, but you cannot stop the emancipation of women."

BAHAI.BE

Masih Alinejad

Iranian activist and award-winning journalist who received the inaugural Women's Rights Award at the Geneva Summit for Human Rights and Democracy for creating "My Stealthy Freedom" Facebook page, inviting women in Iran to post photos of themselves without their headscarves. "These women need their own platform. They want to express themselves [and] they don't have any voice inside Iran."

FACEBOOK

Goli Ameri

First Iranian woman to serve as U.S. Assistant Secretary of State.

WIKIMEDIA.ORG

Maryam Amid-Semnani

Amid-Semnani is considered to be one of the first female journalists in Iran. A leading pioneer of the early women's movement, Semnani was the founding editor of *Shokoufeh* (*Blossom*, 1913), one of the earliest and most influential women's newspapers in Iran.

EN.WIKIPEDIA.ORG

Anousheh Ansari

In 2006, engineer and entrepreneur **Ansari** became the first Iranian woman in space. "I hope to inspire everyone, especially young women and young girls… to not give up their dreams…."

MAXIM MARMUR/COLLECTIONS/GETTY IMAGES

Leila Araghian

An award-winning architect, **Araghian** designed Tabiat Bridge (Nature Bridge, 2014), Iran's largest pedestrian bridge.

REALIRAN.ORG

Parvin Ardalan

Notable Iranian journalist and founding member of the One Million Signature Campaign for Equality was honored in 2007 with Sweden's Olof Palme Prize. Ardalan dedicated her award to "all those who fight for freedom of expression in Iran."

Dr. Marzieh Arfaee

In 1935, **Dr. Arfaee** became the first woman to hold the rank of general in the Iranian military.

"Never underestimate the ripple effect of a random act of compassion."

—NINA ANSARY

Pantea Arteshbod

Arteshbod (559 B.C.) was one of the all time greatest Persian Commanders of the Achaemenid Empire (550–330 BC). The wife of General Aryasb (Achaemenids Arteshbod), she played a crucial role in keeping law and order in Babylonia after the conquest of the Neo-Babylonian Empire in 547 B.C. by Cyrus the Great.

Nafas Asnavandi

Three-year-old Iranian girl who is the first child in Iran to join Mensa, the largest and oldest IQ society in the world.

Golnar Bakhtiar

Iran's most famous female equestrian competed in seventeen national and international competitions. In 1977, Bakhtiar broke the Iranian record by clearing a wall at 2.05 meters.

Rakhshan Bani-Etemad

Referred to as the "First Lady of Iranian Cinema," internationally acclaimed director and screenwriter **Bani-Etemad's** unique cinematic style captures the bitter realities of a suffocating atmosphere for women in post-revolutionary Iran.

IRANREVIEW.ORG

Dr. Ta'lat Basari

In 1965, **Dr. Basari** became the first female vice-chancellor of an Iranian university. She held this post at the Jundishapur University in Ahwaz.

COMMONS.WIKIMEDIA.ORG/WIKI/FILE:TALAT_BASARI.JPG

Simin Behbahani

Referred to as the "Lioness of Iran," this two-time Nobel nominee and recipient of numerous accolades and awards is considered the greatest living female poet and one of the most celebrated figures of modern Persian literature.

ZEYNEP ATAMER / PERSIAN-STAR.NET

Nazanin Boniadi

Prominent Iranian actress, award-winning women's rights activist and official spokesperson for Amnesty International USA, focusing on the unjust conviction and treatment of Iranian women, youth and prisoners of conscience.

NAZANINBONIADI.COM

Sissy Cambis

Cambis (381 BC) was the Empress of Persia and mother of Darius III, the last king of the Achaemenid Empire (336–330 BC). A remarkable Achaemenid noblewoman, she valiantly fought, resisted, and did not surrender to Alexander of Macedonia.

PEREPOLIS.NU

Simin Daneshvar

Daneshvar (1921–2012) was widely regarded as Iran's premier female novelist and the first woman in Iran to publish her collection of short stories. "I wish the world was run by women. Women who have given birth and know the value of their creation."

FA.WIKIQUOTE.ORG

Dr. Parvin Darabi

Born in 1941, **Dr. Darabi** was Iran's first female Ph.D. in Electronics.

EN.WIKIPEDIA.ORG/WIKI/PARVIN_DARABI

Iran Darroudi

Darroudi is considered one of the most renowned contemporary Iranian painters. Darroudi, who studied at École des Beaux-Arts and École du Louvre in Paris, cultivated a unique style that merged elements of Western surrealism with Eastern mysticism. "I have learned the culture of today's painting in France, but I am rooted in my fatherland's culture."

SEBASTIENISRAEL.COM

Sussan Deyhim

Internationally renowned Iranian composer, vocalist and performance artist. Cited as "one of Iran's most potent voices living in exile," Deyhim has an elastic musical approach blurs the boundaries between various vocal traditions.

SUSSANDEYHIM.COM

Azad Deylami

Female guerrilla commander (751 AD), considered to be the symbol of Persian resistance against forced religion by the Arab invaders.

WWW.PERSIA4ALL.COM/ACHMAEMENIDS.HTM]

Sadiqeh Dowlatabadi

Persian feminist activist, journalist and one of the pioneering figures in the women's movement in Iran. In 1918, **Dowlatabadi** opened the first school for girls in Isfahan, Iran. "I will never forgive anyone who visits my grave veiled."

WIKIPEDIA.ORG

Mehrangiz Dowlatshahi

In 1976, social activist and politician **Dowlatshahi** (1919–2008) became Iran's first female diplomat when she was appointed ambassador to Denmark.

FIS-IRAN.ORG

> "Our past is the canvas that illuminates our future."
>
> —NINA ANSARY

Sibel Edmonds

A former FBI agent and founder of the National Security Whistleblowers Coalition (NSWBC). Edmonds is considered the "most classified woman in the U.S." after discovering serious security breaches, cover-ups, and intentional blocking of intelligence.

Dr. Haleh Esfandiari

A feminist scholar and the Director of the Middle East Program at the Woodrow Wilson International Center for Scholars in Washington, DC. In 2007, she endured four months in solitary confinement in Tehran's Evin Prison. "Iranians want evolution not revolution."

Isabelle Eshraghi

Internationally acclaimed award-winning Iranian photographer, **Eshraghi** rediscovers her roots in Isfahan, Iran, through a photographic lens. "My photographs interrogate my roots and question the condition of Iranian culture."

Yasmin Fahimi

In 2014, **Fahimi** became the first Iranian woman Secretary General of the Social Democratic Party of Germany.

Sattareh Farman Farmaian

Widely regarded as the "mother of social work" after establishing the Tehran School of Social Work in 1958. This institution was the first of its kind in Iran.

Zohreh Malileh Farshid

In 1974 **Farshid,** Iran's youngest female architect, designed the Ahwaz Sports Complex.

COMMONS.WIKIMEDIA.ORG/WIKI/FILE:ZOHREH_MALILEH_FARSHID

Forough Farrokhzad

Widely regarded as one of the most influential female poets of 20th century Iran, **Farrokhzad** was a brilliant modernist and iconoclast who broke new ground with her strong feminist voice criticizing social taboos including love, lust and sexuality.

WWW.COMMONS.WIKIMEDIA.ORG/WIKI/FILE:FOROUGH.GIF

Shirin Gerami

Iran's first female triathlete made history in 2013 by competing in the World Triathlon Championships in London.

WARREN LITTLE/COLLECTIONS/GETTY IMAGES

Shadi Ghadirian

Photographer **Ghadirian's** stunning images document the challenges faced by women in Iran trapped between tradition and modernity. Ghadirian's work is represented in numerous major public collections, including the British Museum, the Victoria and Albert Museum, and the Los Angeles County Museum of Art.

SHADI GHADIRIAN / ONEART.ORG

CNN.COM

Roya Hakakian

Acclaimed Iranian author and founding member of the Iran Human Rights Documentation Center. Recipient of the 2008 Guggenheim Fellowship, Hakakian has been highlighted among the "20 most important activists, academics, and journalists of our generation."

KIANA HAYERI / GUERNSEYPHOTOGRAPHYFESTIVAL.COM

Kiana Hayeri

In her 2012 project, "Your Veil Is a Battleground," twenty-six-year-old Iranian-born documentary photographer **Hayeri** captures the dual lives of a new generation of young women in Iran. "Everything that is banned by the government is being practiced, but behind closed doors."

PERSEPOLIS.NU

Iradabama

Iradabama (488 BC): Highly successful Persian businesswoman, most notable for running a flourishing wine and grain business that employed a large workforce during the reign of Xerxes the Great.

Sarvar Kaboli

Kaboli in a performance of *Cinderella* by the Iranian National Ballet Company, Roudaki Opera House, Tehran c. 1970s.

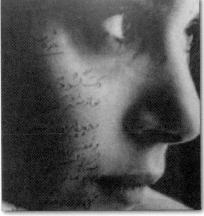

Sheema Kalbasi

Award-winning Iranian poet, human-rights activist, and documentary filmmaker. One of the few literary figures to promote poets of Iranian heritage, Kalbasi's work is distinguished by her passionate defense of ethnic and religious minorities.

Marjan Kalhor

Alpine skier and the first Iranian woman in Winter Olympics history. Leading her country at the 2010 Vancouver Olympics Opening Ceremony, Kalhor stated, "I want women to know if they want to, they can. I want them to know it is possible."

"There is no resolution in war, no glory in violence, and no redemption with injustice."

—NINA ANSARY

Tara Kamangar

World-class Iranian composer and classical pianist. A graduate of Harvard University and London's Royal Academy of Music, Kamangar is renowned for her diverse repertoire, ranging from classical to rarely-heard works by Iranian composers of the past.

Farah Karimi

In 1998, Karimi became the first Iranian woman elected to the Dutch Parliament.

Mahtab Keramati

In 2006, acclaimed Iranian actress **Keramati** was appointed UNICEF Goodwill Ambassador. Keramati has since taken part in the launch of the Global Campaign on Children and AIDS, and more recently chaired a debate on Iranian Women's Day.

Maryam Keshavarz

Critically acclaimed Iranian filmmaker whose 2011 narrative feature *Circumstance* received over a dozen awards, including Best Film at the Rome Film Festival and the coveted Sundance Film Festival Audience Award. "In Iran, anything illegal becomes politically subversive."

ROADSIDE ATTRACTIONS

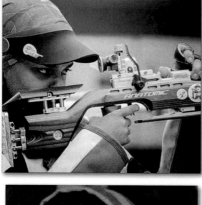

Najmeh Khedmati

In 2014, eighteen-year-old Iranian female sport shooter **Khedmati** won the Gold Medal at the Women's 10m Air Rifle shooting competition at the Asian Games.

Noushin Ahmadi Khorasani

Notable Iranian journalist, women's rights activist and founding member of the One Million Signature Campaign for Equality. "For me the struggle for equality is life itself."

SHAHRGON.COM/FA/WP-CONTENT

Lady Ninjas of Iran

Ninjutsu, a Japanese martial sport, is fast becoming a popular activity with women in Iran, where thousands currently practice in over twenty-two provinces.

SHARQ PARSI

Shahla Lahiji

As the founder of prominent publishing house Roshangaran Press (1985), **Lahiji** was the first Iranian woman to secure a publisher's license in her own name.

IRANIANSTUDIES.CA

Samira Makhmalbaf

In 2000, Iranian filmmaker **Makhmalbaf** was the youngest director ever to compete for the prestigious Palme d'Or at the Cannes Film Festival for her film *Blackboard*.

IRANIANS.KODOOM.COM/EN/SAMIRA_MAKHMALBAF

Dr. Mehrangiz Manouchehrian

In 1947, **Dr. Manouchehrian** becomes Iran's first female lawyer, and in 1963, she was one of two women appointed as the first female senators in Iran.

Arefeh Mansouri

Award-winning Iranian fashion and costume designer, whose "avant-garde masterpieces" have been showcased in major Hollywood productions and featured in fashion magazines including *Vogue, Elle,* and *Marie Claire.* "My designs are created for the unafraid. Decisive women who are non-conforming."

Tahmineh Milani

Feminist Iranian filmmaker **Milani's** numerous controversial features showcase women's lives under an oppressive regime. "When I make a movie, my aim is to challenge society."

Maryam Mirzakhani

In 2014, Iranian mathematician and Stanford University professor **Mirzakhani** became the first woman to ever win the Fields Medal, known as the "Nobel Prize of mathematics." Upon receiving the award, she said, "I will be happy if it encourages young female scientists and mathematicians. . . ."

Mahnaz Mohammadi

In 2014, award-winning Iranian documentary filmmaker and prominent women's rights activist **Mohammadi** began serving a five-year prison sentence. "I am both a woman and a filmmaker: sufficient to be arrested."

Farshid Moussavi

Award-winning Iranian architect recently chosen as one of "Five Women Changing the Face of Architecture," has co-authored numerous critically acclaimed projects, including the mirror-clad Museum of Contemporary Art Cleveland. "Architecture is a creative field ... and my strength is actually my difference."

"You will never find
what lies deep within
if you choose to remain
in shallow waters."

—NINA ANSARY

Dr. Azar Nafisi

Prominent professor and author of the critically acclaimed long-running *New York Times* bestseller *Reading Lolita in Tehran: A Memoir in Books.* Since 1997, Dr. Nafisi has been living in exile in the United States. "I left Iran but Iran did not leave me."

Noora Naraghi

Naraghi is an Iranian motocross racer. In 2009, she won Iran's first-ever female championship in motocross.

Marina Nemat

Author of the international best-selling memoir, *Prisoner of Tehran.* **Nemat** is the recipient of the European Parliament's inaugural Human Dignity Award and Italy's prestigious literary Grinzane Cavour Prize.

Zahra Nemati

First Iranian woman to win a Gold Medal in archery at the 2012 London Paralympic Games. Paralyzed in an earthquake, Nemati dedicated her medal to "all of the people who prayed for me to achieve success."

HARRY ENGELS/COLLECTIONS/GETTY IMAGES

Shirin Neshat

Internationally acclaimed Iranian visual artist and the recipient of numerous accolades and awards for her creations reflecting the paradoxes and complexities of a life in exile. "An artist like myself finds herself in the position of being the voice, the speaker of my own people... art is our weapon, culture is a form of resistance."

SHIRIN NESHAT / EN.WIKIPEDIA.ORG/WIKI/SHIRIN_NESHAT

Mahin Oskouei

A pioneering figure in theater arts, **Oskouei** was Iran's first stage actress and first female theatre director.

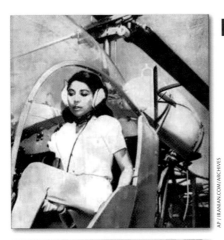

Princess Fatemeh Pahlavi

Half-sister of Mohammad Reza Pahlavi, the late Shah of Iran, was the first woman in Iran to be issued a helicopter license.

Princess Shams Pahlavi

Elder sister of the late Shah of Iran. An international Red Cross leader, she built the Red Lion and Sun Society, Iran's Red Cross. As the country's largest charitable organization, the group supported hundreds of hospitals, orphanages, youth activities, and disaster relief efforts.

Farokhroo Parsa

Iran's first female minister **Parsa** (1922–1980) served as Minister of Education (1962–1979) during the reign of Mohammad Reza Shah Pahlavi.

RAPHAEL GAILLARED/COLLECTIONS/GETTY IMAGES

Zoya Pirzad

In 2014, Iranian novelist **Pirzad** received France's prestigious Chevalier Legion of Honor award.

ZAHRA RAMEZANI / HONARONLINE.IR

Polaris

First all-female Iranian pop band to perform live in concert in Iran since the Islamic Revolution (1979). "We spent three years getting authorization to perform.... We aim to show that Iranian women are also able to work in this field."

JESSICA LUND

Laleh Pourkarim

Iranian singer-songwriter and producer. Since her 2005 debut on the Scandinavian music scene, **Pourkarim** has been awarded multiple Swedish Grammys including Artist of the Year, Newcomer of the Year, and Producer of the Year. "Just because it is black in the dark, doesn't mean there is no color...."

Azita Raji

In 2014, **Raji** became the first Iranian woman, as well as the first female, to be nominated as U.S. ambassador to Sweden.

Sheyma Rashidi

The only female firefighter in the city of Ahvaz, Iran.

Shahla Riahi

In 1956, **Riahi** (1926–present) became the first Iranian woman to direct a feature film, *Marjan*.

"Fight hatred with love, war with peace, and sin with absolution."

—NINA ANSARY

Atoosa Behnegar Rubenstein

Former editor-in-chief of *Seventeen* and the founding editor of *CosmoGirl*. Honored in 2004 by Columbia University as one of the "Top 250 Alumni" through the ages, Rubenstein is a strong advocate for girls to resist the pressure to be perfect. "Your greatness is about the kind of person you are and the contribution you make to humanity."

Shahla Sabet

In 1993, **Sabet** became the first Iranian woman appointed as judge in the United States.

Dr. Pardis Sabeti

Iranian computational geneticist and lead singer of the critically acclaimed alternative rock band *Thousand Days*. A graduate of Harvard Medical School and recipient of *Smithsonian* magazine's Ingenuity Award, Sabeti has been named one of the "Top 100 living geniuses."

EN.WIKIPEDIA.ORG/WIKI/ROOHANGIZ_SAMINEJAD

Roohangiz Saminejad

Iranian actress **Saminejad** (1916–1997) was the star actress in the first sound film made in the Persian language. Famous for playing the heroine Golnar in the film *Lor Girl* (1934), she suffered social ostracism from the conservative culture of the time. She had to change her name and live in anonymity and seclusion.

Pourandokht Sassanid (aka Buran)

First woman to become queen of the Persian Empire (629–632). Daughter of Khosrow Parviz II, the King of the Sassanian Empire (590–628). Pourandokht, who preached egalitarianism, infamously wrote in a letter to her troops, "A monarch, regardless of being a queen or king, must defend his or her land and treat the people with justice."

GRADESAVER.COM

Marjane Satrapi

Academy Award-nominated director and author of the internationally acclaimed best-selling graphic novel *Persepolis*. "It's true that in Iran women have half of the rights that men do. And yet 66% of students are women."

Dr. Fatemeh Sayyah

In 1942, **Dr. Sayyah** became Iran's first female professor when she was awarded the chair of Russian Language and Comparative Literature at Tehran University.

Maryam Sedarati

In 1973, Iranian female high jump star wins the Bronze medal by setting the 1.60-meter record at the Asian Track and Field Championships in Manila, Philippines.

Hila Sedighi

Renowned Iranian poet and female activist. Recipient of the Human Rights Watch's prestigious Hellman/Hammett grant in 2012, Sedighi's poems depict pain, suffering, and oppression in Iran. "But I shall still remain ... in this place, in my homeland.... I am rooted here in this soil."

Neda Shahsavari

The first Iranian woman to compete in table tennis at the 2012 Olympic Games in London. "The fundamental problem facing female national table tennis players is a lack of financial support for (Iran's) Table Tennis Federation."

Mansoureh Shojaee

Leading Iranian women's rights activist and founding member of the 2006 One Million Signatures Campaign for Equality. "We have so many successful women in the fields of art and culture, but for that we cannot say the situation of women is acceptable. We will only accept women's situation when women and men share the same right by law."

Dr. Shahla Solhju

Iran's first professional female astronomer and first codirector of Pahlavi University's Abu Reihan Observatory.

Neda Agha Soltan

A moment of silence for the beautiful and courageous **Soltan** (1983–June 2009), whose shooting death for protest against the 2009 presidential elections made her an iconic symbol of Iran's struggle.

CASPIAN MAKAN/AP

Sura of Parthia

One of the greatest heroines of Persian history. A strategical and military genius, the daughter of Ardavan V, the last king of the Parthian (Ashkanid) Empire, Sura held the rank of Ashkanid's General Sepahbod (Lieutenant General).

CHESS.COM/GROUPS/VIEW/ARTEMIS

Parisa Tabrizi

Google's "Security Princess": As head of security at Google Chrome, Iranian hacker **Tabrizi** protects the tech giant from cybercriminals in a booming industry in which women are vastly underrepresented.

INSPIRALLY

> "Let the desire to make a difference become the opiate of your mind, body, and soul."
>
> —NINA ANSARY

Niloufar Talebi

Award-winning Iranian librettist, poet, and theater artist. The recipient of numerous translation prizes from the international community, Talebi is the creator and visionary behind multimedia projects and theatrical pieces designed to pay homage to the Iranian culture on the world stage.

JOSE DIAZ / MELISSAIMAGES.COM

Newsha Tavakolian

Self-taught photographer **Newsha Tavakolian** began her career as a photojournalist at the age of sixteen, publishing work in *National Geographic*, the *New York Times*, *Le Monde*, *Newsweek*, and *Time* magazine. Tavakolian's captivating images document the evolving role of women in Iran and their struggle to overcome gender-biased restrictions.

NEWSHA TAVAKOLIAN / PRINCECLAUSFUND.ORG

Effat Tejaratchi

In 1939 **Tejaratchi** became the first Iranian woman to earn a pilot license using a Tiger Moth aircraft.

Dr. Alenush Terian

Iran's first female physicist. Referred to as the "Mother of Modern Iranian Astronomy," Dr. Terian was Iran's first female physics professor and founding member of the solar observatory of the Institute of Geophysics at the University of Tehran.

EN.WIKIPEDIA.ORG/WIKI/ALENUSH_TERIAN

Badri Teymourtash

Iran's first female dentist and one of the founding members of Mashad University's School of Dentistry.

COMMONS.WIKIMEDIA.ORG

Iran Teymourtash

A pioneer among women activists, **Teymourtash** was the country's first female editor of an Iranian newspaper.

EN.WIKIPEDIA.ORG/WIKI/IRAN_TEYMOURTASH

Maryam Tousi

Known as "The Fastest Woman in Iran," sprinter **Tousi** is the Iranian record holder in the 400m relay, and Gold Medal winner at the 2012 Asian Indoor Championships. "As a female sprinter, there is no future for me.... You can't hide the discrimination. But I am still hopeful for the future."

Monir Vakili

Celebrated opera singer **Vakili** (1923–1983) started the first opera company in Iran. A pioneer in the true sense, she gave performances as Madame Butterfly, Mimi in *La Boheme,* Violetta in *La Traviata,* and many others in Tehran's famed Rudaki Hall.

Maryam Nayeb Yazdi

The internationally renowned Iranian human-rights activist and heroine to Iran's political prisoners, **Yazdi** is the founder of Persian2English.com, a blog exposing human rights infractions by the Islamic regime to a global audience. In 2013, she was awarded the Queen Elizabeth II Diamond Jubilee Medal in recognition for achievements in social activism.

Irene Zazians

Regarded as the *Elizabeth Taylor* of Iran, "Iren" was the first Iranian actress to appear in a bikini, in the 1959 Persian film *The Messenger from Heaven.*

EN.WIKIPEDIA.ORG/WIKI/IRENE_ZAZIANS

Iranian Girl Scouts prepare for a parade in their uniforms: Tehran, c. 1950s.

IRANIAN.COM/ARCHIVES

Iranian women from Malayer (near Hamadan in the north-west) engage in target practice, c. late 1950s.

SHAHYAR MAHABADI / KAVEHFARROKH.COM

Iran: Women's orchestra, c. 1960.

Female Pilot: Iran, c. 1960s.

Imperial Iranian female police officers: Tehran, c. 1970s.

"Your moral compass should always be pointed in the direction of peace, resolution, and humanity."

—NINA ANSARY

Women parliamentarians of Iran, c.1970s.

Female motorcycle officers: Tehran, c. 1970s.

Imperial Iranian female naval officer, c. 1970s.

Imperial Iranian female military rifle training, c. 1970s.

Imperial female Air Force cadet of the Pahlavi era: Tehran, c. 1970.

The Iranian Women's Fencing Team, winners of the Gold Medal at the 1974 Asian Games.

IRANPOLITICSCLUB.NET

PARSTIMES.COM/SPORTS/WOMEN/HISTORY

Notes

INTRODUCTION

1 K. H. Adams and M. L. Keene, *Alice Paul and the American Suffrage Campaign* (Urbana and Chicago: University of Illinois Press, 2008).

CHAPTER One

1 Clara Rice Colliver, *Persian Women and their Ways* (Philadelphia: J. B. Lippincott Company, 1923), 269, 273, 274, 277.

CHAPTER Two

1 F. M. Mueller, *The Sacred Books of the East* (Oxford: Clarendon Press, 1880), 61.
2 K. Farrokh, "Gender Equality in Ancient Iran (Persia)," *Fezana Journal* 28, no.1 (Publication of the Federation of Zoroastrian Associations of North America), (March/Spring 2014): 105–107.
3 "This is an unknown area that requires further historical research." Cited from E. Sanasarian, *The Women's Rights Movement in Iran: Mutiny, Appeasement, and Repression from 1900 to Khomeini* (Westport, CT: Praeger Publishers, 1982), 10.
4 H. Afshar, "Competing Interests: Democracy, Islamization, and Women Politicians in Iran," in *Women and Fluid Identities: Strategic and Practical Pathways Selected by Women*, ed. H. Afshar (U.K.: Palgrave Macmillan, 2012), 172–173.
5 Parvaneh Pourshariati, *Decline and Fall of the Sasanian Empire: The Sasanian-Parthian Confederacy and the Arab Conquest of Iran* (London and New York: I. B. Tauris, 2008), 204.
6 Maria Brosius, *Women in Ancient Persia, 559-331 B.C.* (Oxford: Clarendon Press, 1998), 140–144.
7 R. N. Frye, *The Golden Age of Persia* (London: Phoenix Press, 1975), 54–57; R. N. Frye, ed., *The Cambridge History of Iran, Vol. 4: The Arab Conquest of Iran and its Aftermath: From the Arab Invasion to the Seljuqs* (Cambridge: Cambridge University Press, 2005), 1–56.

8   E. Sanasarian, *The Women's Rights Movement in Iran: Mutiny, Appeasement and Repression, From 1900 to Khomeini* (New York: Praeger Publishers, 1982), 14.

9   R. Arasteh, *Man and Society in Iran* (Leiden: E. J. Brill, 1964), 23; J. R. Kolayi, "Foreign Education, the Women's Press, and the Discourse of Scientific Domesticity in Early Twentieth-Century Iran," in *Iran and the Surrounding World: Interactions in Culture and Politics*, eds. N. R Keddie and R. P. Mathee (Seattle and London: University of Washington Press, 2002), 183.

10   Arasteh, *Man and Society in Iran*, 6.

11   E. L. Daniel, *The History of Iran* (Westport, CT: Greenwood Press, 2001), 77.

12   E. Sanasarian, *The Women's Rights Movement in Iran: Mutiny, Appeasement and Repression, From 1900 to Khomeini* (New York: Praeger Publishers, 1982), 12–13.

13   Sanasarian, *The Women's Rights Movement*, 13–14.

14   Jack Weatherford, *The Secret History of the Mongol Queens: How the Daughters of Genghis Khan Rescued his Empire* (New York: Crown Publishing, 2010).

15   Weatherford, *Secret History*, xiv.

16   R. J. Abisaab, *Converting Persia: Religion and Power in the Safavid Empire* (London and New York: I. B. Tauris, 2004); A .J. Newman, *Safavid Iran: Rebirth of a Persian Empire* (London and New York: I. B. Tauris, 2006).

17   "Central to the beliefs of Twelver Shia is the story of the hidden Iman, Muhammad al-Mahdi, or simply the 'mahdi, ' meaning 'divinely guided one.' In AD 874, the six-year-old son of the eleventh Iman went into hiding to protect himself from the persecution of the reigning Abbasid empire. The Shia believe that he hid himself in a cave below a mosque in Samarra; this cave is blocked by a gate that the Shia call 'Bab-al Ghayba, ' or the 'Gate of Occultation.' This is one of the most sacred sites in Shi'a Islam, and the faithful gather here to pray for the return of the twelfth Iman. The occultation of the mahdi, known as 'ghaybah' in Arabic, will end with his return to the world for the Last Judgment. This period will be marked by violent upheavals and attacks upon the faithful, but in the end, the mahdi with deliver the world to peace." In "Pilgrimage to Karbala. Who are the Shia?: Hidden Imam" *PBS.org*, March 26th, 2007, http://www.pbs.org/wnet/wideangle/episodes/pilgrimage-to-karbala/sunni-and-shia-the-worlds-of-islam/?p=1737.

18   M. Moojan, *An Introduction to Shi'i Islam* (New Haven and London: Yale University Press, 1985), 114; C. Turner, *Islam Without Allah? The Rise of Religious Externalism in Safavid Iran* (Richmond, Surrey: Curzon Press, 2000), 148–179.

19   The Sunni and Shiite divide is primarily over the succession to the Imamate. The Sunnis claim that the successor to the prophet Muhammad

can be chosen from the Muslim community, whereas Shiites believe that the successor can only be a direct descendant from the Prophet himself.

20   A. Amanat, ed., *Taj Al-Saltaneh: Crowning Anguish. Memoirs of a Persian Princess* (Washington, DC: Mage Publishers, 2003).

21   A. Mango, *Ataturk: The Biography of the Founder of Modern Turkey* (New York: Overlook Press, 1999); P. Kinross, *Ataturk: The Rebirth of a Nation* (London: Phoenix, 2001).

22   S. K. Nawid, *Religious Response to Social Change in Afghanistan 1919–29: King Amanullah and the Afghan Ulama* (Costa Mesa, CA: Mazda Publishers, 1999).

23   Bonnie E. Smith, ed., *Oxford Encyclopedia of Women in World History* (Oxford: Oxford University Press, 2008).

24   S. Effendi, *God Passes By* (New Delhi, India: Bahá'í Publishing Trust, 1971), 75; N. Motahedeh, "The Mutilated Body of the Modern Nation: Qurrat al-Ayn Tahirah's Unveiling and the Iranian Massacre of the Babi's," *Comparative Studies of South Asia and the Middle East* 8, no. 4 (1998): 38–50.

25   H. Javadi and W. Floor, trans., *The Education of Women and the Vices of Men: Two Qajar Tracts* (Syracuse: Syracuse University Press, 2010), 64–65.

26   Ibid.

27   Ibid., 134.

28   A. Amanat, ed., *Taj Al-Saltaneh: Crowning Anguish: Memoirs of a Persian Princess* (Washington, DC: Mage Publishers, 2003), 201.

29   Ibid., 201–202.

30   Clara Rice Colliver, *Persian Women and Their Ways* (Philadelphia: J. B. Lippincott Company, 1923), 94.

31   Ibid., 90–95.

32   Ibid., 92.

33   Ibid., 149.

34   G. Nashat, *Women and Revolution in Iran* (Boulder, CO: Westview Press, 1983), 23; E. Sanasarian, "Characteristics of the Women's Movement in Iran," in *Women and Fluid Identities: Strategic and Practical Pathways Selected by Women*, ed. A. Fathi (Leiden: E. J. Brill, 1985), 86–105.

35   Sanasarian, "Characteristics of the Women's Movement in Iran," 19.

36   *Alliance Israélite Universelle* was the first nationwide Jewish organization through which a number of Jewish schools were founded in Iran. Established in Paris in 1850, the Alliance aimed at unification of Jews. From 1898–1920, schools were founded in Tehran and in the cities of Hamada, Isfahan, and Shiraz. From 1921-1941 (the Reza Shah Pahlavi period), the Iranian community increased its involvement in the Alliance schools.

37   Ibid.

38   The Babi movement, which was violently put down during the mid-1850s, led to the founding of the Baha'i faith, which views the religion of the Bab as its predecessor. The Baha'i religion—a monotheistic religion—is

an outgrowth of Shiism, and emphasizes the unity of God in all world religions as well as the spiritual unity of men and women. The Baha'i religion grew out of the nineteenth-century messianic Shi'ite movement in Iran known as the Babi movement. Many conservative Shiites consider Baha'is as apostates, as they broke away from Shiite Islam and as a result were persecuted for their beliefs and consequently lacked legal status. An intrinsic component of this belief system was its egalitarian premise and the pursuit of knowledge for all regardless of gender. The abatement of restrictions towards this sect in the latter part of the nineteenth century led to the establishment of a number of semi-official Baha'i schools for girls, including the well-known Tarbiyyat School, cited from E. Abrahamian, *A History of Modern Iran* (New York: Cambridge University Press, 2008).

39 Sanasarian, "Characteristics of the Women's Movement," 39.

40 J. Afary, *The Iranian Constitutional Revolution 1906-1911: Grassroots Democracy, Social Democracy, and the Origins of Feminism* (New York: Columbia University Press, 1996), 10; V. Martin, *Islam and Modernism: the Iranian Revolution of 1906* (London: I. B. Tauris, 1989), 3.

41 R. Arasteh, *Education and Social Awakening in Iran* (Leiden: E. J. Brill, 1962), 180.

42 The term *Mullah* is defined by Oxford Dictionary as "A Muslim learned in Islamic theology and sacred law."

43 The International Institute of Social History, http://socialhistory.org/en/collections/s%C3%A9digh%C3%A9-dolatabadi-collection.

44 J. Afary, *The Iranian Constitutional Revolution 1906–1911: Grassroots Democracy, Social Democracy, and the Origins of Feminism* (New York: Columbia University Press, 1966), 187.

45 The International Institute of Social History, http://socialhistory.org/en/collections/s%C3%A9digh%C3%A9-dolatabadi-collection.

46 Ibid.

47 Sanasarian, *The Women's Right Movement*, 32.

48 Ibid., 33–34.

49 Sanasarian, *The Women's Right Movement*, , 35–36.; P. Paidar, *Women and the Political Process in Twentieth-Century Iran* (Cambridge and New York: Cambridge University Press, 1995), 95–97.

50 Sanasarian, *The Women's Right Movement*, 35–36.

51 The Constitutional Revolution was the first time the clerical establishment in Iran became divided. Some wanted to curb royal authority and have it be subject to a system of checks and balances, while others did not deem this necessary. Therefore, the only way to save Iran from government corruption and foreign manipulation was to decree and implement written codes of law—a sentiment leading to the Constitutional Revolution (*Enqelab-e-Mashruteh*) (1906–1911). Mozzafar al-Din Shah was therefore

forced to issue the decree for a constitution and the creation of an elected parliament (Majlis), which not only limited royal power but also led to the establishment of a parliamentary system in Iran.

52 M. Bayat-Philip, "Women and Revolution in Iran, 1905–1911," in *Women in the Muslim World*, eds. L. Beck, and N. Keddie (Cambridge, MA and London, England: Harvard University Press, 1978), 295–308; Afary, *The Iranian Constitutional Revolution 1906–1911*.

53 Sanasarian, *Women's Rights Movement*, 22.

54 Ibid., 20–35.

55 Bayat-Philip, "Women and Revolution," 301.

CHAPTER Three

1   M. Shuster, *The Strangling of Persia* (New York: The Century Co., 1912), 193.

2   The Cossack Brigade was a cavalry unit in the Persian army established in 1879 on the model of Cossack units in the Russian army. The formation of the Cossack Brigade was part of a larger process in which the Persian government, in the late nineteenth and early twentieth centuries, engaged various European soldiers to train units of the Persian armed forces, http://www.iranicaonline.org/articles/search/keywords:Cossack%20Brigade.

3   S. Cronin, ed., *The Making of Modern Iran: State and Society Under Riza Shah, 1921–1941* (London and New York: Routledge, 2003).

4   G. Lenczowski, ed., *Iran Under the Pahlavis* (Stanford, CA: Stanford University Press, 1978); Arasteh, *Man and Society in Iran*, 104–105.

5   R. Mathee, "Transforming Dangerous Nomads into Useful Artisans, Technicians, and Agriculturalists: Education in the Reza Shah Period," in *The Making of Modern Iran*, ed. S. Cronin, 133.

6   I. Sadiq, *Modern Persia and Her Educational System* (New York: Columbia University Press, 1931), 53; A. Banani, *The Modernization of Iran, 1921–1941* (Stanford, CA: Stanford University Press, 1961), 94–95.

7   Sadiq, *Modern Persia*, 57–58

8   Mathee, "Transforming Dangerous Nomads," 126–133.

9   Ibid., 126–133

10 D. Menashri, *Education and the Making of Modern Iran* (Ithaca, NY: Cornell University Press, 1992), 125–130.

11 M. R. Pahlavi, *Mission for My Country* (London: Hutchison & Co., 1960), 231; Noah Feldman, *After Jihad: America and the Struggle for Islamic Democracy* (New York: Farrar, Straus and Giroux, 2004), 104.

12 R .F. Woodsmall, *Muslim Women Enter a New World* (New York: Round Table Press, 1936), 47.

13 Menashri, *Education and the Making of Modern Iran*, 108.

14   H. E. Chehabi, "The Banning of the Veil and Its Consequences," in *The Making of Modern Iran*, ed. S. Cronin, 198.

15   A. Pahlavi, *Faces in a Mirror: Memoirs from Exile* (Englewood Cliffs, NJ: Prentice Hall, 1980), 24–25.

16   Ibid.

17   Chehabi, "Banning of the Veil," 202; C. M. Amin, *The Making of the Modern Iranian Woman: Gender, State Policy, and Popular Culture, 1865–1946* (Tallahassee: University Press of Florida, 2002), 81.

18   L. P. Elwell-Sutton, *Modern Iran* (London: Routledge, 1944), 139; J. S Szyliowicz, *Education and Modernization in the Middle East* (Ithaca and London: Cornell University Press, 1973), 177.

19   Banani, *Modernization of Iran*, 95.

20   Sadiq, *Modern Persia*, 115–116.

21   Menashri, *Education and the Making of Modern Iran*, 109.

22   S. Mahdavi, "Reza Shah Pahlavi and Women," in *Making of Modern Iran*, ed. Cronin, 184; Amin, *Making of the Modern Iranian Woman*, 129.

23   N. R. Keddie, *Modern Iran: Roots and Results of Revolution* (New Haven and London: Yale University Press, 2003), 102.

24   Mahdavi, "Reza Shah Pahlavi," 189; Menashri, *Education and the Making of Modern Iran*, 90, 100.

25   Pahlavi, *Mission for Country*, 47.

26   Sanasarian, *Women's Rights Movement*, 70; A. Tabari, "The Enigma of the Veiled Iranian Woman," (*MERIP Report*, February 1982), 24.

27   Sanasarian, *Women's Rights Movement*, 70; Tabari," Enigma of Veiled Iranian Woman," 24.

28   J. Rostami-Kolayi, "Expanding Agendas for the New Iranian Woman," in *Making of Modern Iran*, ed. S. Cronin, 157–159.

29   Ibid., 169.

30   Sanasarian, *Women's Rights Movement*.

31   Ibid., 67–71.

32   Pahlavi, *Mission for Country*, 255.

33   The Tudeh Party of Iran was formed in September 1941 to continue the work of the banned Communist Party of Iran, http://www.iranchamber.com/history/tudeh/tudeh_party01.php.

34   Lenczowski, ed., *Iran Under Pahlavis*; S. Kinzer, *All the Shah's Men: An American Coup and the Roots of Middle East Terror* (Hoboken, N.J.: John Wiley & Sons, 2008); A.M. Ansari, *Modern Iran Since 1921: The Pahlavis and After* (London and New York: Pearson Education Limited, 2003); E. Abrahamian, *A History of Modern Iran* (New York: Cambridge University Press, 2008).

35   British and Soviet troops had occupied Iran during World War II, as this made it possible to transport much-needed war material to the USSR. The occupation was a strategic move, and one that eventually played a part in

the defeat of Germany. However, this dual occupation proved disastrous for Iran, as it disrupted the Iranian government's ability to exercise effective authority. For example, Iran was still primarily agricultural at that time, and the Russians who had occupied the northern provinces freely exploited the agricultural and industrial resources in that region. To make matters worse, government revenue fell significantly due to the state's inability to collect taxes in the occupied northern region, and agricultural output decreased due to a combination of bad weather and disruption caused by Soviet occupation.

36 Pahlavi, *Mission for Country*, 79–81.

37 The Lend-Lease Act, a proposed plan passed on March 11, 1941, allowed the United States to provide needed supplies to any country whose security was vital to its defense. For a detailed description of this plan, consult B. Rubin, *Paved with Good Intentions: The American Experience in Iran* (New York: Oxford University Press, 1980). In 1949, President Truman proposed a worldwide policy of economic aid and technical assistance for underprivileged nations, which came to be known as the Point Four Program. For a more concise documentation refer to W.E. Warne, *Mission for Peace: Point 4 in Iraq* (Bethesda, MD: Ibex, 1999).

38 Pahlavi, *Mission for Country*, 89, 138, 181. The history of development planning in Iran dates back to the mid-1920s, when Reza Shah's government formulated its industrialization policy, mainly with contributions from the British Anglo-Iranian Oil Co. (AIOC). The plan was ambiguous, with narrow focus on the public sector and inadequate enumeration of concrete policy objectives. Development projects came to a standstill with the Allied invasion and occupation of Iran (1941) and the subsequent abdication of Reza Shah. "Actual" planning in Iran began in 1948, when the government of Mohammad Reza Pahlavi began to rebuild and expand its industries through the initiation of two consecutive seven-year cycles. For a more detailed summary, consult R. Looney, "Origins of Pre-Revolutionary Development Strategy," *Middle Eastern Studies* 22, no. 1 (1986): 104–119 and F. Daftary, "Development Planning in Iran: A Historical Survey," *Iranian Studies* 6, no. 4: 176–228.

39 Pahlavi, *Mission for Country*, 181.

40 F. Bostick and G. Jones, *Planning and Power in Iran: Ebtehaj and Economic Development Under the Shah* (London: Frank Cass Publishers, 1987), 122, 143; G. Baldwin, *Planning and Development in Iran* (Baltimore: Johns Hopkins Press, 1967), viii, 50; Third National Development Plan (1962–1968), Plan Organization (Tehran: Office Press Inc.).

41 Fourth National Development Plan (1968–1972), Plan Organization (Tehran: Office Press Inc.), 263.

42 Ibid., 262–265.

43 Fifth National Development Plan (1973–1978), Plan Organization (Tehran: Office Press Inc.), 199–215.

44 Fourth National Development Plan, 259.

45 Menashri, *Education and the Making of Modern Iran*, 164.

46 F. Sabahi, "The Literacy Corps in Pahlavi Iran (1963–1979): Political, Social, and Literary Implications." (Ph.D. diss. School of Oriental and African Studies (SOAS), University of London, 2002), 220–222; Menashri, *Education and the Making of Modern Iran*, 173; Arasteh, *Education and Social Awakening in Iran*, 191.

47 Arasteh, *Education and Social Awakening in Iran*, 70.

48 Menashri, *Education and the Making of Modern Iran*, 139.

49 S. Hamadhaidari, "Education During the Reign of the Pahlavi Dynasty (1941–1979)," *Teaching in Higher Education* 13, no. 1 (Feb. 2008): 17–28.

50 Pahlavi, *Mission for Country*, 262.

51 A. Doerr, "An Assessment of Educational Development: The Case Study of Pahlavi University in Iran," *The Middle East Journal*, no. 3: 200–213.

52 Pahlavi, *Mission for Country*, 236.

53 Ibid., 232.

54 F. R. Woodsmall, *Women and the New East* (Washington, DC: The Middle East Institute, 1960), 84.

55 M. R. Pahlavi, *The White Revolution of Iran* (Teheran: The Imperial Pahlavi Library, Keyhan Press, May 1967), 109.

56 Pahlavi, *White Revolution*, 22.

57 Ibid., 101.

58 Ibid., 99.

59 Ibid., 103–125; K. Watson, . "The Shah's White Revolution: Education and Reform in Iran," *Comparative Education* 12, no. 1: 23–36.

60 Sabahi, "Literacy Corps," 212–224; C. Prigmore, *Social Work in Iran Since the White Revolution* (Tuscaloosa, AL: The University of Alabama Press, 1976), 24–37.

61 Discrepancies found in researching the mandate for coeducational facilities during this period prompted confirmation with Abdolmajid Majidi, who served as Minister of State for Agricultural and Consumer Affairs (1968), Minister of Labor (1969–1972), and Minister of State and Director of the Plan and Budget Organization (1972–1977). In an interview conducted in Sausalito, California, on January 8, 2013, Dr. Majidi confirmed that in the aftermath of the White Revolution and the mandate for free and compulsory education, it simply became economically more feasible to have an integrated school system.

62 Sabahi, "Literacy Corps," 177–195.

63 Economic Report of the Central Bank of Teheran, 1978.

64 P. J. Higgins and P. Shoar-Ghaffari, "Sex-Role Socialization in Iranian Textbooks," *NWSA Journal* 3, no. 2 (Spring 1991): 213–232.

65 D. Coleman, *Emotional Intelligence* (New York and London: Bantam Books, 2005), 193–194.

66 J. W. Santrock, *Adolescence*, 14th edition (New York: McGraw Hill, 2010), 128–161; C. P. Edwards, *Promoting Social and Moral Development in Young Children* (New York: Teachers College, Columbia University, 1986).

67 G. Handel, S. E. Cahill, and F. Elkin, *Children and Society: The Sociology of Children and Childhood Socialization* (New York and Oxford: Oxford University Press, 2006), 131–182.

68 E. Durkheim, *Les Regles de la Monde Sociologique* (Paris: Presses Universitaires de France, 1992), 95; E. Durkheim, *Education et Sociologie* (Paris: Librairie Félix Alcan, 1922), 51; E. Durkheim, *Moral Education* (Mineola, NY: Dover Publications Inc., 2002), 223–251.

69 A. Kroska, "Conceptualizing and Measuring Ideology as an Identity," in *Gender and Society* 14, no. 3 (June 2000): 368–394; G. Ritzer and J. M. Ryan, eds., *The Concise Encyclopedia of Sociology* (United States and England: Wiley-Blackwell, 2011), 249.

70 S. N. Davis, "Gender Ideology: Components, Predictions and Consequences," *Annual Review of Sociology* 35 (August 2009): 87–105; G. Kaufman, "Do Gender Role Attitudes Matter? Family Formation and Dissolution Among Traditional and Egalitarian Men and Women," *Journal of Family Issues* 21, no. 1 (January 2000): 128–144; J. E. Cameron and R. L. Lalonde, "Social Identification and Gender Related Ideology in Men and Women," *British Journal of Social Psychology* 40, no. 1 (March 2001): 59–77; L. Kramer, *The Sociology of Gender: A Brief Introduction* (New York and Oxford: Oxford University Press), 2011.

71 Farsi Grade I textbook (Tehran: Ministry of Education, 1974), 4, 42, 52.

72 Ibid., 51, 58, 59, 81.

73 Ibid., 73, 74.

74 Ibid., 47; Farsi Grade 2 textbook (Tehran: Ministry of Education, 1974), 1, 72.

75 Farsi Grade 5 textbook (Tehran: Ministry of Education, 1974), 18.

76 Pahlavi, *Mission for Country*, 236.

77 E. Abrahamian, *Iran Between Two Revolutions* (Princeton, NJ: Princeton University Press, 1982), 434.

78 A. Pahlavi, *Faces in the Mirror: Memoirs from Exile* (Englewood Cliffs, NJ: Prentice Hall, 1980), 155–156.

79 Ibid., 155–157.

80 Sanasarian, *Women's Rights Movement*, 73–79; Woodsmall, *Women and New East*, 80–83; S. Vakili, *Women and Politics in the Islamic Republic of Iran: Action and*

Reaction (London and New York: Continuum International Publishing Group, 2011), 35.

81   Kermit Roosevelt Jr., *Countercoup: The Struggle for the Control of Iran* (New York: McGraw-Hill, 1979).

82   History: This Day in History, "CIA-Assisted Coup Overthrows Government of Iran," http://www.history.com/this-day-in-history/cia-assisted-coup-overthrows-government-of-iran.

83   Pahlavi, *Mission for Country*, 138–139; J. Gaslorowski and M. Byrne, *Mohammad Mossadegh and the 1953 Coup in Iran* (Syracuse and New York: Syracuse University Press, 2004).

CHAPTER Four

1   "Ayatollah Ruhollah Khomeini," The Biography.com website, accessed Mar 03 2015. http://www.biography.com/people/ayatollah-ruhollah-khomeini-13680544.

2   S. Abrahamian, *A History of Modern Iran: Clergy-State Relations in the Pahlavi Period* (New York: State University of New York Press, 1980).

3   Ibid. (Citation from *Velayet-e-Faqih*, a series of lectures published as a book, became a handbook for revolution.) (NOTE: In his book *The Reign of the Ayatollahs*, historian Shaul Bakhash states that the Iranian revolution derived specifically from Iranian conditions and Iranian historical and religious tradition.)

4   S. Bakhash, *The Reign of the Ayatollahs: Iran and the Islamic Revolution* (New York: Basic Books, 1990).

5   Ansari, *Modern Iran Since 1921.*

6   Shirin Ebadi, *Iran Awakening: A Memoir of* Revolution (New York: Random House, 2006), 33–34.

7   Pahlavi, *Faces in a Mirror*, 25–26.

8   Ibid., 27.

9   Ibid., 194.

10   Ibid., 195.

11   Ibid., 205.

12   Ansari, *Modern Iran Since 1921*, 219; A. Matin-Asgari, *Iranian Student Opposition to the Shah* (Costa Mesa, CA: Mazda Publishers, 2001).

13   Nashat, *Women and Revolution*, 1.

14   In 1979, Khomeini referred to the veil as "the flag of the revolution," cited in *Persian Mirrors: The Elusive Face of Iran*, E. Sciolino (New York: The Free Press, 2000), 134; F. Azari, "Islam's Appeal to Women in Iran: Illusions and Reality," in *Women of Iran: The Conflict with*

Fundamentalist Islam, ed. F. Azari (London: Ithaca Press, 1983); Ansari, *Modern Iran Since 1921,* 222–223.

15   Ansari, *Modern Iran Since 1921,* 219–221.

16   M. K. Shavarini, "The Feminization of Iranian Higher Education," *Review of Education* 51 (2005): 329–347.

17   Ayatollah Khomeini, *Der Spiegel,* interview conducted in Paris, November 7, 1979.

18   Ayatollah Khomeini, *Guardian,* interview In Paris, November 6, 1978.

19   Orianna Fallaci, "Iran: Khomeini and the Veiled Lady," *Time,* October 22, 1979.

20   Ayatollah Seyyed Ruhollah Mousavi Khomeini, "Precepts of a Permanent Contract," in *A Clarification of Questions,* unabridged trans. J. Boroujerdi (Boulder and London: Westview Press, 1984), 318.

21   S. Ebadi and A. Moaveni, *Iran Awakening—From Prison to Peace Prize: One Woman's Struggle at the Crossroads of History* (Canada: Random House, 2006), 38, 43.

22   D. Brumberg, *Reinventing Khomeini: The Struggle for Reform in Iran* (Chicago and London: Chicago University Press, 2001), 154; Hamid Algar, translator and annotator, *Islam and Revolution: Writings and Declarations of Imam Khomeini (1941–1980)* (Berkeley: Mizan Press, 1981); S. Akhavi, *Religion and Politics in Contemporary Iran: Clergy-State Relations in the Pahlavi Period* (Albany: State University of New York Press, 1980), 64-166; R. Takeyh and N. K. Gvosdev, *The Receding Shadow of the Prophet: The Rise and Fall of Radical Islam* (Westport, CT: Praeger Publishers, 2004), 24.

23   Bakhash, *Reign of the Ayatollahs.*

24   On November 5, 1979, Khomeini referred to the United States as the "great satan … the wounded snake," cited in "1979: Iran's Islamic Revolution," *New York Times,* May 27, 2007; R. De Zoysa, "America's Foreign Policy: Manifest Destiny or Great Satan," *Contemporary Politics* 11, nos. 2–3 (2005): 133–156.

25   L. Halper, "Law and Women's Agency in Post-Revolutionary Iran," *Harvard Journal of Law and Gender* 28 (2005): 85–138; H. Moghissi, "Public Life and Women's Resistance," in *Iran after the Revolution: Crisis of an Islamic State,* eds. S. Rahnema and S. Behdad (New York and London: I. B. Tauris, 1996), 251–267; Z. Mir-Hosseini, "Women and Politics in

Post-Khomeini Iran: Divorce, Veiling and Emerging Voices," in *Women and Politics in the Third World, ed.* H. Afshar (London: Routledge, 1996), 145–173; N. Ramazani, "Women in Iran: The Revolutionary Ebb and Flow," *Middle East Journal* 47, no. 3 (1993): 409–428; S. Haeri, "Temporary Marriage: An Islamic Discourse on Female Sexuality in Iran," in *Women and Islam: Critical Concepts in Sociology, ed.* H. Moghissi (New York: Routledge, 2005), 166–183.

26   Elaine Sciolino, "Love Finds a Way in Iran: Temporary Marriage," *New York Times,* October 4, 2000.

27   Constitution of the Islamic Republic of Iran.

28   Ibid.

29   Mohammad Hossein Nayyeri, *Gender Inequality and Discrimination: The Case of Iranian Women* (New Haven, CT: IHRDC Iran Human Rights Documentation Center).

30   Ibid.

31   In 1980, veiling was enforced in the public domain, with any deviation punishable by seventy-four lashes. For additional information regarding this mandate, consult Nashat, *Women in Revolution,* 121–123. The quotation appears in Nashat, *Women and Revolution,* 195; Z. Mir-Hosseini, *Islam and Gender* (Princeton, N.J.: Princeton University Press, 1999), 61; Vakili, *Women and Politics,* 51–52.

32   Ebadi and Moaveni, *Iran Awakening,* 106.

33   Ibid., 109.

34   M. Satrapi, *Persepolis: The Story of a Childhood* (New York: Pantheon Books, 2003), 5.

35   A. Nafisi, *Reading Lolita in Tehran: A Memoir in Books* (New York: Random House, 2003), 101, 165.

36   F. El-Guindi, *Veil: Modesty and Resistance* (New York and Oxford: Berg Publishers, 1999), 176, 176.

37   S. Behdad, "The Islamization of Economics in Iranian Universities," *Journal of Middle Eastern Studies,* 27 (1995): 193.

38   J. Al-i Ahmad, *Occidentosis: A Plague from the West* (Berkeley: Mizan Press, 1984), 64, 70.

39   Ayatollah Khomeini, *Keyhan Newspaper,* December 18, 1980, Interview.

40   Article 30, Constitution of the Islamic Republic of Iran.

41   K. Sobhe, "Education in Review: Iran's Cultural Revolution Duplicating the Chinese Cultural Revolution?" *Comparative Education* 18, no. 3 (1982):

271–280; Rebecca Barlow, "Women's Rights in the Islamic Republic of Iran: The Contribution of Secular-Oriented Feminism," in *Islam and Human Rights in Practice: Perspectives Across the Ummah,* eds. S. Akbarzadeh and B. Macqueen (New York and London: Routledge, 2008), 42.

42   H. Godagzar, "Islamic Ideology and Its Formative Influence on Education in Contemporary Iran," *Economia, Sociedad y Territorio* 3, numero 10 (2001), 321–326; Bakhash, *Reign of the Ayatollahs,* 110–114.

43   R. Sedgewick, "Education in Post-Revolutionary Iran," *World Education News and Reviews* 13, no. 3 (2000): 128–139; B. Mohsendouri, "Philosophy of Education in Post-Revolutionary Iran," *Comparative Educational Review* 23, no.1 (1988): 76-86; N. Entessar, "Educational Reform in Iran: Cultural Revolution or Anti-Intellectualism?" *Journal of South Asian and Middle Eastern Studies* 8 (1984): 47–64.

44   "Ayatollah Khomeini in an Interview with Committee Members of the *Ettela'at* newspaper," *Ettela'at,* October, 1979, interview (*Ayatollah Khomeini Dar Molaghat Ba Azaye Komiteh-ye Rooznameh-ye Ettela'at*).

45   D. Menashri, *Education and the Making of Modern Iran,* 319; A. M. Riazi, "The Four Language Stages in the History of Iran," in *Decolonization, Globalization, Language in Education Policy and Practice,* eds. Angel M. Y Lin and P. W. Martin (U.K. and Clevedon: Multilingual Matters, 2005), 100–116; H. Farhady, H. Sajadi, and H. Hedayati, "Reflections on Foreign Language Education in Iran," *The Electronic Journal for English as a Second Language* 13, no. 4 (2010): 1–18.

46   J. Amuzegar, *Iran's Economy Under The Islamic Republic* (London and New York: I. B. Tauris, 1993), 125.

47   Literacy Movement of Iran, The Activities of the Literacy Movement (*Fa'aliyatha-ye Nehazat-e Savad-e Amuzi*) (Tehran: Office of Planning and Statistics, 1987); G. Mehran, "The Paradox of Tradition and Modernity in Female Education in the Islamic Republic of Iran," *Comparative Education Review* 47, no. 3 (2003): 269–286.

48   The First Economic, Social and Cultural Development Plan of the Islamic Republic of Iran (1983–1988) (*Barname-ye Aval Tose'eh-e Eqtesadi-ye Ejtemai'i-e Farhangi Jomhuri-ye Islami-ye Iran*) (Teheran: Planning and Budget Organization, 1983).

49   "Objectives of the SCCR."

50   Paidar, *Women and the Political Process,* 320–321; SCCR: Goals and Duties/Principles of the Cultural Policies.

51   K. Aryan, "The Boom in Women's Education," in *Women, Power and Politics in 21st Century Iran,* eds. T. Povey and E. R. Povey (Burlington, VT: Ashgate Publishing Co., 2012), 41; IRI Ministry of Culture and Higher Education—Guide for the Selection of Fields in Higher Education (*Rahname-ye Reshteha-ye Tahseelee Baraye Daneshgaha va Moassesate Aliyeye Keshvar*), 1986.

52   IRI—The General Plan of the System of Education in the Islamic Republic of Iran, 1988.

53   Tehran Ministry of Education, 1988; The First Economic, Social, and Cultural Development Plan of the Islamic Republic of Iran (1983–1988) (*Barnameye Avaaliye To'she Eqtesadi Ejtemai va Farhangi-ye Iran*), 277, 37, 66, 72.

54   UNESCO—World Survey of Education V: Educational Policy, Legislation and Administration, 1971.

55   Ibid.

56   Menashri, *Education and the Making of Modern Iran,* 302.

57   P. Paidar, "Feminism and Islam in Iran," in *Gendering the Middle East: Emerging Perspectives,* ed. D. Kandiyoti (London: L. B. Tauris, 1996), 51–68.

58   Ayatollah Khomeini, speech cited in F. Rajaee, *Islamic Values and World View: Khomeini on Man, the State, and International Politics,* Vol. XIII, (Lanham: University Press of America, 1984), 36.

59   J. M. Henslin, *Sociology: A Down-to-Earth Approach,* 11th edition (Upper Saddle River, NJ: Pearson, 2010), 85, 373.

60   J. W. Santrock, *Adolescence,* 14th edition (New York: McGraw Hill, 2010), 162–182; C. E. Bidwell, "School as Context and Construction: A Social Psychological Approach to the Study of Schooling," in *Handbook of the Sociology of Education,* ed. M. T. Hallinan (New York: Springer Science and Business Media, 2006), 15–35; E. H. McEneaney and J. W. Meyer, "The Content of the Curriculum: An Institutionalist Perspective," in *Handbook of the Sociology of Education,* M. T. Hallinan, ed., 189–211; B. Schneider, "Social Systems and Norms: A Coleman Approach," in *Handbook of Sociology of Education,* ed. M. T. Hallinan, 365–386.

61   J. Karabel and A. H. Halsey, *Power and Ideology in Education* (US: Oxford University Press, 1977), 551.

62   Ibid; J. Shepard, *Sociology*, 10th edition (Belmont, CA: Wadsworth 2010), 345–356.

63   E. Durkheim, *Les Regles de la Monde Sociologique* (Paris: Presses Universitaires de France 1992), 95; E. Durkheim, *Education et Sociologie* (Paris: Librairie Félix Alcan, 1922), 51; E. Durkheim, *Moral Education* (Mineola, NY: Dover Publications, Inc., 2002), 223–251.

64   A. Kroska, "Conceptualizing and Measuring Ideology as an Identity," *Gender and Society* 14, no. 3 (June 2000): 368–394; G. Ritzer and J. M. Ryan, *The Concise Encyclopedia of Sociology* (Hoboken, NJ and Oxford: Blackwell Publishing), 2011, 249.

65   S. N. Davis, "Gender Ideology: Components, Predictions and Consequences," *Annual Review of Sociology* 35 (August 2009): 87–105; G. Kaufman, "Do Gender Role Attitudes Matter? Family Formation and Dissolution Among Traditional and Egalitarian Men and Women," *Journal of Family Issues* 21, no. 1 (January 2000): 128–144; J. E Cameron and R. L. Lalonde, "Social Identification and Gender Related Ideology in Men and Women," *British Journal of Social Psychology* 40, no. 1 (March 2001): 59–77; L. Kramer, *The Sociology of Gender: A Brief Introduction* (New York and Oxford: Oxford University Press, 2011).

66   IRI, Reading and Writing Farsi *(Khandan va Neveshtan-e Farsi)* Grade 1, Tehran Ministry of Education, 1986, 3, 13, 39; Reading Farsi—Grade 2, Tehran Ministry of Education, 1988, 68.

67   IRI, Reading and Writing Farsi *(Khandan va Neveshtan-e Farsi)* Grade 5, Tehran Ministry of Education, 1988, 155, 199.

68   IRI, Reading Farsi—Grade 2, Tehran Ministry of Education, 1988, 157.

69   Ibid., Grade 1, pages 2, 4, 38, 49, 68, 76; Ibid., Grade 2, pages 25, 31; Ibid., Grade 3, page 14.

70   Ibid., Grade 1, pages 27, 46, 83; Ibid., Grade 2, page 5.

71   Ibid., Grade 2, pages 155, 157.

72   Ibid., Grade 1, page 24; Ibid., Grade 3, page 72.

73   Ibid., Grade 2, page 10; Ibid., Grade 3, page 14.

74   Ibid., 71.

75   Ibid., 6.

76   Ibid., 26.

77   Ibid., cover page, 63, 64, 119; Ibid., Grade 5, page 147.

78   Ibid., Grade 2, page 23.

79   Ibid., 154.

80   IRI, Science *(Ulum-e Tajrobi)* Grade I, Tehran, Ministry of Education, 1988, 8, 35.

81   Ibid., 12.

82   IRI, Gifts From Heaven *(Hediye-hay-e Asemani)* Grade 4, Tehran Ministry of Education, 1988, 2.

83   Ibid., Grade 4, pages 108, 109.

84   Ibid., 111, 112.

85   IRI, Reading and Writing Farsi, Grade 5, Tehran, Ministry of Education, 1974, 18.

86   IRI, Reading and Writing Farsi, Grade I, Tehran, Ministry of Education, 1988, 37; Farsi Grade 2, Tehran, Ministry of Education, 1974, 53.

87   J. M. Henslin, *Sociology: A Down-to-Earth Approach,* 11th edition (Upper Saddle River, NJ: Pearson, 2010), 85, 373.

88   N. C. Chesler and M. A. Chesler, "Gender-Informed Mentoring Strategies for Women Engineering Scholars: On Establishing a Caring Community," *Journal of Engineering Education* (January 2002): 49–55.

89   G. Mehran, "The Paradox of Tradition and Modernity," *Comparative Education Review* 47, no. 3 (2003): 269–286.

90   Vakili, *Women and Politics,* 111.

91   H. Sedghi, *Women and Politics in Iran: Veiling, Unveiling and Re-veiling* (New York: Cambridge University Press, 2007), 225.

92   Ibid.

93   J. Brooks-Gunn and A. Peterson, *Girls at Puberty* (New York: Plenum Press, 1983), 110.

94   R. Simmons and D. Blyth, *Moving into Adolescence: The Impact of Pubertal Change and the School Context* (Piscataway, NJ: Aldine Transaction, 1987), 72–125.

95   *AAUW Report* (Washington, DC: American Association of University Women, 1990), 32, 147.

96   B. M. Solomon, *In the Company of Educated Women and Higher Education in America* (New Haven, CT: Yale University Press, 1985).

97   M. Sadker and D. Sadker, *Failing at Fairness: How Our Schools Cheat Girls* (New York: Touchstone, 1994), 18.

98   Ibid.

99   Ibid.

100   Ibid., 51.

101   Sadker and Sadker, *Failing at Fairness;* AAUW *Report,* 1990.

102   Sadker and Sadker, *Failing at Fairness* ; C. Riordan, *Boys and Girls in School: Together or Separate?* (New York: Teachers College, Columbia University, 1990); AAUW Report, *How Schools Shortchange Girls* (New York: Marlowe & Co., 1992).

103   Sadker and Sadker, *Failing at Fairness*, 233.

104   L. M. Brown and C. Gilligan, *Meeting at the Crossroads: Women's Psychology and Girls' Development* (New York: Ballantine Books, 1992); C. Gilligan, "Teaching Shakespeare's Sister," in *Making Connections: The Relational Worlds of Adolescent Girls at Emma Willard School*, eds. C. Gilligan, N. Lyons, and T. Hammer (Cambridge: Harvard University Press, 1990), 10; S. J. Hekman, *Moral Voices, Moral Selves: Carol Gilligan and Feminist Moral Theory* (Hoboken, NJ, and Oxford: Blackwell Publishers, 1995), 12.

105   Interview with Carol Gilligan, "Restoring Lost Voices," *The Phi Delta Kappan* 81, no. 9 (May 2000): 701–704.

106   C. Gilligan, *Joining the Resistance* (Cambridge, MA: Polity Press, 2011), 109.

107   Sadker and Sadker, *Failing at Fairness.*

108   Ibid.

109   Ibid.

110   Ibid., 1

111   Ibid.

112   Ibid., 235

113   Ibid.

114   AAUW , *How Schools Shortchange Girls: The AAUW Report: A Study of Major Findings on Girls and Education* (New York: Marlowe & Co., 1995).

115   Ibid.

116   Riordan, *Boys and Girls in School.*

117   C. Riordan, "Early Implementation of Public Single-Sex Schools: Perceptions and Characteristics," prepared for The United States Department of Education: Office of Planning, Evaluation and Policy Development, 2008, 21, 24, 27.

118   Gilligan, *Joining the Resistance*; Gilligan, *Joining the Resistance*; Sadker and Sadker, *Failing at Fairness*.; AAUW , 1990; C. Riordan, "What Do We Know about the Effects of Single-Sex Schooling in the Private Sector? Implications for Public Schools," in *Gender in Policy and Practice: Perspectives on Single-Sex and Coeducational Schooling*, A. Datnow and

L. Hubbard (New York: RoutldgeFalmer, 2002), 10–30; L. Sax, *Why Gender Matters: What Parents and Teachers Need to Know about The Emerging Science and Sex Differences* (New York: Random House, 2005).

119   UNESCO Institute for Statistics, *UNESCO Statistical Yearbook and World Survey of Education* (Montreal: UNESCO Institute for Statistics).

120   Statistical Center of Iran, 2007.

121   M. K. Shavarini, "The Feminization of Iranian Higher Education," *Review of Education* 51 (2005): 329–347; World Bank, "The Road Travelled: Education Reform in the Middle East and North Africa," 2008.

122   F. Harrison, "Women Graduates Challenge Iran," *BBC News*, September 19, 2006.

123   P. Paidar, "Gender of Democracy: The Encounter Between Feminism and Reformism in Contemporary Iran," Program Paper No. 6, Democracy, Governance and Human Rights, U.N. Research Institute for Social Development (UNRISD), October 2001, 1–47; G. Mehran, "Doing and Undoing Gender: Female Higher Education in The Islamic Republic of Iran," *International Review of Education* 55 (2009): 541–599; G. Mehran, "The Paradox of Tradition and Modernity," *Comparative Education Review* 47, no. 3 (2003): 269–286; G. Mehran, "Lifelong Learning: New Opportunities for Women in a Muslim Country," *Comparative Education* 35, no. 2 (1999): 201–215.

124   Sedghi, *Women and Politics*, 222.

125   A. Rabassa, M. Waxman, E. Larson, and C. Y. Marcum, *The Muslim War after 9/11* (Santa Monica, CA: The Rand Group), 2004, 226.

126   Vakili, *Women and Politics*, 85

127   Elaheh Rostami-Povey, "Women and Work in Iran (Part I)," *State of Nature: An Online Journal of Radical Ideas* (September 19, 2005): 7, http://www.stateofnature.org/?p=5243.

128   Ibid., 8.

129   "Rosie the Riveter," History.com, 2010, http://www.history.com/topics/world-war-ii/rosie-the-riveter.

130   M. Kar, "Women's Strategies in Iran from the 1979 Revolution to 1999," in *Globalization, Gender, and Religion: The Politics of Women's Rights in Catholic and Muslim Contexts*, eds. J. Bayes and N. Tohidi (New York: Palgrave, 2001), 177–203.

131   M. Kar, "Women's Strategies," 96.

132 Note: "Popular class" is not an American term. It refers to religious conservative women of the middle class who constitute the majority of women in Iran.

133 L. Halper, "Law and Women's Agency in Post-Revolutionary Iran," *Harvard Journal of Law and Gender* 28 (2005): 117.

134 Z. Mir-Hosseini, "Islam, Women and Civil Rights: The Religious Debate in the Iran of the 1990's," in *Women, Religion and Culture in Iran*, eds. S. Ansari and V. Martin (Richmond, Surrey: Curzon Press, 2002), 169–188.

CHAPTER Five

1 P. Paidar, "Gender and Democracy: The Encounter Between Feminism and Reformism in Contemporary Iran," *U.N. Research Institute for Social Development, Program Paper 6* (October 2001): 64.

2 Iranian State Television, February 18, 1988.

3 "Conservative or Conservative? A Pitiful Narrowing of Choice for Iranians and the World," *The Economist*, March 19, 2008; Sedghi, *Women and Politics in Iran*, 327–330.

4 M. Poya, *Women, Work & Islamism* (New York: St. Martin's Press, 1999); P. Paidar, *Women and the Political Process*; V. Moghadam, "Islamic Feminism and Its Discontents: Toward a Resolution and Debate," *Journal of Women in Culture and Society* 27, no. 4 (2002); V. Moghadam, *Modernizing Women: Gender and Social Change in the Middle East*, 2nd edition (Boulder, CO: Lynne Rienner Publishers, 2003); J. Afary, *Sexual Politics in Modern Iran* (New York: Cambridge University Press, 2009.); Vakili, *Women and Politics*.

5 R. K. Ramazani, *Revolutionary Iran: Challenge and Response in the Middle East* (Baltimore, MD: Johns Hopkins University).

6 Menashri, *Education and the Making of Modern Iran*, 327.

7 Ibid., 327.

8 Ibid., 315.

9 Moghadam, *Modernizing Women*, 208.

10 F. Roudi-Fahimi, "Iran's Family Planning Program Responding to a Nation's Needs," MENA Policy Brief (Washington, DC: Population Reference Bureau), 2002.

11 2006 Iran Census; U.N. Population Fund (UNFPA), *Country Report on Population Reproductive Health and Family Planning Program in the*

Islamic Republic (Tehran: Family Health Department, Undersecretary for Public Health, Ministry of Health and Medical Education, 1988).

12 *Encyclopedia Britannica,* last updated June 25, 2014, http://www.britannica.com/EBchecked/topic/489481/Hashemi-Rafsanjani.

13 Paidar, "Gender and Democracy," 18–24.

14 N. Keddie, *Modern Iran: Roots and Results of Revolution* (New Haven: Yale University Press, 2003), 294; Sedghi, Women and Politics in Iran, 242–272; Brumberg, *Reinventing Khomeini.*

15 Vakili, *Women and Politics,* 140–143; J. Kadivar, "Women Working as Judges and Making Judicial Decisions," in *Women, Power and Politics in 21st Century Iran,* eds. T. Povey and E. Rostami-Povey (London: Ashgate, 2012), 115.

16 C. De Bellaigue, *The Struggle for Iran* (New York: New York Review of Books, 2007), 8–9; E. Sciolino, "Daughter of the Revolution Fights the Veil," *New York Times,* April 2, 2003, 213; Vakili, *Women and Politics,* 119–140.

17 M. Kar, "Standing on Shifting Ground: Women and Civil Society in Iran," in *On Shifting Ground,* ed. F. Nouraie-Simone (New York: Feminist Press, 2005), 218–234; Samira Makhmalbaf, interview, May 15, 2012, *BBC News,* <http://www.bbc.co.uk/films/2000/12/19/samira_makhmalbaf_part2_191200_interview.shtml; H. Naficy, "Veiled Visions/Powerful Presences: Women in Post-Revolutionary Iranian Cinema," in *In the Eye of Storm, Women in Post-Revolutionary Iran,* eds. M. Afkhami and E. Friedl, (New York, 1994), 131–134.

18 G. Kiabany and A. Sreberny, "The Women's Press in Contemporary Iran: Engendering the Public Sphere," in *Women and Media in the Middle East: Power Through Self-Expression,* ed. N. Sakr (New York: I. B. Tauris, 2007); M. Poya, *Women, Work and Islamism* (New York: St. Martin's Press, 1999); Kar, "Standing on Shifting Ground," 218–234.

19 Z. Mir-Hosseini, "Debating Women: Gender and the Public Sphere in Post-Revolutionary Iran," in *Civil Society in the Muslim World: Contemporary Perspective ,* ed. A. B. Sajoo (New York: I. B. Tauris, 2002), 95–122; G. Khiabany, "Politics of the Internet in Iran," in *Media, Culture and Society: Living with Globalization and the Islamic State,* ed. M. Semati (New York: Routledge, 2007), 17–36.

20 The Guardian Council or the Council of Guardians of the Constitution (*Shoray-ye Negahban-e-Qanun-e-Assassi*) is the most influential body

in Iran currently controlled by the conservative faction. According to the Iranian Constitution, the council must be composed of six theologians (Islamic faqihs—experts in Islamic law) appointed by the Supreme Leader—who are "conscious of the present needs and issues of the day" and six jurists "specializing in different areas of law." The jurists are nominated by the Head of the Judicial Power (who incidentally, yet not surprisingly, is also appointed by the Supreme Leader) and elected by the parliament (Majlis) (Article 91 of the Islamic Constitution). The council has the authority to interpret the Iranian Constitution (Article 98), supervise elections, and approve candidates by "ensuring ... compatibility ... with the criteria of Islam and the Constitution" (Articles 94, 96, and 98). Furthermore, the Iranian Parliament derives its legal status from this council, and therefore all bills passed by the Parliament are subject to the approval of the council (Article 94). With respect to judicial authority, the council also functions in a similar manner as that of a constitutional court in that it has the authority to interpret the Constitution (Article 98).

21   "Iran Parliament Bid To Ease Press Curbs Quashed," *Los Angeles Times,* April 7, 2000; A. Soroush, "2001 World Press Freedom Review," *http:// www.drsoroush.com*; S. Patterson, *Let the Swords Encircle Me: Iran—A Journey Behind the Headlines* (New York: Simon & Schuster, 2010), 265; J. Campagna, *Iran Briefing*, Committee to Protect Journalists, May 2000.

22   De Bellaigue, *Struggle for Iran*, 5.

23   Moghadam, *Modernizing Women,* 218; "Profile: Mohammad Khatami," *BBC News,* June 17, 2009.

24   Mohammad Khatami, interview, May 1997, "What does Khatami Have to Say About Women?" (*"Khatami Dar Bar-re-ye Zanan Che Migouyad?"*) *Zanan,* no. 34, 2–5.

25   D. Menashri, *Post-Revolutionary Politics in Iran: Religion, Society and Power* (London: Routledge, 2001), 96; "Profile: Mohammad Khatami," *BBC News,* June 6, 2001.

26   Afary, *Sexual Politics,* 330.

27   S. Vakili, *Women and Politics,* 139; J. Afary, *Sexual Politics,* 329.

28   Ansari, *Modern Iran Since 1921,* 248; "Profile: Mohammad Khatami," *BBC News,* June 6, 2001.

29   A. Gheissari and V. Nasr, *Democracy in Iran: History and the Quest for Liberty* (New York: Oxford University Press, 2006), 135.

30   J. Howard, *Inside Iran: Women's Lives* (Washington, DC: Mage Publishers, 2002); Moghadam, *Modernizing Women*; Poya, *Women, Work and*

Islamism; Mir-Hosseini, *Islam and Gender*; Afary, *Sexual Politics*; Vakili, *Women and Politics*; H. Afshar, *Islam and Feminism: An Iranian Case Study* (New York: St. Martin's Press, 1998).

31   *The Concise Oxford English Language Dictionary*, 11th edition (New York: Oxford University Press, 2004), 522.

32   N. Tohidi, "The Issues at Hand," in *Women in Muslim Societies: Diversity Within Unity*, eds. N. Tohidi and H. L. Bodman (Boulder, CO: Lynne Rienner Publishers, 1998), 283–285.

33   Z. Mir-Hosseini, *Islam and Gender* (Princeton, NJ: Princeton University Press, 1999); Z. Mir-Hosseini, "Women and Politics in Post Khomeini Iran: Divorce, Veiling and Emerging Feminism," in *Women and Politics in the Third World*, ed. H. Afshar (London and New York: Routledge, 1996), 145–174; Z. Mir-Hosseini, "Stretching the Limits: A Feminist Reading of the Sharia in Post-Khomeini Iran," in *Islam and Feminism: Legal and Literary Perspectives*, ed. M. Yamani (London: Ithaca Press, 1996), 285-319; Paidar, "Gender and Democracy," 18–24.

34   H. Moghissi, *Populism and Feminism in Iran: Women's Struggle in a Male-Defined Revolutionary Movement* (New York: St. Martin's Press, 1996); H. Moghissi, *Feminism and Islamic Fundamentalism: The Limits of Post-Modern Analysis* (New York: St. Martin's Press, 2002); H. Moghissi, "Women, Modernity, and Political Islam," *Iran Bulletin* (Autumn/ Winter 1998); H. Shahidian, "The Iranian Left: The Woman Question: The Revolution of 1978–1979," *International Journal of Middle Eastern Studies* 26, no. 2: 223-247; H. Shahidian, "Islamic Feminism Encounters Western Feminism: Towards an Indigenous Alternative?" (paper presented to the Feminism and Globalization Seminar, Illinois State University, Springfield, IL: February 12, 1998); H. Shahidian, *Women in Iran: Gender Politics in the Islamic Republic* (Westport, CT: Greenwood Press, 2002); H. Shahidian, *Women in Iran: Emerging Voices: The Women's Movement* (Westport, CT: Greenwood Press, 2002); H. Afshar, "Feminist Voices," in *Women and Politics in the Third World*, ed. H. Afshar (London and New York: Routledge, 1996), 142–169; H. Afshar, "Islam and Feminism: An Analysis of Political Strategies," in *Islam and Feminism*, ed. M. Yamani, 197–217; S. Mojab, "Islamic Feminism: Alternative or Contradiction," in *Women and Islam: Critical Concepts in Sociology*, ed. H. Moghissi (London and New York: Routledge, 2005), 320–325; Tohidi, "The Issues at Hand," in *Women in Muslim Societies*, eds. Tohidi and Bodman,

277–294; N. Tohidi, "Gender and Islamic Fundamentalism: Feminist Politics in Iran," in *The Politics of Feminism*, eds. C. T. Mohanty, A. Russo, and L. Torres (Bloomington: Indiana University Press, 1991), 251–267; N. Tohidi, "Modernity, Islamization and Women in Iran," in *Gender and National Identity: Women in Politics in Muslim Societies*, ed. V. Moghadam (London: Zed Books, 1994), 110–147; Moghadam, "Islamic Feminism and Its Discontents," 1135–1171; V. Moghadam, *Women, Work, and Economic Reform in the Middle East and North Africa* (Boulder, CO: Lynne Rienner Publishers, 1998); A. Najmabadi, "Power, Morality and the New Muslim Womanhood," in *The Politics of Social Transformation in Afghanistan, Iran and Pakistan*, eds. M. Weiner and A. Banuazizi (Syracuse, NY: Syracuse University Press, 1994), 366–389; M. Najmabadi, "Feminism in the Islamic Republic: Years of Hardship, Years of Growth," in *Gender and Social Change in the Muslim World*, eds. Y. Haddad and J. Esposito (New York: Oxford University Press, 1994), 59–84; Z. Mir-Hosseini, "Sexuality, Rights and Islam," in *Women in Iran From 1800 to the Islamic Republic*, eds. L. Beck and G. Nashat (Champaign, IL: University of Illinois Press, 2004), 204–217.

35   Moghadam, *Islamic Feminism*, 1154.

36   Afshar, *Islam and Feminism*, 18.

37   Mojab, *Islamic Feminism*, 325.

38   H. Shahidian, "Feminism in Iran: In Search of What?" *Zanan*, no. 46 (1998): 32–38.

39   Shahidian, "Islamic Feminism Encounters Western Feminism," 11–12.

40   Poya, *Women, Work & Islamism*, 122; Vakili, *Women and Politics*; Afshar, *Islam and Feminism*; Moghadam, "Islamic Feminism and Its Discontents"; Kar, *Women's Strategies in Iran*; Halper, "Law and Women's Agency."

41   Mir-Hosseini, "Sexuality, Rights, and Islam," 212.

42   E. Addley, "Zahra Rahnavard: Wife Who Urges Protesters On," *Guardian*, theguardian.com, June 15, 2009, http://www.theguardian.com/world/2009/jun/15/zahra-rhanavard-iran-elections-presidential.

43   Jamileh Kadivar, "Women and Executive Power" in *Women, Power and Politics in 21st Century Iran*, eds. T. Povey and E. Rostami-Povey (Burlington, VT: Ashgate Publishing Co., 2012).

44 Jenny Cleveson, "Interview with Parvin Ardalan," *New Internationalist*, 440, March 1, 2011. *http://newint.org/columns/makingwaves/2011/03/01/interview-parvin-ardalan/*.

45 Arash Karami, "Faezeh Rafsanjani: Prison Was the Best Time of My Life," *Iran Pulse*, August 19, 2013, *http://iranpulse.al-monitor.com/index.php/2013/08/2637/faezeh-rafsanjani-prison-was-the-best-time-of-my-life/*.

46 "Azam Taleghani Scolds the Iranian Parliament for Straying Far from People (and Islam)," August 29, 2009, *http://iranfacts.blogspot.com/2009/08/azam-taleghani-scolds-iranian-clerics.html*.

47 M. Kar, "Death of a Mannequin," in *My Sister, Guard Your Veil; My Brother, Guard Your Eyes: Uncensored Iranian Voice*, ed. Lila Azam Zanganeh (Boston, MA: Beacon Press, 2006), 37.

48 *Asharq Al-Awsat*, "Shahla Lahiji: Iran's First Female Publisher," May 2, 2007, *http://www.aawsat.net/2007/05/article55262845*.

49 "Shirin Ebadi: Who Defines Islam?" Shirin Ebadi in conversation with Deniz Kandiyoti, opendemocracy.net, March 21, 2011, *https://www.opendemocracy.net/5050/shirin-ebadi/shirin-ebadi-who-defines-islam*.

50 *Asharq Al-Awsat*, "Inside Iran: Interview with *Zanan* magazine's editor, Shahla Sherkat," May 11, 2007, *http://www.aawsat.net/2007/05/article55262756*.

51 "The Receipt and Expansion of Women's Rights," *("Qabz va Bast-e Hoquq-e Zanan")*, interview with Abdolkarim Soroush, *Zanan*, no. 59, January 2000, 32–38.

52 D. Kandiyoti, "Bargaining with Patriarchy," *Gender and Society* 2, no. 3 (Sept. 1988): 274–290.

53 I. Lichter, *Muslim Women Reformers: Inspiring Voices Against Oppression* (New York: Prometheus Books), 2009; Mir-Hosseini "Debating Women," in *Civil Society in the Muslim World*, ed. Sajoo, 95–122; Vakili, *Women and Politics*; Afary, *Sexual Politics*; Poya, *Women, Work & Islamism*; Sedghi, *Women and Politics in Iran*; Moghadam, *Islamic Feminism*; Moghadam, *Modernizing Women*; Howard, *Inside Iran*; H. Nikanashi, "Power, Ideology and Women's Consciousness in Post-Revolutionary Iran," in *Women in Muslim Societies: Diversity Within Unity*, eds. H. Bodman and N. Tohidi (Boulder, CO: Lynne Rienner Publishers, 1998), 83–100; Shahidian, *Women in Iran*; E. Rostami-Povey, "Feminist Contestations

of Institutional Domains in Iran," *Feminist Review* 69, no. 1 (2001); Mir-Hosseini, *Islam and Gender*; A. Samiuddin and R. Khanum, "Gender Politics in Iran and Afghanistan," in *Muslim Feminism and Feminist Movements*, eds. A. Samiuddin and R. Khanum *(Central Asia)* (Delhi, India: Global Visions Publishing House, 2002), 45–81; H. Shahidian, *Journalism in Iran: From Mission to Profession* (London and New York: Routledge, 2007).

54 Moghadam, *Modernizing Women*, 177.

55 Nikanashi, "Power, Ideology and Women's Consciousness," 97; Vakili, *Women and Politics*, 85.

56 G. Khiabany, *Blogistan: The Internet and Politics in Iran* (London and New York: I. B. Tauris, 2010), 97; Poya, *Women, Work & Islamlism*, 139.

57 Vakili, *Women and Politics*, 117.

58 Mir-Hosseini, "Debating Women" in Sajoo, ed., *Civil Society in the Muslim World*, 102.

59 Shahidian, *Women in Iran*, 41; G. Khiabany and A. Sreberny, "The *Women's Press* in Contemporary Iran: Engendering the Public Sphere," in *Women and Media* in the Middle East, ed. N. Sakr (London: I. B. Tauris, 2004), 30; Khiabany, *Blogistan*, 103.

60 Khiabany and Sreberny, "Women's Press," 31–32.

61 Moghadam, *Modernizing Women*, 219.

62 Khiabany, *Blogistan*, 103; Khiabany and Sreberny, "Women's Press," 30–32.

63 Vakili, *Women and Politics*, 122.

64 Lily Farhadpour, "Women, Gender Roles, Media and Journalism," in *Women, Power and Politics in 21st Century Iran*, eds. Tara Povery and E. Rostami-Povery (Surrey, UK and Burlington, VT: Ashgate Publishing, 2012), 98.

65 Mir-Hosseini, "Debating Women," 114.

66 Ibid., 113.

67 Howard, *Inside Iran*, 47–51; Khiabany and Sreberny, "Women's Press," 35–36, Mir-Hosseini, "Debating Women," in Sajoo, ed., *Civil Society in the Muslim World*, 113–115; Z. Mir-Hosseini, "Islam, Women and Civil Rights: The Religious Debate in the Iran of the 1990s," in *Women, Religion, and Culture in Iran*, eds. V. Martin and S. Ansari (Surry: Curzon Press, 2002), 116.

68 Khiabany and Sreberny, "Women's Press," 35.

69   Mir-Hosseini, "Islam, Women and Civil Rights" in Martin and Ansari, eds., *Women, Religion and Culture in Iran,* 137; Khiabany and Sreberny, "Women's Press," 33.

70   Howard, *Inside Iran,* 151–212.

71   Rostami-Povey, "Feminist Contestations," 58.

72   "Iranian Newspaper Banned," *BBC News,* April 7, 1999.

73   "Iran Jails Former President Rafsanjani's Daughter," *BBC News,* January 3, 2012.

74   H. Esfandiari, "The Politics of the 'Woman Question' in the Islamic Republic, 1979–1999," in *Iran at the Crossroads,* eds. J. Esposito and R. Ramazani (New York: Palgrave, 2001), 110.

75   Afary, *Sexual Politics,* 317.

76   Mir-Hosseini, "Debating Women," 109; Nikanashi, "Power, Ideology, and Women's Consciousness," 85–86; Mir-Hosseini, *Islam and Gender,* 86.

77   Afary, *Sexual Politics,* 310

78   Vakili, *Women and Politics,* 120.

79   Afary, *Sexual Politics,* 316; Khiabany, *Blogistan,* 90–97; Vakili, *Women and Politics,* 87; Khiabany and Sreberny, "Women's Press," 19; Shahidian, *Women in Iran,* 82–85.

80   Mir-Hosseini, "Debating Women," 103–105; Khiabany and Sreberny, "Women's Press," 34–35; Keddie, *Modern Iran;* Mir-Hosseini, *Islam and Gender,* 215.

81   Poya, *Women, Work & Islamism,* 140.

82   P. Ardalan, "The Year 77—The Best and Worst Year for Women" ("*Sal-e Haftado Haft—Behtarin va Badtarin Baraye Zanan*"), *Zanan* 9, no. 51 (March 1999).

83   "Where are they now? Noushin Ahmadi Khorasani," *New Internationalist,* March 2013, http://newint.org/features/2013/03/01/noushin-ahamdi-khorasani/.

84   Moghadam, *Modernizing Women,* 217; Howard, *Inside Iran,* 13.

85   Moghadam, "Islamic Feminism," 1156; A. Samiuddin and R. Khanum, "Gender Politics in Iran and Afghanistan," in *Muslim Feminism and Feminist Movements (Central Asia),* eds. A. Saiuddin and R. Khanum (Delhi, India: Global Vision Publishing House, 2002), 236; Afshar, "Islam and Feminism," 214.

86   "Iran Hardliners Push for Family Law Bill That Activists Say Further Erodes Women's Rights," *Los Angeles Times,* August 26, 2010.

CHAPTER Six

1   Deborah Campbell, "Iran's Quiet Revolution: A Feminist Magazine, a Nobelist, and a Rising Generation Try to Promote Women's Equality," *msmagazine.com*, Winter 2007, http://www.msmagazine.com/winter2007/iransquietrevolution.asp.

2   Nina Ansary, "Iranian Women's Magazine *Zanan* Makes Comeback" *Women's eNews*, May 28, 2014, http://www.trust.org/item/20140528202132-hlfws/.

3   Golnaz Esfandiari, "Iranian women's magazine editor accused of promoting feminist views," *theguardian.com*, September 5, 2014, http://www.theguardian.com/world/iran-blog/2014/sep/05/iran-editor-feminist-views.

4   Afary, *Sexual Politics*, 317.

5   Khiabany, *Blogistan*, 102.

6   *Fiq'h* is an Arabic term, which literally translated means "full comprehension, to know, to understand." It is the human understanding of the Sharia, which has been expanded through interpretation of the Koran by Islamic jurists and the process of gaining knowledge of Islam through jurisprudence.

7   As quoted in H. Shahidian, *Women in Iran: Emerging Voices in the Women's Movement* (Santa Barbara, CA: Praeger, 2002), 71.

8   "Inside Iran: Interview with 'Zanan' Magazine's Editor Shahla Sherkat," *Asharq al-Awsat*, May 11, 2007.

9   Afary, *Sexual Politics*, 316–317; Lichter, *Muslim Women Reformers*, 196; Kar, "Standing on Shifting Ground," 225.

10 Lichter, *Muslim Women Reformers*, 133.

11 Lichter, *Muslim Women Reformers*, 197; Poya, *Women, Work & Islamism*, 141; Interview with Mohammad Khatami, *Zanan*, no. 34, 6th year, 2–5, May 1997; F. Sadeghi, "Bypassing Islamism and Feminism: Women's Resistance and Rebellion in Post-Revolutionary Iran," in *Revue des Mondes Musulmans et de la Méditeranée*, December 2010, 218.

12 Howard, *Inside Iran*, 142–144; Rostami-Povey, "Feminist Contestations," 59; Moghadam, *Islamic Feminism*, 219; Lichter, *Muslim Women Reformers*, 140; Shahidian, *Women in Iran*, 40–41; A. Najmabadi, "Feminism in an Islamic Republic," in *Transitions, Environments and Translations: Feminism in International Politics*, eds. J. Scott, C. Kaplan, and D. Keates (London and New York: Routledge, 1997), 390–399.

13 A. Najmabadi, "Feminism in an Islamic Republic," in *Transitions, Environments and Translations: Feminism in International Politics*, eds. C. Scott Kaplan and D. Keates (London and New York: Routledge, 2001), 71.

14 Afary, *Sexual Politics*, 320; Mir-Hosseini, "Stretching the Limits," 285–309.

15 Vakili, *Women and Politics*, 105–106.

16 *Zanan*, June 1994, no. 18, cover; August 1994, no. 19, 68–72; November 2003, no. 104, 2–6; April 2006, no. 131, 65; April 2007, no. 143, 2–5; July 2007, no. 146, 23–24; October 2007, no. 149, 2–5; March 1995, no. 23, 46–55; February 1992, no. 2, 26–31; November 1994, no. 20, 66–67; August 2007, no. 147, 82–85.

17 *Zanan*, August 2007, no. 147, 82–84; February 1992, no. 1, 40–51; May 1998, no. 43, 4–10.

18 *Zanan*, July 1997, no. 35, 28–35.

19 *Zanan*, February 1994, no. 22, 36–38; November 1992, no. 8, 42–44; April 1994, no. 17, 18–20; December 1995, no. 27, 22–23.

20 *Zanan*, November 1992, no. 8, 42–44.

21 *Zanan*, April 1994, no. 17, 18.

22 *Zanan*, December 1995, no. 27, 22–23.

23 *Zanan*, February 1994, no. 22, 36.

24 J. Syfers, "Why I Want a Wife," *Ms.* magazine, Spring 1972; "Why I Want a Wife," *("Man Ham Zan Mikhaham")*, *Zanan*, December 1999, no. 58, 44–45.

25 D. H. Currie, *Girl Talk: Adolescent Magazines and Their Readers* (Toronto: University of Toronto Press, 1999), 56.

26 Currie, *Girl Talk*, 7.

27 J. J. Arnett, "Adolescents' Uses of Media for Self-Socialization," *Journal of Youth and Adolescents* 24, no. 5 (1995): 520–523; C. Gilligan, *In a Different Voice* (Cambridge, MA: Harvard University Press, 1993); M. Pipher, *Raising Ophelia: Saving the Selves of Adolescent Girls* (New York: Riverhead Books, 1994); D. Gauntlett, *Media, Gender and Identity: An Introduction* (London and New York: Routledge, 2008).

28 Arnett, "Adolescents' Uses of Media," 523; S. W. Bowling, T. S. Zimmerman and K. C. Daniels, "Empower: A Feminist Consciousness-Raising Curriculum for Adolescent Women," *Journal of Child and Adolescent Group Therapy* 10, no. 1 (2000): 3-28.

29 Pipher, *Raising Ophelia*, 38–42.

30 N. H. Barazangi, "Self-Identity As a Form of Democratization," in *Democratization and Women's Grassroots Movement*, eds. M. Bystydzienski and J. Sekhon (Bloomington and Indianapolis: Indiana University Press, 1999), 146.

31 Moghadam, *Islamic Feminism*, 177; Mir-Hosseini, "Sexuality, Rights and Islam," 214; Z. Mir-Hosseini, "The Conservative–Reformist Conflict over Women's Rights in Iran," *International Journal of Politics, Culture and Society* 16, no. 1 (Fall 2002): 37–53; F. Jahanbaksh, *Islam, Democracy and Religious Modernism in Iran (1953–2000): From Bazargan to Soroush* (Boston: Brill Leiden, 2001).

32 Vakili, *Women and Politics* (quotations appear on 106); Shahidian, *Women in Iran*, 35; Afary, *Sexual Politics*, 320; Mir-Hosseini, "Sexuality, Rights and

Islam," 204; A. Ashraf and A. Banuazizi, "Iran's Tortuous Path Toward Islamic Liberalism," *International Journal of Politics, Culture and Society* 15, no. 2 (Winter 2001}: 237–256.

33   S. Macleod, "The 2005 Time 100: The Lives and Ideals of the World's Most Influential People," *Time*, April 18, 2005.

34   N. Keddie, *Modern Iran: Roots and Results of Revolution* (New Haven and London: Yale University Press, 2003), 250.

35   C. Kurzman, *Liberal Islam* (New York and Oxford: Oxford University Press, 1998), 244; Mir-Hosseini, *Islam and Gender*, 218; F. Jahanbakhsh, "Religion and Political Discourse in Iran: Moving Towards Post-Fundamentalism," *Brown Journal of World Affairs* IX, issue 2 (Winter/Spring 2002/2003): 243–254.

36   A. Soroush, M. Sadri, and A. Sadri, *Reason, Freedom and Democracy in Islam: The Essential Writings of Abdolkarim Soroush* (New York: Oxford University Press, 2000).

37   Afary, *Sexual Politics*, 320–321.

38   A. Soroush, "The Receipt and Expansion of Women's Rights," *Zanan*, January 2000, *(Qabz va Bast-e Hoquq-e Zanan)*, no. 59, 32–38.

39   Mir-Hosseini, *Islam and Gender*, 215.

40   F. Vahdat, "Post-Revolutionary Islamic Discourses on Modernity in Iran: Expansion and Contradiction of Human Subjectivity," *International Journal of Middle Eastern Studies* 35 (2003): 599–631.

41   Fatma Saqir, "Islam Is a Religion, Not a Political Agenda," interview with Mohammad Mujtahid Shabestari, en.qantara.de, July 11, 2008.

42   R. Wright, *Dreams and Shadows: The Future of the Middle East* (US: Penguin Press, 2008), 296.

43   "A Scholar and Dissident," *The Chronicle: The Independent Daily at Duke University*, December 2, 2011.

44   R. Eftekhari, "Zanan: Trials and Successes of a Feminist Magazine in Iran," in *Middle Eastern Women on the Move: Openings for and the Constraints on Women's Political Participation in the Middle East*, proceedings of a conference of the Middle East Project at the Woodrow Wilson International Center for Scholars, October 2 and 3, 2001, published 2003, 18.

45   Mir-Hosseini, "Stretching the Limits," 296.

46   Ibid.

47   Eftekhari, "Zanan: Trials and Success," 17–18.

48   Halper, "Law and Women's Agency," 136; Mir-Hosseini, *Islam and Gender*, 24.

49   Halper, "Law and Women's Agency," 138.

50   Mehrangiz Kar, http://www.mehrangizkar.net/english/biography.php.

51   Kar, "Women's Strategies, "178–193 .

52   Ibid., 199.

53   Ibid., 191–194.

54   Ibid., 193.

55   Ibid., 194.

56   Mir-Hosseini, "Stretching the Limits," 296.

57   Kar, "Stretching the Limits," 194–195.

58   Shahidian, *Women in Iran*, 41.

59   Mir-Hosseini, *Islam and Gender*, 248–249.

60   Lichter, *Muslim Women Reformers*, 199.

61   Afary, *Sexual Politics*, 48–49.

62   Khiabany and Sreberny, "Women's Press," 31.

63   Sedghi, *Women and Politics in Iran*, 260–269.

64   Ibid., 259.

65   Lichter, *Muslim Women Reformers*; Afary, *Sexual Politics*; Vakili, *Women and Politics*.

66   "Inside Iran: Interview with *Zanan* Magazine's Editor Shahla Sherkat," *Asharq al-Awsat*, May 11, 2007.

67   S. Sherkat, "Telling the Stories of Iranian Women's Lives," *Neiman Report*, Neiman Foundation for Journalism, Harvard University, Nov. 2009.

68   Lichter, *Muslim Women Reformers*, 140.

69   Vakili, *Women and Politics*, 189.

70   Sciolino, *Persian Mirrors*, 121.

71   Lichter, *Muslim Women Reformers*, 198.

72   Interview with Mohammad Khatami, *Zanan*, no. 34, May 1997, 2–5.

73   Z. Mir-Hosseini, "The Conservative-Reformist Conflict over Women's Rights," *International Journal of Politics, Culture and Society* 16, no. 1 (Fall 2002): 37–53 (quotation appears on 38).

74   Sedghi, *Women and Politics in Iran*, 268.

75   "Shutting Down *Zanan*," *New York Times*, February 7, 2008; "Iran: Closure of Women's Rights Publication *Zanan*," *Frontline*, February 5, 2008; Lichter, *Muslim Women Reformers*, 197–198.

76   Vakili, *Women and Politics*, 189.

77   F. Farhi, "The Attempted Silencing of Zanan," *Informed Comment: Global Affairs* (blog), February 1, 2008.

78   S. Sherkat, "Telling the Stories of Iranian Women's Lives," *Neiman Report*.

79   Howard, *Inside Iran*, 143.

80   Ibid.

81   Ibid., 144–145.

82   Sedghi, *Women and Politics in Iran*, 268; Lichter, *Women and Politics in Iran*, 196; Khiabany, *Blogistan*, 100.

83   Mir-Hosseini, *Islam and Gender*, xv; M. Khatami, *Islam, Liberty and Development* (Global Academic Publishing, 1998), 82.

CHAPTER Seven

1   Lichter, *Muslim Women Reformers*, 148–149.

2   *Euronews*, interview with Mansoureh Shojaee, July 7, 2013, http://www.euronews.com/2013/06/07/iran-s-women-discriminated-against-by-law/.

3   J. Estrim, "Your Veil Is a Battleground," interview with Kiana Hayeri, *New York Times*, May 29, 2012, http://lens.blogs.nytimes.com/2012/05/29/your-veil-is-a-battleground/?_r=0.

4   E. Sciolino, "Daughter of the Revolution Fights the Veil," *New York Times*, April 2, 2003.

5   G. Smythe, "Iran's Khatami Strikes Back," *Guardian*, September 20, 2013, http://www.theguardian.com/world/iran-blog/2013/sep/20/iran-khatami-revenge-rouhani-victory.

6   "Iran Leader Introduces Plan to Encourage Population Growth by Paying Families," *New York Times*, July 27, 2010, http://www.nytimes.com/2010/07/28/world/middleeast/28iran.html.

7   "Ahmadinejad Offers Iranian Couples Cash to Have Babies," *BBC News*, July 28, 2010.

8   "In a Death Seen Around the World: A Symbol of Iranian Protest," *New York Times*, June 22, 2009.

9   Abbas Milani, "The Green Movement," *The Iran Primer*, United States Institute of Peace, http://iranprimer.usip.org/resource/green-movement.

10   Jenny Cleveson, "Interview with Parvin Ardalan," *New Internationalist* magazine, Issue 440, March 1, 2011, http://newint.org/columns/makingwaves/2011/03/01/interview-parvin-ardalan/.

11   Haleh Esfandiari, "The Women's Movement" *The Iran Primer*, United States Institute of Peace. http://iranprimer.usip.org/resource/womens-movement.

12   Shirin Ebadi, *Campaign for Equality*, October 15, 2006, http://nobelwomensinitiative.org/2006/10/campaign-for-equality/.

13   "One Million Signatures: The Battle for Gender Equality in Iran," https://tavaana.org/en/content/one-million-signatures-battle-gender-equality-iran

14   Sussan Tahmasebi, "The One Million Signatures Campaign: An Effort Born on the Streets," *International Civil Society Action Network*, September 14, 2013, http://www.icanpeacework.org/the-one-million-signatures-campaign-an-effort-born-on-the-streets/.

15   "Iran's Banned Press Turns to the Net," *BBC News*, August 9, 2002.

16   Khiabany, *Blogistan*, 75.

17   Lichter, *Modern Muslim Reformers*, 139; Nouraie-Simone, "Wings of Freedom," 69; Khiabany, *Blogistan*, 51–107.

18 Lichter, *Modern Muslim Reformers*, 151; Azadeh Moaveni, "Slamming Its Doors on the World," *Time*, January 15, 2006.

19 "Women driven out of social life in southern port city," December 6, 2006, Kanoun-e Zanan website, Women's UN Report Network, http://www.wunrn.com/.

20 Lichter, *Modern Muslim Reformers*, 139.

21 Jila Baniyaghoob, "A Letter of Hope, Courage and Love from Evin to Rajai Shahr Prison," October 17, 2012, http://we-change.org/site/english/spip.php?article962.

22 Nouraie-Simone, "Wings of Freedom," 62–80.

23 Khiabany, *Blogistan*, 5, 76.

24 Kar, "Standing on Shifting Ground," 219; Povey and Povey, eds., *Women, Power, and Politics*, 55.

25 S. Bakhtavar, *Iran: The Green Movement* (US: Parsa Enterprises, 2010), 206.

26 "Iran's Youth: The Protests Are Not Over," *US Institute of Peace, Peace Brief*, No. 36, June 8, 2010.

27 Bakhtavar, *Iran: The Green Movement*, 9–10.

28 "Iran's Youth: The Protests are Not Over," *U.S. Institute of Peace, Peace Brief*, No. 36, June 8, 2010, 3; Bakhtavar, *Iran: The Green Movement*, 47–48.

29 Ali Samadi Ahadi and Oliver Stoltz , *The Green Wave*, 2010 documentary film on Iran's 2010 Green Revolution, directed by Ali Samadi Ahadi, 2010.

30 "Mission and History," Tavaana: E-Learning Institute for Iranian Civil Society, *tavaana.org.* https://tavaana.org/en/content/mission-history-0.

31 Erin Banco, "Iran's Internet Repression Draws Yet Another Division Between Hardliners and Rouhani Supporters As Arrests Increase," *International Business Times*, December 6, 2014, http://www.ibtimes.com/irans-internet-repression-draws-yet-another-division-between-hardliners-rouhani-1736825.

32 "Iran Protest Biggest Since Revolution," *Washington Times*, June 16, 2009; "Post-Election Clampdown," *BBC News*, June 15, 2009; "Iran Continues to Crack Down on Women's Rights Advocates," *Ms.* magazine, Winter 2010.

33 Khiabany, *Blogistan*, 1; "Iranian Women Protesters Sentenced to Jail," *Reuters Press*, April 18, 2007.

34 S. Sayyati, "Parvin Ardalan Wins the Olof Palme 2007 Award," *Payvand Iran News*, February 14, 2008.

35 "Women's Rights Activist Missing in Iran," *Guardian*, June 22, 2011; M. Sahim, Frontline Tehran Bureau, June 30, 2011 (source of the quotation).

36 2007 Interview with Tahmineh Milani posted on YouTube.

37 "Faezeh Rafsanjani: Prison Was the Best Time of My Life," *Iran Pulse*, August 19, 2013, http://iranpulse.al-monitor.com/index.php/2013/08/2637/faezeh-rafsanjani-prison-was-the-best-time-of-my-life/.

38   J. Baniyaghoob, *Women of Evin: Ward 209* (Bloomington, IN: Xlibris, 2013), 40.

39   Ibid., 41.

40   Khiabany and Sreberny, "Women's Press," 35.

41   Ibid, 36.

42   L. Farhadpour, "Women, Gender Roles and Journalism in Iran," (presentation, Development Studies Association, Women and Development Study Group, York University, UK, May 6, 2006, 6).

43   L. Gemholtz and F. Sanei, "Iran's Islamicisation Program Threatens Civil Society," *Public Service Europe*, October, 5, 2012.

44   Ibid.

45   Ibid.

46   Afary, *Sexual Politics*; P. Mahdavi, *Iran's Sexual Revolution: Passionate Uprisings* (Stanford, CA: Stanford University Press, 2009).

47   Afary, *Sexual Politics*, 322–337; Mahdavi, *Iran's Sexual Revolution*, 36.

48   Afary, *Sexual Politics*, 322.

49   "Throwing off the covers: An official report blows the lid off the secret world of sex," *The Economist*, August 9, 2014, *http://www.economist.com/news/middle-east-and-africa/21611117-official-report-blows-lid-secret-world-sex-throwing*.

50   "Iran's Persecution of Gay Community Revealed," *Guardian*, May 17, 2012.

51   Ibid.

52   "Iran Curtails Female Education," interview with Haleh Esfandiari, U.S. Institute of Peace, August 20, 2012.

53   Ibid., 33–35; D. Bagchi and D. Steinmetz, *The Cambridge Companion to Reformation Theology* (Cambridge and New York: Cambridge University Press, 2004).

54   R. Wright, "An Iranian Luther Shakes the Foundations of Islam," *Guardian*, February 1, 1995; R. Wright "Islam and Liberal Democracy: Two Visions of Reformation," *Journal of Democracy* 7, no. 2 (1996): 64–75.

55   "Who Wrote the Koran?" *New York Times*, December 5, 2008.

56   Interview with Mohsen Kadivar in the 2010 documentary *The Green Wave*.

57   P. Fritzsche, *Nietzsche and the Death of God: Selected Writings* (Boston and New York: Bedford/St. Martin's, 2007), 2; C. Lindberg, *The European Reformations*, 2nd edition (U.K: Blackwell Publishing, 2004); J. Dillenberger, ed. *Martin Luther: Selections from his Writings* (New York: Anchor Books, 1962).

58   C. Kurzman and M. Browers, "Introduction: Comparing Reformations," in *An Islamic Reformation?*, eds. M. Browers and C. Kurzman (New York and London: Lexington Books, 2004), 6.

59   Rex Welshon, *The Philosophy of Nietzsche* (Montreal: McGill-Queen's University Press, 2004), 40.

60 F. Nietzsche, *The Gay Science* (Mineola, NY: Dover Publications, 2006), Section 125, 90–91.

61 *New World Encyclopedia,* http://www.newworldencyclopedia.org/entry/Death_of_God .

62 Ibid.

63 P. Van Buren, *The Burden of Freedom: Americans and the God of Israel* (New York: Seabury Press, 1976), 976, 56; R. Rubenstein, *After Auschwitz: History, Theology, and Contemporary Judaism,* 2nd edition (Baltimore and London: Johns Hopkins University Press, 1966), 293–294

64 Mohammad Khatami, quoted in A. Bayat, *Making Islam Democratic: Social Movements and the Post-Islamist Turn* (Stanford, CA: Stanford University Press, 2007), 85.

65 Ibid., 34, 84, 93

66 Kar, "Women's Strategies," 194–196.

67 Amin, *Making of the Modern Iranian Woman,* 246.

68 Khatami's oft-quoted claim, cited in *The Intellectual Bases of the Khatami Phenomenon in Iran* (New York: Middle East Institute, Columbia University, 1999), 7.

69 H. Moghissi, *Populism and Feminism in Iran* (New York: St. Martin's Press, 1996), 183.

70 Saeed Kamali Dehghan, "Iranian Media Banned from Mentioning Former President Mohammad Khatami," *Guardian,* February 17, 2015, *http://www.theguardian.com/world/2015/feb/17/iranian-media-banned-from-mentioning-mohammad-khatami.*

71 An abridged version to Karl Marx's infamous proverb, "Religion is the sigh of the oppressed creature, the heart of the heartless world, and the soul of soulless conditions. It is the opiate of the masses." In "A Contribution to the Critique of Hegel's Philosophy of Right," K. Marx, first published in *Deutsch-Französiche Jahrbücher* 7 and 10, February 1844.

Index

The Book Cover Artist

Born in Ahwaz, Iran in 1985, **Morteza Pourhosseini** has been the recipient of numerous accolades and awards, and his paintings have sold at Sotheby's London auction house and the Metropolitan Museum of Art in New York.

A child of the revolution who has never left Iran, Pourhosseini courageously expresses the denigration of women in Iran today and captures the foundational precepts of a patriarchal order enshrined since the ascension of the Safavid Dynasty (1501-1722) and the declaration of Shi'ite Islam as the official state religion.

The dagger, emblematic of this sixteenth-century ruling dynasty and their doctrinal justification for women's diminished capacity, is a metaphor whose ripple effects continue to contaminate the soul of Iran.

About the Author

Born in Tehran, Iran, Nina Ansary left her country of birth at the onset of the 1979 Islamic Revolution and has not returned since. Growing up in New York City, she received her BA in Sociology from Barnard College and her MA in Middle Eastern Studies from Columbia University. Most recently, Ansary completed her doctoral studies at Columbia University, earning a Ph.D. in history. Inspired by her scholarly journey into the feminist movement in post-revolutionary Iran, she seeks to rectify the stereotypical assumptions and the often misunderstood story of women in Iran today.

In 1996, Ansary moved to Los Angeles and, following her family's long and distinguished record, began to pursue her passion for humanitarian causes. As an avid philanthropist, she serves on the Middle East Institute Advisory Board at Columbia University,

Columbia University's Global Leadership Council, the Board of Trustees of the Iranian American Women's Foundation (IAWF), and the Advisory Board of the Pacific Youth Foundation. Ansary is an elected member of the Everychild Foundation and the Pacific Council on International Policy, and a member of the American Association of University Women (AAUW), the National Organization for Women (NOW), and the U.S. National Committee for U.N. Women (USNC)—organizations dedicated to public policy and supporting education, charitable and gender-related causes.

Ansary is one of the "Top Influencers" on Iran on Twitter, and a regular contributor to the Daily Beast, the Huffington Post, and Women's eNews, an award-winning news website which recently honored her as one of the "21 Leaders of the 21st Century."